The Golden Hind

The
Golden Hind

T. W. E. Roche

History Book Club

This Edition published by
The History Book Club,
St. Giles' House, 49/50 Poland Street., London W1A 2LG
by arrangement with Weidenfeld and Nicolson

Printed in Great Britain by
Redwood Press Limited, Trowbridge, Wiltshire

Contents

Illustrations

Acknowledgements
Acknowledgements are due to the following for permission to reproduce illustrations in this book: the Radio Times Hulton Picture Library, London; the Victoria and Albert Museum, London; the National Portrait Gallery, London; the National Maritime Museum, London; the Pepys Collection, Magdalene College, Cambridge; the Mansell Collection, London; the British Museum, London; Buckland Abbey, Devon; the Bancroft Library, University of California; the London Library; the Bodleian Library, Oxford; Tom Molland, Plymouth; Berkeley Castle, Gloucestershire; Robert Chapman; and Douglas Allen, Bridgwater, Somerset.

The picture of Drake on the back of the jacket is reproduced by courtesy of the Radio Times Hulton Picture Library.

Author's Foreword

I must confess to having had great innate advantages in the preparation of this book. The golden hind was familiar to me from early childhood, for my mother was a Hatton, christened Dorothy after Sir Christopher's sister, from whom she was descended. Sir Christopher Hatton, whose crest was a 'hind statant or' in heraldic parlance, was the friend and patron of Sir Francis Drake, and it was in his honour, as I explain more fully later in this book, that Drake's ship was named *Golden Hind*. On the mantelpiece in my grandfather's dining-room stood some of the family silver with the Hatton crest engraved upon it – my eldest daughter has it still – while my grandmother enclosed her letters in envelopes bearing on the flap an embossed golden hind with the motto *Quid ni tandem*. Above the fireplace hung an engraving of the portrait of Sir Christopher with his dog at his feet, the original of which hangs in the Inner Temple, where my grandfather was once a bencher. When I was two and a half a cousin arrived on the scene and he was christened Christopher.

Birth and upbringing in Devon made me, like all Devonians, an unswerving partisan of my county. From my earliest years the name and exploits of Drake were familiar; boyhood holidays at Lydford led me to Tavistock, his statue, his birthplace, the splendid Dartmoor river Tavy by which he was born. An occasional treat was a visit to Plymouth, where one would stand on the Hoe beside the replica of the Tavistock statue, close to the spot where he played his famous game of bowls, and gaze out across the Sound to his island where he had lain discreetly in *Golden Hind* until he knew the queen's mind towards him.

Ever and anon a ship of the modern navy, whose fortunes and traditions Drake had done so much to form, would come swiftly by on her way to or from Devonport; when Plymouth Navy Week was held I would seize the opportunity to go and, as often as not, there would come sailing into the basin beside the modern battleships and aircraft-carriers a model of *Golden Hind*, manned by sailors superbly attired in Elizabethan dress, which would make a spirited and of course successful attack upon a supposed Spaniard, to the accompaniment of loudly banging cannon.

My daily route to school in Exeter by train led along the coast and up the Exe estuary, across which one could see Nutwell Court, one of Drake's houses, which had replaced an earlier castle and in which his drum was housed prior to its removal to Buckland Abbey; a minute later and we were abreast of the entrance to the Exeter ship canal, the construction of which Drake had so greatly influenced. It supplied the chief city of the county with access to the sea again, denied it for three centuries after its quarrel with Isabella de Fortibus, Countess of Devon, who had blocked it with her famous Countess Wear. But Drake had found a way round it and as one passed along St Martin's Lane in Exeter one beheld the Ship Inn bearing the inscription 'Next to mine own shippe I do most love that Shippe in Exon', while a stone's throw from it, just in the cathedral close, stood Mol's Coffee House. In both of these Drake and his fellow-Devonians like Hawkins, Gilbert, Davis and Raleigh had been wont to sit over their wine, discussing voyages that lay ahead or astern.

After all this it seems almost superfluous to add that at school I eventually became head of Drake House, which numbered a Drake among its members, and that from school I gravitated to Exeter College, Oxford, with its many Devonian associations and portraits of Devon worthies, whence it was but a step into the Bodleian Library.

Author's Foreword

In Devon, in addition to Mr Cole at Appledore, Mrs Hazel Berriman, art assistant at the Plymouth City Museum and Art Gallery, went to great trouble to provide me with the illustrations I required and to display the Drake Cup for my benefit; my particular thanks are due to her and to Mr Andrew Cumming FMA, the curator. Through them I was put in touch with Mr Robert Powers of Nut Tree, California, himself the author of a forthcoming book on the *Golden Hind* and Drake's landing in New Albion; he holds the copyright of the Hondius map and kindly allowed me to reproduce it. My thanks also go to my own colleague, Mr Peter Richards of Plymouth, to whose energy and interest on my behalf I owe a great deal, including researches in Tavistock and obtaining the Drake excerpt from the marriage register of St Budeaux church, which is reproduced by kindness of the Plymouth City Library.

I have, I hope, acknowledged my indebtedness for the reproduction of other illustrations at the appropriate place in the book and I apologize if any have been omitted by oversight. Canon Frith of All Saints, Long Stanton, very kindly allowed my son-in-law, Mr Campbell Gordon, to take photographs of the Hatton monuments in the church. I am also grateful to the master and fellows of Corpus Christi, Cambridge, and in particular to the librarians, Dr Paige and Mrs Rolfe, for providing facilities for research in the Matthew Parker Library, despite the difficulties caused them by repairs to the structure; likewise to Mr Claydon, senior under-librarian at the University Library, Cambridge, for granting me an alumnus of 'the other place', reading facilities there.

The typing of the manuscript I owe, as with previous books, to Mrs R. E. Green, whose uncomplaining readiness to shoulder this burden has been a great source of relief to me. To my editors, Mr Christopher Falkus who has fired me with enthusiasm from the start, and Miss Barbara Littlewood who went to untold trouble to obtain illustrations, go my grateful thanks for their unceasing kindness and encouragement. Finally my family have, as always, espoused my cause and helped by their enthusiasm and forbearance; two particularly associated with the book are my aunt, Lady Rachel Hatton, and my

Introduction

Some years ago there was published a bibliography of a hundred books relating to Sir Francis Drake – a figure now well exceeded. It is hardly surprising that the man who was a legend in his own lifetime should generate such an interest, contemporary and subsequent; what is surprising is that his famous ship *Golden Hind* should have been the subject of virtually no literature at all. Modern passenger liners like *Aquitania* and *Queen Mary* have inspired their own biographies, but *Golden Hind* rates little more than a couple of articles some twenty-five years ago – one significantly entitled 'The Mystery of the Tonnage of the *Pelican/Golden Hind*'.

She is of course mentioned in every book on Drake as the vehicle of his success, but to obtain even an imperfect impression of her one must seek beyond the accounts of the circumnavigation given by his officers and relatives and consult the evidence of his prisoners – Spanish captains like San Juan de Anton and Don Francisco de Zarate and in particular the Portuguese pilot Nuño da Silva.

The object of this book then is to redress the balance, to describe the ship and her exploits. The story must of course begin in Devon, with the birth in 1541 in a farm beside the Tavy of a son to a shearman employed by the Russells. Francis Russell, the future Duke of Bedford, stood godfather to the new baby, for his father, Edmund Drake, was a strong

Protestant and a trusted retainer of the new lords of Tavistock seeking to fill the vacuum left by the dissolution of the great abbey.

Young Francis was only eight, however, when the Prayer Book Rebellion in the west forced his parents to flee from Devon and find a home in a hulk on the Medway. Edmund became a preacher to the navy in Chatham and young Francis acquired his thirst for the sea: at fourteen he shipped along with the old master of a small east coaster, trading to near continental ports and became such a good seaman that when the skipper died he left Drake his ship. Luckily for such a strong Protestant he was at sea throughout the years of Marian persecution and it was only after Elizabeth's accession, when he was twenty-four, that he returned to the west country and sailed under the command of his kinsman John Hawkins.

So we follow these two to the Spanish Main and later to the disastrous encounter with the Spaniards at San Juan de Ulua, the consequences of which were incalculable. English seamen, including the master of Hawkins's *Jesus of Lübeck*, captured as a result of Spanish treachery, were sent to the galleys or shipped over to Spain to perish in the flames of the Inquisition. For Drake such unforgivable treachery inspired a personal crusade against Philip II, whereby the unknown Devon farmer's son was to become *El Draque*, the Dragon, singeing the king of Spain's beard in his home ports, giving oppressed men and nations new hope that tyranny could be overthrown.

Before the great days of Cadiz and the Armada, however, Drake was to reach a pinnacle of fame in *Golden Hind*. For over a hundred years the initiative in voyages of exploration had lain with the Portuguese – inspired by Henry the Navigator, whose English mother had learnt something of navigation from Chaucer – and the Spaniards. The English, in Hakluyt's phrase, had remained 'sluggishly secure'. Then, suddenly, an Englishman proved that he could equal and indeed better their exploits, his circumnavigation inspiring a whole series of great voyages of the Elizabethan age.

The ship in which he did it was a far cry from his two-man east coaster trader. We sail with her then from Plymouth in the late autumn of 1577, down to the coast of Africa and the

Cape Verde Islands, seizing Portuguese prizes and the useful old pilot Nuño da Silva. Across to Brazil and down the South American coast sailed the flotilla, the discord between Drake and Thomas Doughty growing till the latter's head was to fall as a traitor in the bay of Port St Julian, where Drake called his crews together, demanded that 'the gentlemen must haul with the seamen', and offered any who feared to follow him a passage home. But something more was needed to give the enterprise new purpose, and at that spectacular spot, the eastern entrance to the Magellan Straits, he renamed his flagship *Golden Hind* in honour of his friend and patron, Sir Christopher Hatton. Young John Drake, the admiral's artistic nephew, was set to rekindle enthusiasm and rally spirits by adorning the stern with the new red and yellow of Hatton's livery and the fourteen quarterings of his arms, while the pelican figure-head was replaced by a spirited golden hind, his crest.

The book investigates the reason for Drake's thus honouring Hatton – a subject neglected by historians – and concludes that not only was he a prime promoter of the voyage, but that it was he who first introduced Drake into the queen's presence and so brought him her favour for his enterprise.

The most perilous part of the *Golden Hind*'s voyage now began: once clear of Magellan Straits she was blown by the gales as far south as fifty-seven degrees latitude but saw no sign of *Terra Australis*, the imagined southern continent. Happily *Golden Hind* was as efficient as she was graceful – all Drake's later prisoners agreed that she sailed well and handled excellently, though liable to leak when labouring into the wind.

We do not know for certain where she was built; surprisingly, no English shipwright boasted that she was his work. The Portuguese pilot Nuño da Silva described her as 'French fashion' but not specifically as 'French built'. She carried an impressive array of canvas – topgallants above her main and fore topsails, spritsails, a lateen sail on the mizzen – and an equally impressive array of armaments. Nuño da Silva saw seven gun ports on each side; there were also two cannon on the poop and almost certainly eighteen guns in all. Below decks was a veritable arsenal of fighting equipment.

Her crew were estimated at about eighty-five, of whom nine were 'gentlemen, younger sons of English noble families' and approximately fifty 'real fighting men'. Estimates of her tonnage varied wildly from fifty to four hundred, the latter being a Spanish version designed to excuse the surrender to a supposed leviathan – waters in which the viceroy's scribes and the Inquisition's clerks were pretty well lost.

Eventually, though the other members of the little fleet were dispersed, Drake made his way up the Pacific coast, where the Spaniards never dreamt to see an English sail. All the way they attacked and plundered Spanish ships and harbours – even Callao, the port of Lima itself; at last they caught up with their greatest prize, the treasure ship *Nuestra Senora de la Concepcion*, called in rude sailors' Spanish *Cacafuego*. Her capture financed the entire voyage and gave the queen and its other promoters a huge dividend on their investment. Drake, on setting free her captain, sent with him a message to the viceroy of Peru threatening massive reprisals should he execute any more Englishmen – for Drake's fellow-Devonian, John Oxenham, and three of his officers were then in prison in Lima.

A graphic account of the next and last major capture exists in the report of Don Francisco de Zarate to the viceroy of New Spain – how he was under way from Acapulco to Panama when in the moonlight an hour before dawn he suddenly beheld a strange ship beside him and in a trice found himself a prisoner on board *Golden Hind*. He was well received by Drake – who reserved his threats for the viceroy himself, as cause of the treachery at San Juan de Ulua – and ate with him from his own silver plate in the great cabin to the accompaniment of minstrels' viols. Drake took from Don Francisco a gold falcon with an emerald in its breast, which he said was for his wife; then, after despoiling his ships he let him go. At Guatulco he sacked the port and put ashore the unfortunate Nuño da Silva, setting a course northwards where the Spaniards never sought to follow him, seeking the North-West Passage back to Europe. Having reached the latitude of modern Vancouver, and finding the coast trending ever north-westwards, he put about and sought a convenient anchorage to careen *Golden Hind* before making the long crossing of the Pacific that was now his only way home.

In the vicinity of modern San Francisco he found what he sought, a sheltered bay with white cliffs reminiscent of Kent. The local Indians worshipped the English as gods and prevailed upon Drake to accept their land in the name of his queen, which he did, setting up a plate of brass on a 'great and firm post' to commemorate his acceptance of 'New Albion'. Controversy has raged to this day as to the exact site of Drake's landing – the more fiercely since a brass plate answering in every description was discovered thirty-five years ago much nearer San Francisco Bay than the area called Drake's Bay and Drake's Cove behind Point Reyes.

Eventually, after five weeks' repairs safe from prying Spanish eyes, *Golden Hind* set sail westwards, despite the weeping Indians' pleas to Drake to remain. With little to report she winged her way across the Pacific, coming safely to the Spice Islands and a profitable trading agreement with the Sultan of Ternate – the first breach in the all-embracing Portuguese hold on the Far East.

Sailing on homeward, well down with Spanish booty and Moluccan cloves, *Golden Hind* ran aground on a reef off Celebes. Desperate efforts were made to free her by lightening her cargo and at this inopportune moment Francis Fletcher, the chaplain, proclaimed that *Golden Hind*'s misfortune was a judgement of God on their sins, notably Drake's execution of Doughty. One did not criticize the absolute commander thus; after a lucky shift of wind had freed *Golden Hind* Drake had Fletcher manacled before him on deck and sitting on a sea-chest 'with a pair of pantouffles in his hand' declared, 'I excommunicate thee out of the Church of God' and compelled him to wear a placard naming 'Francis Fletcher, the falsest knave that liveth'. Despite such tyrannies, Drake's men had told the Spaniards they adored him.

Thereafter *Golden Hind* made a swift and unmolested passage across the Indian Ocean, round the Cape of Good Hope and up the west coast of Africa to water in Sierra Leone. Then eventually on 26 September 1580 she stood in towards the dark mass of Rame Head backed by the towering bulk of

Dartmoor. Drake called down from the poop to some Plymouth fishermen to ask if the queen were alive and well.

She was, but her attitude to his activities was uncertain. So instead of entering the Cattewater *Golden Hind* dropped anchor discreetly behind St Nicholas Island – thereafter to bear Drake's name – and out came the mayor of Plymouth with Mary Newman, Drake's Cornish wife for whom he had taken Don Francisco's jewel. The mayor bade him lie low; diplomatically he dispatched some 'samples' of his voyage to the queen. Soon the summons came to sail *Golden Hind* round to the Thames for a royal inspection. There at Deptford on 4 April 1581 the climax of the great voyage was attained when Drake knelt on her deck to receive the honour of knighthood.

A special dock was built at Deptford to preserve *Golden Hind* for all to see and there she remained nearly a hundred years to the days of Pepys, who went aboard her. On New Year's Day 1582 the queen presented Drake with a silver goblet to commemorate his voyage, bearing one of the only two representations of the ship to survive from her day – it is now in the Plymouth City Museum. Nearby at Drake's home, Buckland Abbey, is his famous drum from *Golden Hind* and the banners which flew at her topmasts; a chair from her survives in the Bodleian library at Oxford and a table in the Middle Temple Hall. Her name was borne by the largest ship in Sir Humphrey Gilbert's ill-fated expedition to Newfoundland in 1583. It has inspired generations of Englishmen since.

So much for the story of the ship herself, but what of the deeper significance for religion and politics which the voyage held? In this ecumenical age of ours, when every step towards Christian unity must be hailed by men of goodwill but when religious discord leads to civil unrest on our very doorstep, it may seem retrograde and anachronistic to applaud an undertaking aimed directly at the power of the Roman Catholic Church. But men in all ages react to the circumstances in which they find themselves and the first Elizabethan age was vastly different from the second; in the former, religion and politics were closely interwoven.

It was plain for all in England to see, from the queen to her humblest subject, however much at times Elizabeth and her ministers might have affected not to, that Philip of Spain was determined to conquer England as part of his grand design to restore all Europe to the Catholic faith; and in this he was unquestionably the strong right arm of successive popes in Rome. The doctrines of Luther and the spread of Protestantism had alerted the Catholic Church to the dangers in which its former supreme authority now stood; the rebellious children must be chastized and brought back into the fold – such was the reasoning, and an agent was ready to hand in the shape of Philip of Spain.

His forces already invested the Netherlands, where the Duke of Alva was engaged in suppressing Protestantism with great cruelty. Philip had hoped to gain England by more peaceable means through marriage to Mary Tudor and she, eager to please the man whose child she could not bear, embarked in the third year of her reign on a campaign of repression and burning of heretics which, far from having the desired result, succeeded in alienating her subjects so that they welcomed her Protestant half-sister Elizabeth to the throne with open arms. Consequently Philip was forced back on two alternatives – subversion and conquest – and until he built up his maritime strength he relied mainly on the former.

What then of Drake? Our cynical and embittered age will surely go down in history as the great period of the debunker and it is fashionable to topple national heroes from their pedestals and denigrate their motives. Drake, we are told, was merely a pirate lining his own pockets, devoid of high principles. Yet the evidence points to the fact that he was very much acting on the queen's orders, albeit covertly, and that however much he might strike at the wealth of Spain he always treated his prisoners with humanity and released them alive – sometimes acting against his own best interests in doing so. Elizabeth had told him she would fain be revenged on the king of Spain for divers injuries done her and Drake had replied that he could not yet attack his main base in Spain but that the best way to do it was 'to annoy him in his Indies'. The raids on the Spanish Main and in the Caribbean, followed by the raids during the circumnavigation, illustrated how brilliantly Drake was able to annoy.

Hawkins and he had come back with bitter recollections of Spanish treachery from San Juan de Ulua, but what really horrified England was the treatment meted out to those of their crews unfortunate enough to fall into the Spaniards' hands. For any English prisoner ran a double risk of religion and politics, the spiritual and the temporal powers, ecclesiastic and secular, combining against him; having run the risk of the forces of nature in his cockle-shell craft he then had to run the gauntlet of Spanish guns and swords, and if captured not only the justice of the Spanish royal courts but of the devious cruelty of the Inquisition, whose holy offices had recently been set up throughout the Spanish dominions in the New World.

The master of the *Jesus of Lübeck* was conveyed from Mexico to Spain to be burnt at Seville, while others of his crew were lashed through the streets of Mexico City and then sent to the galleys as slaves for many years. Even youths were thus sentenced to perpetual captivity. The appalling feline cruelty of the Inquisitors awoke a burning resentment throughout the Protestant communities of Europe and terror in Spain herself and her dominions, so that men and women dared not show their own revulsion. Thus a two-headed monster, the finest fighting force of Europe and the repressive churchmen, threatened to destroy men's minds and bodies and to enslave the whole of Christendom. It is a story too familiar from our own bloody century, but then as now there were men who, irrespective of the risk, were not prepared to be enslaved.

In August 1572, by the design of Queen Catherine de Medici, the massacre of St Bartholomew's Day had taken place in France and the flower of the Huguenots was killed. Burning with resentment, the Huguenot captain Le Testu set out to attack the power of the chief oppressor, Spain, and when about to make a raid in the Isthmus of Panama encountered none other than Francis Drake. Together they launched the attack on the treasure-train at Nombre de Dios which has gone down to history. The Cimaroons, descendants of the cruelly-oppressed slaves of the Spaniards suddenly found new allies. Then, five years later, the impossible happened; into the Pacific, the great South Sea which Spain regarded as her private ocean, sailed a single, cheeky, little English ship, striking blow after blow at

King Philip's power, appearing unpredictably, her indomitable captain threatening the viceroy of Peru from his own port of Callao. Then, leaving a trail of chaos and demoralization astern of her, *Golden Hind* vanished as suddenly as she had come and months later, deep laden with Philip's gold and silver, returned in triumph to Plymouth Sound.

The oppressed breathed again. Books extolling the achievement appeared all over Europe. Though the struggle ahead was long and bloody, the monster's power was weakened irretrievably, both physically and psychologically. We have seen in our own tortured age how one brilliant stroke could encourage the oppressed of occupied Europe; so it was in the sixteenth century, and in this breaching of a monstrous tyranny lay the great significance of the voyage of *Golden Hind*.

Prologue

To commemorate Sir Francis Drake's historic, round-the-world voyage in the *Golden Hind* nearly 400 years ago, an authentic replica has been built at the yard of J. Hinks and Sons in Appledore, North Devon, to designs prepared by Christian Norgaard, a naval architect from Marin County in California where Drake was the first white man to set foot in 1579.

The new *Golden Hind* will sail from Plymouth in autumn 1974, retracing Sir Francis Drake's original route across the Atlantic to Panama and from there along the west coast of America to her final berth at Fisherman's Wharf, San Francisco. Her plans are the result of more than three years' research, and since sixteenth-century shipwrights built solely from ratios of length to depth to width, no plans or blueprints from the period exist. The reconstruction is, therefore, based on a meticulous study of contemporary paintings and careful inspection of accounts of the voyage and every other scrap of recorded evidence.

On the basis of Norgaard's research the *Golden Hind* has been interpreted as a classic example of a mid-sixteenth-century warship built along Venetian lines and representing the transition from carrack to galleon. Over 100 feet long and twenty feet wide, the replica will have five decks and carry three masts. The hind figurehead and a lion for the top of the rudderpost are to be made by two marine carvers from Fishbourne on the Isle of Wight, and eighteen cannons, complete with loading and priming gear, are being specially cast. The interior will be fitted with all the items that would have been carried in the original ship. The timbers used are English oak, elm, pine and fir and the 4,150 square feet of sail are being made of hand-sewn flax. The two cabins – the 'Great Cabin' on the main deck and 'Drake's cabin' on the half deck – will be furnished throughout to authentic Tudor designs, as a complete floating museum.

The ship will be exhibited in Britain at Plymouth and other south coast ports, then in London from September 1973 before setting sail for Panama under the command of Captain Adrian Small.

Dimensions

Length of keel	60 ft	Foremast	46 ft
Length of waterline	75 ft	Fore topmast	25 ft
Length overall	102 ft	Mainmast	59 ft
Mean draft	9 ft	Top mainmast	29 ft
Breadth to outside		Mizzen mast	36 ft 6in
of planking	20 ft	Sail area	4,150 sq ft

1

Where Tavy flows

All around is the desolation of the vast peat-bog, hills worn with great fissures dug by centuries of rain, the only sounds the breath of the wind and the occasional croak of Dartmoor's grim raven. Alone in all this wilderness of black-brown peat and purple heather rises the great green height of Fur Tor, firm turf amid the upland bog, her brow crowned with mighty grey piles of granite, in whose upper crevices the ravens have built their nests.

On the southern flanks of Fur Tor are the springs of Tavy, a tiny hollow in one of the loneliest fastnesses of England. For a while her course is westward, first little more than a peaty runnel, then, as rivulets ooze to her from the surrounding bog she grows, until she becomes wider and boulder-strewn and real tributaries add to her. Past the hut circles of primeval man she flows, then as she receives the Rattlebrook she turns abruptly southwards and enters the spectacular Cleave.

High tors crowd close above the hurrying waters that form countless falls, dropping over wide shelves of pink granite that form the river bed. At times of spate the narrow ravine is filled with the river's cry and her spume of spray. Round a sharper nose of granite she swings, entering a great defile below the towering Ger Tor, which soars up, with a stream of clitter, or disintegrated granite blocks, cascading from it to the river bank. Beyond, where the flanks of Standon on the opposite side fall back to let in the sunlight, come the first thin fingers of cultivation, the meagre intakes of ancient farms. Then woodland, and soon the crocketed towers of Mary Tavy and Peter Tavy rise above the wider stream. Though the moor is still at hand the meadows grow lusher, the trees more frequent and Tavy, a Dartmoor stream still even if somewhat civilized, washes the walls of the green town which has taken her name.

Over the weir she foams, under the bridge which the monks built, along the curtain wall of the ancient abbey of Tavistock. Founded by St Rumon in the days of Dunstan, it grew to wealth and prosperity until it owned wide lands all over Devon. To this abbey, across the trackless moor from Buckfast, monks and merchants trod the Abbot's Way, marked here and there by granite crosses. So Tavistock, built of its green volcanic stone, held sway until the reign of Henry VIII, when the king's commissioners came, assessed its wealth, stripped it of its fittings and destroyed some of its buildings.

The district suddenly experienced a vacuum, a centre of life was gone. Someone or something must replace it and as the king bestowed monastic lands on trusted noblemen and gentry so the wide lands of Tavistock Abbey fell to the Russells, sometime Dukes of Bedford. They were strong Protestants, and needed as yet to go carefully, as subsequent events would show, in introducing the new faith into the conservative west-country. They needed the support of those of like mind to themselves. Such a one was Edmund Drake, sometime 'sayler' turned tenant farmer and shearman in Lord Russell's service, occupying part of the farm of Crowndale which stood above the right bank of the Tavy a mile downstream from the still visible towers of Tavistock Abbey. Edmund attracted his lord's attention and the relationship between the two grew cordial. So when in 1541, two years after the abbey's dissolution, Edmund Drake's wife presented him with a son, it was Lord Russell's son Francis who stood godfather to him at the font in St Eustace's Church in Tavistock and whose name the new baby received – an honour which in other circumstances a shearman's child would have been unlikely to enjoy.

Below the farm of Crowndale Tavy still brawls, though less fiercely than in her moorland reaches. She now enters a deeply wooded stretch, hills crowding in close upon her; in a mile or two the Cistercian abbey of Buckland, founded in the thirteenth century by the Lady Amicia de Clare, Countess of Devon, rose high upon the eastern bank. Here the monks exercised some of their fishing rights in the Tavy and lower down where the river grew tidal the salmon fishers cast their nets; here the de Ferrers' manor and village stood high upon the western side and Tavy debouches into her greater sister Tamar. They flow together with Devon on the one hand and Cornwall on the other to join with Lynher to form the Hamoaze and then with Plym to enter the great cliff-bordered sweep of Plymouth Sound and so merge with the limitless sea.

Such were the surroundings in which Francis grew up, the voice of the Tavy and the cries of the farm animals the first sounds he heard. The movement of water was thus borne upon his infant consciousness and as his eyes focused on distance the silhouette of the tors which gave his river birth became familiar. During his early years his father would take him up on to the moor seeking sheep and ponies, while in the other direction boyhood explorations would lead to the tidal waters. Dartmoor and the Tavy became his familiars; something of their characters washed off on him and was to last the rest of his life.

He was not to enjoy it long, however. In 1549 the government of Edward vi proclaimed that Cranmer's new prayer-book should be read from every pulpit; this did not please the conservative west, which still clung doggedly to the old faith. 'In a week the West was in a flame'; supporters of the new beliefs were forced to flee. The rebellion broke out at Sampford Courtenay, to the north of Dartmoor and some twenty-five miles from Crowndale. The Drakes could no longer rely on Lord Russell's protection – indeed, though the king sent him down to Devon to restore order, he could get no nearer to his estates than Honiton before the rebels barred his path.

So Edmund Drake with his wife and young sons Francis and Robert were forced to leave their native land as fugitives and by devious routes make their way to Kent where they had

3

friends but where the best accommodation they could afford was the hulk of an old ship lying in the Medway near Gillingham. So at the age of eight Francis came to live on water and not merely beside it, to hear, instead of the lowing of cattle, the creak and groan of a ship and the bubble of the ebb-tide. His father obtained part-time work as a preacher to the crews of naval ships in the dockyard, but it was clear that as soon as he was old enough young Francis must stand on his own feet too.

At the age of twelve or thirteen, when Mary Tudor had just ascended the throne, he was apprenticed to the master of a tiny coasting vessel and these two, man and boy, sailed her from the ports of Kent and the Thames estuary across to those of Holland; Drake learnt to know wind and tide, channel and shoal, and to navigate the tricky harbours of the east coast, places like Whitstable or Wells-next-the-Sea. It was lucky for such a strong Protestant as Drake had become that his most ebullient years should have been spent thus at sea out of harm's way, while Marian persecutions raged ashore and hundreds of his co-religionists were burnt alive. Though he prospered as a seaman Drake naturally hankered after his native west and the great voyages in which his kinsmen, William and John Hawkins of Plymouth, were already achieving fame. In 1558, when he was seventeen, Mary Tudor died and her half-sister Elizabeth took her place, to the delight and relief of the great majority of her subjects.

In the short intervening space of nine years since the Prayer-Book Rebellion the whole religious complexion of the west had changed and the population at large, taking their cue from the great landowners, had become staunch Protestants. The time was ripe for Drake to return but as yet he had not the funds to do so. His old skipper however died soon after and so impressed had he been with Drake's seamanship that he left the young man his ship in his will. Drake was now the owner and master in his own right, albeit of a very small craft. He yearned for something larger, with blue water under his keel, but he resolutely carried on until in 1564, at the age of twenty-three, he sold the ship and made his way 'downalong' to offer his services to William and John Hawkins. From this moment his true career as a Devon navigator began, from which he was never to look back; in thirteen years he would progress to the command of *Golden Hind* and to the circumnavigation of the world.

Few of his biographers have been Devonians and therefore few have stressed the significance of the locality of his birth and circumstances of the first eight years, the exile which drove him to return. Camden, one of the earliest, wrote rather scathingly *'natus est loco mediocri in comitate Devoniense'*, but though Crowndale was no nobleman's castle it was a firm enough foundation and Drake was now once more based at home, ready to launch upon the great western seas that had always beckoned him. His first voyage out of Plymouth may have been as purser in an English ship sent to convey an English bride to Spain, but it is certain that he sailed in November 1566 with John Lovell, one of Hawkins's captains, in a fleet of three ships. The prime object of the voyage was to pick up Negro slaves in West Africa and convey them across the Atlantic for sale to the Spanish settlers on the mainland of South America – the fabled Spanish Main. Lovell had a brush with the Portuguese, who drove him away from the West African coast, but he turned the tables at the Cape Verde Islands, where he captured some Portuguese ships laden with slaves, transhipped the human cargo and sailed away to the west.

Having called at a number of Spanish trading posts they came to Rio de la Hacha, where the treasurer of the town, one Miguel de Castellanos, was out of favour with the Spanish viceroy, Ponce de Leon, who was investigating his alleged financial irregularities. It was not a propitious moment for English traders to turn up and try to barter slaves, however much the labour-hungry Spanish Main might need them. Castellanos needed to justify himself in his superior's eyes and what better way than to outwit the heretics? Lovell's advent provided him with a golden opportunity. After some haggling Lovell was tricked into landing his last ninety slaves, but Castellanos then declined to pay for them. Lovell did not dispute this trickery by force of arms, as Hawkins proceeded to do in the same place a mere twelvemonth later and as Drake would doubtless have done had he not been a subordinate. Instead they sailed for home. Drake however had had his first taste of Spanish methods and was soon to learn again first-hand that their code regarded it as no dishonour to break their word to a mere heretic. He made a mental note of Castellanos's perfidy and was to refer to it in later years. The ships returned to Plymouth in August 1567 with him thirsting for more adventure and the chance to teach the Spaniards a lesson.

As Hawkins was even then fitting out a larger fleet for a voyage to the Spanish Main he very readily gave his young relative his first deep-sea command, so that Drake remained a mere two months ashore in his home port. While Hawkins's preparations were only partly advanced however, an incident took place which, but for his immediate defence of the queen's interests and his own, might have had very nasty consequences. The English ships were in Sutton Pool, below the castle and to the north of the entrance to the Cattewater, the estuary of the Plym. The castle guard sent Hawkins an urgent message that strange ships had entered the Sound. They proved to be a squadron from the Spanish Netherlands under the command of a Flemish admiral, De Wachen. By all the custom of the sea, foreign ships entering a port would strike their ensigns and veil their topsails as a mark of courtesy and respect. De Wachen did neither but sailed steadily on, heading for the narrow entrance between the Hoe and Mount Batten. Did he mean to sail in and attack the English ships in harbour, or lay the town waste? Either possibility looked likely but John Hawkins did not wait to find out.

One ship of his fleet was nearly ready for sea and he cast off in her at once, dashing out with a fair wind between the head-lands towards the tacking Flemish flagship and sending a shot through her rigging which brought down her mainsail. Then he roared alongside and demanded to know why the stranger thus dared insult the queen. Protestations of innocence by the Fleming followed, but when harmony was restored he contrived to get a message off to the Spanish ambassador, who immediately protested to the queen of Hawkins's unprovoked aggression. Cecil and others whispered to her that she was in no state to conduct open war with Spain and a severe reproof for Hawkins sped westwards. But he did not care; he knew what the Spanish fleet had really been up to and he had prevented it. Where Plym, Lynher, Tamar and Tavy flowed was his preserve and woe betied any alien who thought to swashbuckle therein. It was a timely lesson for both sides, for the forthcoming voyage was to show both Hawkins and Drake just how deeply the tides of Spanish treachery could run.

2

San Juan de Ulua

The year 1568 was a milestone in Drake's career, when he suffered such treachery at the hands of the viceroy of Mexico as to infuse him with a burning desire for revenge and a determination to attack the King of Spain and rob him of his wealth wherever it might be propitious to do so, so that Europe beheld the astonishing spectacle of a Dartmoor farmer's son taking on almost single-handed its principal military power.

The fleet commanded by John Hawkins sailed out of Plymouth on 2 October 1567. It consisted of six ships, with 408 men aboard, the flagship being the queen's vessel *Jesus of Lübeck*. As her name implied, she had formerly belonged to the Hanseatic League, from whom Henry VIII had bought her; she was therefore well over half a century old, clumsy and high-sided, a far cry from the lean, swift ships which Hawkins was to develop and Drake to use with such deadly effect. The second ship was named *Minion*, the third – generally reckoned the best in the fleet – *William and John* after the Hawkins father and son who owned her. Drake's command, *Judith*, was smaller still and the two tiniest were *Angel* and *Swallow*.

'So sailing in company until the 10th, an extreme storm took us near Cape Finisterre, which lasted four days. It separated our ships and our general finding the *Jesus* to be but an ill case, was in mind to give over the voyage and return home. However, when the sea became calm and the wind was fair for us, he changed his mind.'

This was again to be a slaving voyage, a trade in which Hawkins was doing fairly well with the Spanish colonists in the New World albeit they had been prohibited officially from doing any trading with anyone but Spain. Still they needed the labour to mine the king of Spain's silver and carry it to the ports and the sixteenth century was not troubled by any sense of racial equality. The ships came together again at the Canaries, where they took water and sailed again on 4 November. A fortnight later they anchored off Cape Verde and Hawkins

> landed about 160 men to seek for negroes. They continued going up-country for about six miles ['up-country' is still common westcountry parlance for the rest of Great Britain!] encountered a great number of negroes who hurt a number of our men with their poisoned arrows, so that they were forced to retire to their ships. In the conflict they captured a few negroes, but seven or eight of our men who were hurt died in a very strange manner. Their mouths shut and we were forced to put sticks and other things to keep them open. These unfortunates were doubtless the victims of lockjaw.

Hawkins's plans fared none too well. A local chief tricked him out of eight hundred slaves promised – but eventually managed to round up about four hundred, 'so our general thought it best to stay no longer, but to depart for the West Indies with what we had'. In parentheses it may be observed that slaving was by no means purely a white man's traffic but the native chiefs, by capturing and selling men of other tribes, did well out of it. Then another misfortune occurred; they lost in a storm the *William and John* 'of which we had no tidings during the rest of our voyage'.

It was 3 February 1568 when the rest of the ships sailed away from the African coast, 'the weather somewhat tempestuous, which made our voyage hard'. They were fifty-two days in passage till they 'came in sight of an island called Dominica in the West Indies' on 27 March. 'From thence we coasted from place to place, making traffic with the Spaniards and

Indians with difficulty, because the King of Spain had charged all his subjects not to trade with any but Spaniards. Nevertheless during April and May we had reasonable trade and courteous entertainment in several places, until we came to Rio de la Hacha, a place from which the pearls come.' Drake had already experienced trouble here, as we have seen and now 'the governor would not by any means permit us to trade, nor yet allow us to take fresh water'. It was the latter unreasonable refusal which really stuck in Hawkins's throat. Drake reminded the treasurer, Miguel de Castellanos, of their presence by sending a shot very neatly through his house. 'Thereafter our general was compelled to land about two hundred men and to obtain by force what he could not get by fair means. So we took the town with the loss of two of our men. After which there was a secret trade, the Spaniards coming by night and buying two hundred negroes and other goods also.'

In the hopes of more trade, Hawkins sailed along the coast to the city of Cartagena, the principal place on the Main and in later years the scene of much of the Inquisition's cruelty. Here his reception was as blank as at Rio de La Hacha and he had not the force to overthrow such a strong citadel. Therefore he decided 'to leave the coast to avoid the dangerous storms called hurricanes which usually began there about that time of the year'. On 24 July he set sail on a northward course, passing to the west of Cuba. 'But as we sailed towards Florida, on the 12th August an extreme tempest arose and lasted for eight days. Our ships were most dangerously tossed and beaten, so that we were in continual fear of being drowned, and in the end we were compelled to flee for succour to the port of San Juan de Ulua.'

On 11 September they had sighted the Triangles, coral reefs about fifty miles off the coast of the northward-facing peninsula of Yucatan. Next day they captured a small Spanish ship, whose captain, Francisco Maldonado, was brought aboard the *Jesus of Lübeck* and told Hawkins that the only port for repairs was San Juan, four days' sailing away. San Juan de Ulua lies on the east coast of Mexico, the port of the modern city of Vera Cruz, much frequented nowadays by American tourists who go to see the island fortress where the Spaniards made their last stand against the Mexican rebels and their allies. In the sixteenth century San Juan de Ulua was the principal port of landing and embarkation for Mexico City, and provided the only good haven for miles. To it came the annual *flota*, the treasure fleet from Spain to load silver and take it back to increase the wealth of Philip II; it also conveyed important passengers and a most important one, the new viceroy of New Spain, Don Martin Enriquez, was now due to arrive to take up his appointment in Mexico City. Maldonado told Hawkins that the *flota* was due to arrive some time before the end of September; the English ships could indeed hardly have arrived at a more unpropitious moment.

The coastline hereabouts was low lying, with sand dunes covered with coarse grass. 'A desolate but necessary harbour' was how they described San Juan, which lay fifteen miles from the settlement of Vera Cruz, 'an unhealthy town of some three hundred households', named to commemorate the planting of the true cross in the soil of Mexico. The harbour of San Juan de Ulua was formed by a low shingle bank some two hundred yards long called the Arrecife de la Gallega, sheltering it from the ocean; there was deep water immediately on the lee side of the bank and ships could lie up against it, moored by head-ropes and stern anchors to prevent them swinging. There was no permanent settlement on the island; a few fortifications, a chapel and some warehouses fulfilled the needs of the Spanish garrison of fifty and their force of a hundred and fifty Negro slaves, all of whom were under the command of one Captain Delgadillo.

'In the port were twelve ships which by report had in them treasure to the value of two hundred thousand pounds, all of which our general had the power to take, but did set at liberty.' Hawkins also released the passengers he had taken from the small Spanish ship captured outside the port, 'not taking from them one groat' but keeping only as hostages

two men of credit, one named Don Laurenzo de Alva and the other Don Pedro de Rivera. Then our general sent to the Viceroy of Mexico, sixty leagues away, telling him of our arrival there by force of weather, and asking that he would furnish us with victuals and allow us quietly to repair our ships. Further because of the expected arrival of the Spanish fleet, our general requested His Excellency to make some special order to this fleet that the peace might be kept. This message was sent on the day of our arrival there.

Of course it never reached Mexico and even had it done so it seems unlikely, with the new viceroy approaching, that anyone would have dared to answer it on his behalf. Meanwhile the treasurer of the town, Francisco de Bustamente and the deputy mayor, Martin de Marcana, had come out in a small boat thinking to welcome their new viceroy and finding to their chagrin that their visitor was the heretic Hawkins. Captain Delgadillo was likewise as yet undeceived and had his shore batteries fire a salute, which the *Jesus of Lübeck* returned. She and *Minion* were both within a cable's length of the island before their true identity was realised and a cry of 'The Lutherans are upon us!' echoed across the harbour, the majority of Delgadillo's men deserting their posts and hastily rowing to the mainland. Only eight remained loyally beside him and once the English ships were safely moored with headropes and kedge anchors astern the master of the *Jesus of Lübeck*, Robert Barrett, came ashore to speak to Delgadillo. This Devon man and kinsman of Hawkins, an able seafarer, had a fluent command of Spanish, a fact which was ultimately to prove his undoing. He apologised for the stir their unexpected arrival had caused, explained that they had only been driven in by force of weather for urgent repairs and would merely place a guard on their mooring ropes. 'The next morning, the 17th September, we sighted thirteen great ships approaching the port. As soon as our general knew it was the expected Spanish fleet, he sent to advise the Spanish Ambassador of our presence in the harbour. For it was necessary that some understanding should be made for the keeping of the peace.' Hawkins had however been forestalled by Delgadillo who had gone out in a sloop to the Spanish admiral Francisco de Luxan to warn him of the disconcerting presence in the harbour of the English ships. Hawkins had also asked him to act as his emissary to the admiral, suggesting that the two fleets should remain in harbour amicably until his repairs were complete. Unfortunately Delgadillo had gone primarily on his own errand and equally unfortunately it was not the Spanish admiral who had the final word, but his superior, the viceroy, a fanatical aristocrat who, about to enter his new kingdom, found his principal port invested by the heretics.

Don Martin Enriquez had instantly assumed supreme command, ordered all the captains to report aboard the flagship and announced that he intended to sail into the harbour and attack the English as they lay at their moorings. Don Francisco de Luxan explained the topography of San Juan to the viceroy, who had never been there and said that as Hawkins had control of the island a direct attack would not work. He prevailed upon Don Martin to accept Hawkins's proposal for an exchange of hostages, but even at this stage the viceroy's mind was bent on trickery. He did not want to waste his gentlemen as hostages and decided to dress up some seamen in gentlemen's clothes. He was however dissuaded by the vice-admiral, Juan de Ubilla, not from any motives of honour but because he thought Hawkins would smell a rat. The written requests which Hawkins had sent by the hand of Delgadillo read:

1. That we might have victuals for our money and licence to sell such wares as might pay for our wants; 2. That we might be suffered peacefully to repair our ships; 3. That the island might be in our possession during our stay there, and that no Spaniard should land on the island bearing arms; 4. That to guarantee these terms, twelve gentlemen of credit from either side should be exchanged as hostages.

Hawkins was indeed faced with many problems.

At this time our general was in much perplexity. He was well able to prevent the fleet from entering the port; but, if he did prevent it, on that dangerous coast the fleet might be wrecked, and its value amounted to one million and eight hundred thousand pounds. On the other hand, he felt sure that if he permitted the fleet to enter, the Spaniards would use all manner of means to betray him. Also, if they came in, the ships would have to ride hard aboard one another, because the harbour was so small.

Moreover, no sea-captain of Elizabeth's could fail to have a weather eye over his shoulder for that remarkable woman. 'Also he saw that, if their fleet did perish because he had kept them out, he must stand in great favour of the Queen's displeasure. Therefore he did choose the lesser evil, which was to let them in under an assurance of peace, but at the same time to stand upon his guard in case they practised treason.'

Delgadillo meanwhile returned to the *Jesus of Lübeck* and some further haggling about the number of hostages ensued; eventually it was agreed to reduce the number to ten from each side and that number of volunteers from among the English officers, gentlemen and merchants went out to the Spanish fleet, now hove to off the port. All seemed set fair; but while professing friendship and preparing a flowery reply to Hawkins the viceroy had already sent a pinnace to Vera Cruz carrying his most valuable treasure and his ten-year-old son, together with a message to the mayor, Don Luis Zegni, to recruit as many men capable of bearing arms as possible. As a result some two hundred men were rounded up and secretly ferried aboard the Spanish ships.

Don Martin's letter to Hawkins reads:

I well believe that your honour's arrival in the port was forced by the great need your honour had of subsistence and other things, as your honour writes me. So also I am certain that, as your honour says, your honour has not maltreated any vassal of His Majesty's, not done any damage with your fleet in those ports or parts where it has called, but that your honour has engaged solely in bartering slaves and other merchandise carried, paying in the same for the subsistence taken at its just value; and further that your honour had paid the dues payable to His Majesty's royal revenues. Wherefore I am content to accept the proposal which your honour makes in your letter, asking me to deliver hostages and to enter the port in peace, although I was determined to the contrary. Therefore I send ten principal persons and rely upon what your honour states, that those your honour sends me are similar persons. I well believe that although the people of this fleet enter without arms into the island, they will not be prevented from going about their affairs, nor harassed in any fashion. And I am very confident that, when we meet, friendship will augment between the fleets, since both are so well disciplined.

'These conditions were agreed by the Viceroy with his hand and sealed'; ten 'well-attired' Spaniards were sent to San Juan in a pinnace. 'It was further decided that the two generals should meet and give faith to each other for the performance of the contract. All of which was proclaimed with the sound of trumpets.' On Tuesday 21 September the wind dropped and the Spanish fleet entered San Juan de Ulua, while the guns roared a salute – 'thus at the end of three days the fleet entered the port, the ships saluting each other after the manner of the sea.'

No less than thirty ships now crowded into the small harbour; Hawkins had wisely insisted that the English ships should occupy the southernmost berths, nearest the entrance, while *Minion* was nearest the Spanish ships and between her and them lay the hulk of a carrack used as a storeship. By the evening of Wednesday 22 September the mooring of all the ships was complete. 'However, as the sequel showed, the Spaniards meant nothing like this [i.e. great friendship]. For the Viceroy and governor had secretly assembled on land a thousand men, meaning at Thursday dinner time to assault us,' wrote Miles Phillips, then aged thirteen.

The viceroy held a secret council of war aboard his flagship and arranged to hide two hundred men aboard the hulk.

The same Thursday morning some appearance of this showed itself, as shifting weapons from ship to ship and positioning their guns toward our men that guarded the island. This caused our general to send to the Viceroy to know what was meant. To which the Viceroy replied that the guns should be moved, and that he would be our defence against treachery. Our general was not satisfied, seeing that they had secretly taken a great number of men aboard a great hulk which was riding near the *Minion*. He therefore sent Robert Barrett, master of the *Jesus* who could speak Spanish very well, to ask that these men should be moved from the hulk again. The Viceroy then saw that their treason was known. He seized Robert Barrett, sounded a trumpet and gave the order that his men upon all sides should charge upon our men.

At dinner on board the *Jesus of Lübeck* one of the Spanish hostages was observed concealing a dagger in his sleeve. Hawkins dashed up on deck and descried the Spanish vice-admiral, Ubilla, in the bows of the nearby hulk, about to wave a white napkin, which was the agreed signal for the attack on the heretics. He hailed Ubilla and asked him what he was doing; the Spanish vice-admiral in his embarrassment gave the signal and replied that the ships were forfeit. Hawkins fired a crossbow at him but missed. Then the Spaniards attacked from all sides.

'This struck such amazement and fear among us that were ashore that many gave way and tried to get back to the ships. Then Spaniards hidden in ambush on land were quickly brought to the island in longboats and slew without mercy all our men they could find.' Fortunately, as the preparations had been visible from *Minion*, her crew was not caught entirely unawares and they were able to haul off. The two hundred or so Spaniards who had been concealed in the hulk then tried to board *Jesus*, where 'there was a cruel fight and many of our men slain. But our men fought well and kept them out, so the *Jesus* also got loose and joined *Minion*, and the fight waxed hot on all sides. But they, having captured our great guns, which were on shore, did greatly annoy us.'

Two Spanish ships were sunk and one set on fire; then the Spaniards decided to use two more of their vessels as fireships in retaliation, 'which came directly down on us and bred among our men a marvellous fear. The *Minion*, which had her sails ready, shifted for herself without orders from our general or from her own captain and master.' Hawkins himself managed with great difficult to get aboard her, roaring encouragement to his men; the *Jesus of Lübeck* raked by fire from her own guns now ashore, with her mainmast shot away, unwieldy and cumbersome, could not get under way and most of her crew took to the boats and followed *Minion* 'but those

16

who could not get into the boat were cruelly slain by the Spaniards'.

Only *Minion* and *Judith* escaped the holocaust; Drake took advantage of his southernmost moorings and put to sea at Hawkins's command, to wait for *Minion* at the harbour mouth.

> The same night the *Judith* lost us, we being in great trouble and forced to anchor within two bow shots of the Spanish fleet. Next morning we weighed anchor, and came to an island a mile north from the Spaniards. Here a storm took us, with a north wind, in which we were greatly distressed, having but two anchors and two cables left; for in the conflict we had lost two anchors and three cables.

They had also lost Paul Hawkins, John's nephew and page, who had been unwittingly left behind on board the *Jesus of Lübeck*, and the others left in the Spaniards' hands suffered appallingly, as we shall see, so that the name of San Juan de Ulua on English lips was to become synonymous with treachery of the deepest dye.

Minion struggled on, grossly overcrowded, carrying the survivors of the *Jesus of Lübeck* as well as her own.

> The next day we set sail, being many men with but little store of food, so that we feared we should perish of famine, and some of us were of a mind to surrender to the Spaniards. Others thought it better we should yield ourselves to the savages. Thus we wandered in unknown seas for some days, and hunger compelled us to eat hides, cats and dogs, mice, rats, parrots and monkeys. In short, our hunger was so great that everything seemed sweet and savoury.

Thus graphically did the thirteen-year-old Miles Phillips describe their predicament. 'On the eighth day we came to land again in the bottom of the Bay of Mexico.' They hoped they might obtain food from the natives and be able to repair the badly damaged *Minion* 'for she was so badly bruised that our weary arms were scarce able to keep the water out of her. Oppressed with famine on the one side and danger of drowning on the other, we began to be in a wonderful despair.'

Some of them went to Hawkins and begged to be put ashore. To their surprise he agreed to land half his complement 'for it would lessen his numbers and add to the safety of the rest. . . . But on that it was a wonder to see how men's minds changed. They who a little while ago had begged him to set them on shore, now begged to be allowed to stay in the ship.' Hawkins, however, his mind made up, went firmly about choosing between the shore party and those to stay. First he chose every man needed for working the ship, then he selected those he could most easily spare and set them ashore in a boat, Miles Phillips among them, promising to return within a year, 'or send someone else to fetch us home. But it would have melted a stony heart to hear the pitiful moans that many did make, being so loth to go.'

With reason, for the story of their sufferings is a saga of horror with few parallels. Reaching Tampico on foot, they were forced to march all the way to Mexico City, a young Spanish guard constantly hitting the stumbling men in the back with a javelin so violently that they fell down, while he drove them on with shouts of 'March on, you English dogs! March, heretics and enemies of God!' Those who had been left behind in San Juan de Ulua fared just as badly. 'It is certain that when they had captured some of our men ashore, they hung them up by their arms on high posts until the blood burst out of their finger ends.'

The men with Miles Phillips were at first treated better in Mexico. They were put in hospital on arrival 'and were visited by virtuous ladies and gentlemen who brought us such comforts as sweets and marmalade'. Evidently the Spanish gentlefolk themselves bore the English no ill will. They were left in hospital six months and those who survived recuperated fully for their next ordeal. 'After this we were sent to the town of Tescuco, eight leagues from Mexico. In this town there are certain houses of correction, like our Bridewell in London.' Here they were imprisoned and 'almost famished' though their slender diet was eked out by an expatriate Englishman, Robert Sweeting, who brought them food. After two months they escaped, but were recaptured, taken to Mexico and brought before the viceroy, who threatened to hang them. However, they were spared for the moment, and set to work in his garden for four months, having but 'two sheep allowed every day for meat between a hundred men.' In the garden they briefly encountered the English gentlemen who had been kept hostage on board the Spanish flagship at San Juan de Ulua, together with Robert Barrett, master of the *Jesus of Lübeck*, before these unfortunates were removed to a prison near the viceroy's house. The rest, however, were allotted to the households of Spanish gentlemen as servants 'for in that country no Spaniard will serve another. They are served only by Indians and negro slaves.' The Englishmen were in general well treated; others were sent to the mines to be overseers of Indians and Negroes. 'In the mines many of us did profit greatly, being paid almost 300 pesos a year, which is about sixty pounds.'

The gentlemen hostages however were kept prisoner for a further four months and then shipped off to Spain. 'I have heard than many of them died there at the hands of the Inquisition.' Robert Barrett was kept in prison in Mexico for a further year, then sent to the Holy House in Seville and there condemned to be burnt to death; this savage sentence was duly carried out in the market place. Thus perished an extremely able young man whose only faults were that he was an Englishman, a Protestant and was fluent in Spanish – and because of the latter talent the Spaniards seemed to have singled him out for particular cruelty.

As news of this leaked back to England the reaction was one of boundless fury. Drake meanwhile, having lost touch with *Minion*, had arrived safely in Plymouth Sound in *Judith* on 22 January 1569. Hawkins had some bitter things to say about his kinsman at first, accusing him of leaving him in the lurch, but apparently Drake had thought *Minion* lost and that therefore his only duty was to set course for home and save his men. *Minion*, lightened of half her complement, had eventually got away from the Mexican coast on 16 October 1568 and limped into Pontevedra in Galicia on the last day of the year. The dangers of entering a port in mainland Spain were only too obvious but Hawkins could go no further without provisions. He hoped to be mistaken for a trader and disguised himself as a passenger, but the English factor in the port, Edward

Boronel, who came aboard swiftly realized who was really in command. Later, when the Spaniards realized belatedly who had slipped through their fingers, some of the Pontevedrans who had seen Hawkins were asked to describe him. 'Youthful, well-dressed with velvet trunk-hose, knitted stockings and a scarlet leather jacket embellished with silver trimmings' they said. He was also wearing 'a pelisse lined with marten's fur and a gold chain' and was 'of medium height and somewhat dark complexion'. We can still recognise the description if we compare Zucchero's portrait which hangs in the Drake draw-ing-room at Buckland Abbey to this day, for despite all the privations of the voyage John Hawkins still contrived to look smart and elegant The factor warned him that he had been recognized and Hawkins weighed anchor and sailed off to Vigo where, surprisingly enough, he obtained permission to stay for a few days and replenish *Minion*'s stores.

Luckily for him there were a number of other English mer-chant ships in Vigo harbour and Hawkins applied to their captains who readily lent him a dozen seamen to make good deficiencies in his crew. *Minion* sailed from Vigo on 20 January and limped into Mounts Bay in Cornwall on the twenty-fifth, three days after Drake in *Judith* had reached Plymouth and announced that to the best of his belief Hawkins was lost. Even so, *Minion*'s crew had had enough. Evidently an easterly was blowing and they were too weak to sail her against the wind for the last stage up the Cornish coast from 'the guarded Mount' to Plymouth. Hawkins for his part believed *Judith* lost and wrote to Burghley saying that disaster had overtaken his expedition; he also wrote to William Hawkins in Plymouth asking him to send a relief crew down to Mounts Bay to sail *Minion* home. This was eventually done and she was sailed round to the Medway for repairs.

Financially, all was not so disastrous for Drake and Hawkins. *Judith* was safe and the profits of the voyage amounted to no less than 25,000 pesos. It required four laden pack-horses to carry the spoils from Plymouth to London where the Spanish ambassador gloweringly observed their arrival. The real loss was in men and far away in Mexico Miles Phillips and his comrades were soon to be faced with a far worse foe than the Spanish soldiery. To give him his due, Don Martin Enriquez had done all in his power to prevent the Inquisition getting a foothold in New Spain but despite his influence with King Philip the churchmen were too strong for him. They arrived in force in 1574 and finding the colonists by their standards fallen into lax ways decided to make an example of the easiest and handiest victims – the remnants of Hawkins's crews. As Miles Phillips put it:

> Now after we had been in the Indies six years, in the year 1574 the Inquisition came to be established in the Indies. This was very much against the wishes of the Spaniards themselves, for never since the first conquest had they been subject to that bloody and cruel Inquisition.
>
> Then, deciding they must make a good beginning in Mexico, to put terror into the whole country, they thought it best to put us Englishmen first to the question. So now began our sorrows afresh, for we were soon taken and all our goods seized and were committed to prison in dark dungeons, never more than two of us together.

They spent eighteen months like this while the sophisticated interrogators of the Inquisition played with them with feline cruelty.

> During this time we were often called before the Inquisitors one at a time. We were severally examined about our faith. We were commanded to say the Paternosters and the Ave Maria and the Creed in Latin, which God knows many of us could not say except in English. Then they demanded of us what we did believe of the Sacrament, and whether any bread or wine remained after the consecration, yes or no, and if the host which the priest raised was truly the body and blood of Christ, yes or no. To which, if he answered no, there was nothing for us but death.

Many of Hawkins's simple, rough westcountry seamen were no match for the snares of the smooth Inquisitors who now had their penultimate brutal card to play. 'Within three months we were all put upon the rack, where some were forced to utter things against themselves that afterwards cost them their lives.' Now the stage was set to make an example of the English and the Inquisitors arranged it all with their full, dia-bolical panoply.

Then having got sufficient for them to proceed to judgement, they made a large scaffold in the market place. That done, for fourteen days they called people with the sound of drum and trumpet to come to hear sentence passed on the English heretics. The night before the appointed day, officers of the Inquisition brought us certain fools' coats which they call San Benitos, made of yellow cotton with red crosses on them. The next morning we were each given for our break-fast a cup of wine and a slice of bread fried in honey.

They were going to need this, for the familiars of the In-quisition had given them no sleep, rehearsing them all night to make sure nothing went wrong on the great day.

Then at about eight o'clock we set forth, each in his yellow coat with a halter round his neck and a great green candle in his hand, unlighted. So we marched to the scaffold, and found so great a throng of people there that officers on horseback had to clear a way for us. Then we went up some steps and found seats ready for us.

Presently the inquisitors came up other stairs, and the viceroy and chief justices, and also a great number of friars, white, black and grey, about three hundred. Then was sil-ence commanded, and presently their cruel judgement be-gan. The first man called was one Roger, chief armourer of the *Jesus*. He was condemned to receive three hundred lashes on horseback and afterwards to go to the galleys as a slave for ten years. After him were called others who were condemned to one or two hundred lashes, and to serve in the galleys for six, eight or ten years.

Then I, Miles Phillips, was called and was ordered to serve in a monastery for five years, without any lashes. [This 'clemency' was no doubt due to the fact that Miles had been only thirteen when he had sailed with Hawkins.] Six others were also ordered to serve in a monastery, without lashes, for three or four years, and to wear the San Benito for all

22

that time. Which being done – George Rively, Peter Monfrey and Cornelius the Irishman were called and were condemned to be burnt to ashes. They were immediately sent to a place a little way from the scaffold, where they were quickly burnt. Sixty-eight of us were taken back to prison for the night.

Next day the sentences on those to be whipped were carried out: Miles Phillips provides a horrifyingly graphic description. The wretched men were flogged round Mexico City on horseback, the mob – anxious to curry favour with the Inquisition – jeering at them when they made periodical stops, almost fainting on the backs of their horses. They arrived back in prison in an appalling condition, to spend a short time there while their more fortunate compatriots tried to comfort them and soothe their sores, before they were driven off to the coast and the living tomb of the galleys.

Miles reported:

I and the six with me were sent to certain religious houses, where I was appointed overseer of Indian workmen who were building a new church. Among them I learned the Mexican tongue, and found them to be a courteous and gentle people. They hate the Spaniards, who have used horrible cruelties against them. Thus we served the years for which we were condemned, and I must confess the friars used us very well. Every one of us had his chamber with bedding and food, and everything clean and neat. For many Spaniards, even the friars themselves, do hate and abhor the Inquisition, though they stand in such fear of it that they do not let the left hand know what the right is doing.

This last sentence puts the position in a nutshell, but the oppression of the Spaniards themselves by the Inquisition was no consolation to the English sufferers nor to the many families in both lordly and humble houses in the westcountry which had lost their menfolk, either for ever or for long years of misery in the galleys from whence they might never return. The sense of outrage as the news of the Inquisition's cruelties seeped through permeated even to the queen's court in London.

23

Elizabeth, with all too recent memories of the fires of Smithfield in her sister's time, was furious that her Englishmen should be so served. She was as yet too weak for a full-scale confrontation but she looked about her for a tool for revenge.

As for Drake, he had already sworn to be avenged on the viceroy of Mexico for his treachery at San Juan de Ulua; now he had ample reason to assault the king of Spain. In later years Spanish officials were to complain bitterly at what they regarded as sacrilege by Drake's seamen and depredations by Drake himself; but the dragon's seed sown by Don Martin Enriquez and by the Inquisitors in Mexico germinated and grew until the sowers very deservedly found themselves assaulted by a small stocky Devonian in a ship called *Golden Hind*.

3

First sight of the Pacific

Although Drake and Hawkins had returned to Plymouth in January 1569 very much the worse for wear, at least for Drake that year was to offer something very much better on the personal front. In the library at Plymouth is still preserved the sixteenth-century marriage register of the church of St Budeaux and there, in the parson's elegant hand, is shown '1569 – 4 July – ffrancis Drake and Mary Newman'.

St Budeaux church, dedicated to St Budoc, had then only recently been built, replacing the older mediaeval church down by Budockhead Creek, an inlet of the Tamar estuary. The new St Budeaux stood high, facing Cornwall across the wide river which divides it from Devon. It was perhaps fitting that the greatest of westcountry seamen, himself a Devonian, should marry a Cornish wife and that Mary Newman should be rowed across from her native town of Saltash to St Budeaux on her wedding day. It is uncertain when they met, whether in Drake's early youth or when he may have anchored off Saltash on the return from an earlier voyage than that from San Juan de Ulua, though it is thought that Mary's brother Harry was a member of the crew of *Judith*. Francis Drake and Mary Newman were to be married fourteen years until her untimely death, but in all that time they were able to spend remarkably few months together because of his long absences at sea.

Hawkins meanwhile had not stayed at home long; in March

1569 he had taken some ships to La Rochelle to assist the Huguenots against the king of France, while the Devonian gentry, incensed at the treatment of their French co-religionists, raised a body of horse for service under the Huguenot leader, Admiral Coligny. Among the horsemen was Walter Raleigh, then aged seventeen. Early the following year an event added to English Protestant anger when Pope Pius v issued a bull excommunicating Queen Elizabeth, 'that incestuous bastard begotten and born in sin'. This was dangerous stuff by any yardstick and the king of Spain, as the Pope's champion, was soon to feel the force of English anger at the insult.

The lure to the English was the mule-trains of treasure which crossed the Isthmus from Panama itself, where the treasure was discharged from the ships which had brought it up the Pacific coast from the mines of Peru, where it had been loaded at ports like Arica after being brought overland from Potosi and elsewhere. The mules bore the silver and gold across the Isthmus to the small port of Nombre de Dios on the Caribbean coast whence it was shipped annually to Spain in the galleons of the *flota*, or treasure fleet. The route from Panama to Nombre de Dios lay through deep jungle, inhabited by the Cimaroons or *Cimarones*, mainly people of mixed Indian and Negro blood, descendants of escaped slaves of the Spanish. This country was and is an almost impenetrable jungle of mountain and tropical forest – in our own time we have seen a British motorized expedition struggling through 'the most difficult country in all America' even though equipped with all modern devices, and its safe emergence hailed as a great achievement. In the sixteenth century an adventure into the Cimaroon country was fraught with the greatest uncertainty and danger, though at least an Englishman might expect a welcome from the Cimaroons as an enemy of Spain. It was to this challenging target, the despoliation of which would not only enrich England but impoverish the king of Spain, that Drake now addressed himself.

He was as yet unable to fit out a ship of his own, but his kinsman John Hawkins gave him command of his ship *Swan*. Drake's and Hawkins's differences over San Juan de Ulua were evidently submerged in the latter's appreciation of Drake's seamanship. The *Swan*'s tonnage, a bare twenty-five, indicates the incredible daring of the Elizabethan seaman, who would embark on a transatlantic crossing for a destination in enemy country in the merest cockle-shell. Drake sailed from Plymouth in the late autumn of 1570 on what was primarily a reconnoitring expedition, a dress rehearsal for the real attack to come. In February 1571 he arrived off the Spanish Main in the vicinity of Nombre de Dios and captured several Spanish ships. Landing on the Isthmus he contacted the Cimaroons, with whom the Huguenots already had a very satisfactory working agreement in the common cause against Spain. Drake then penetrated the Rio Chagres, down which the bulkier cargoes were shipped part-way to Nombre de Dios from the small port of Venta Cruces, though the treasure itself came by mule-back over the jungle paths.

Drake learned much from the Cimaroons, much from his Spanish prisoners, acquiring a photographic knowledge of the layout of Nombre de Dios, the location of its treasure-house, governor's residence and strong points. He cruised along the coast eastwards nearly to Cartagena and some two hundred miles east of Nombre de Dios lighted upon a small and secret cove, uninhabited but sheltered, with jungle down to the water's edge, an ideal raider's lair. This would suit him nicely as a base on the occasion of his next visit and he buried some stores there in readiness; unfortunately he still had his Spanish prisoners on board when he did so and though he landed them unharmed later they rewarded him by not keeping their mouths shut. He sailed for home again in the summer of 1571 and entered Plymouth Sound in the autumn, his head full of exciting plans to lay before Hawkins.

In his absence relations with Spain had deteriorated still further; a Genoese treasure ship, sent to increase the Duke of Alva's finances in his oppression of the Protestant Netherlands, was pursued by Huguenot ships and had actually taken refuge in an English harbour. By order of the queen its cargo was seized; she told the Spanish ambassador she would return it some day but must first be satisfied that it was not intended to finance a Spanish army to invade England. Philip, outraged,

27

infiltrated his subversive agents into England; Elizabeth re-
taliated by expelling De Gueras, the Spanish ambassador.
Finally Hawkins, as a former servant of the king of Spain, had
had some success in reversing the fortunes of San Juan de Ulua
by securing by trickery the release from Seville of some of the
Englishmen taken prisoner from the *Jesus of Lübeck*, though
this came too late to save poor Robert Barrett.

So the momentous year of 1572 dawned. On 24 May Drake
sailed once again from the Sound; he had two ships this time,
the *Swan* as before and a larger vessel, of seventy tons, named
Pasco, the Cornish word for Easter. It was a truly westcountry
expedition, with three Drakes on board – Francis and his
younger brothers John and Joseph – and an ebullient and up-
and-coming young fire-eater, John Oxenham from South Tawton to the north of Dartmoor – the total crew numbering
seventy-three men. The voyage went well; with favourable
winds they headed south-south-west past the Canaries, then
crossed the Atlantic with the benefit of the north-east trades
and put in for water at Guadeloupe in the West Indies. Then
they sailed south direct to Drake's secret cove, which because
of the plentiful game birds his crew called Port Pheasant. To
his annoyance he found his stores gone and a message from
John Garrett, a Plymouth man who had been there five days
before him. Garrett had discovered that the Spaniards, informed
by some of their compatriots released by Drake, had dug up the
hidden stores and therefore knew of his projected hiding-place.
Fortunately they had no idea when he was coming so nothing
daunted he used the place to assemble the pinnaces which he
had brought out from England in sections for shallow water
work. Then he sailed westwards along the coast to his victim
port.

The descent upon Nombre de Dios was a 'commando raid'
reflecting very detailed planning and brilliant in its execution.
Exactly two months after they had left Plymouth they
anchored out of sight behind a promontory to the east of the
harbour and launched their pinnaces. Then on 28 July 1572, in
the small hours and by the light of the moon, Drake led his
men into the sleeping town. 'I have brought you to the mouth
of the Treasure House of the world', he told them; that they

were now to leave it empty-handed was due to bad luck. His piecing together of information beforehand had given him a precise knowledge of the place albeit he had never set foot in it. He knew just where the battery would be and the lone gunner on night duty was rapidly seized and his guns heaved over on to the beach. Drake had meanwhile sent his brother John and John Oxenham off to attack the town from the opposite side and so create a diversion. He knew just where the Spaniards would put up some resistance – in the market-place, but after a brief encounter they joined the majority, who had fled at the first alarm into the hills.

Unerringly Drake led his men into the treasure-house. It was stacked high with bars of silver, the like of which they had never before seen, but at the moment he would not let them touch them. To the governor's house, he cried, where the gold was – but at that moment a tropical thunderstorm broke and the attackers were forced to shelter, a tantalizing half-hour's delay, so as not to let their bow-strings and musket primings get wet. When it stopped they had lost valuable time and knew that not only were the Spaniards massing for a counter-attack but – so their Cimaroons told them – had sent post-haste for reinforcements from Panama. So to the governor's house they dashed, as if they had had a street map before them; but it was empty – the Spaniards had kept the gold in Panama. And at that precise moment, to the horror of his men, Drake collapsed from loss of blood. He had been wounded in the leg earlier in the action but had given no sign. Without their captain they could not and would not go on; his horrified men carried him to the boats and, although once he regained consciousness he protested vehemently, they conveyed him on board *Pasco*.

Fortunately his iron constitution soon effected a recovery; the Spanish governor sent an officer out in a boat ostensibly to enquire after his health, but in reality to report back whether the English were so weakened as to be easy prey. The officer also asked what cure they could advise for poisoned arrow wounds, as they understood the English arrows were poisoned and a number of Spaniards had been hurt. To this Drake answered indignantly that he was Captain Francis Drake and no poisoner. The Spanish officer returned to the governor and reported that, far from being weak, the English were in first-class fighting spirit and their captain well on the way to recovery.

His Cimaroon allies now told Drake the sad truth; there would be no more treasure until the arrival of the *flota* early in the New Year. Lesser men would have been daunted and turned for home; not so Drake. He told his men they would wait and that meanwhile he would take a party of some half their number and reconnoitre the whole Isthmus with the aid of their Cimaroon guides, going to the outskirts of Panama itself and finding out exactly where the mule-tracks ran and where were the most advantageous points to attack. The ships meanwhile would remain hidden and could be careened and repaired. Thus he would pass the intervening months.

So, by tortuous paths through the tropical forest his faithful allies led him until on 11 February 1573 they came to a tall tree crowning a ridge, in which the Cimaroons had cut notches for hand- and footholds. They invited Drake to climb it and from its summit pointed out to him the blue Caribbean waters of the Atlantic far to the north whence he had come, while to the south his eyes beheld for the first time the blue of the 'great South Sea', the famous Pacific which the Spaniards regarded as their private ocean. There he prayed 'Almighty God in his goodness to give him life and leave to sail once in an English ship upon that sea.' How his prayer was answered is the story of *Golden Hind*.

The Cimaroons led him to a distant view of Panama – they saw the treasure ships arriving from Peru, for the *flota* had by now come to Nombre de Dios. Drake planned a perfect surprise attack on a heavily laden mule-train but 'the gaff was blown' by one of his seamen who, full of brandy, reeled into the path of a lone Spanish horseman going in the opposite direction and he warned the captain of the mule-train that something was wrong. The latter wisely kept the mules with the gold and silver back so that when the English attacked they found only mules laden with bales of taffeta and silk. Worse still, the Spaniards now had a rough idea of where Drake was, but fortunately, owing to the impenetrable nature of the jungle, only a rough one. The English were still empty-handed and after so many dangers and so long a wait it was demoralizing for them.

To keep up their spirits Drake planned a raid on Venta Cruces, the small port on the Rio Chagres where the bulkier cargoes were embarked for the second stage of their journey, but although ably executed it did not provide much treasure. Again many Spaniards fled and Drake, with that 'born courtesy' which Queen Elizabeth so much admired in her men of Devon, made a point of calling on the frightened ladies left behind and assuring them that he would do them no ill. The sight of this stocky, red-faced English heretic in the middle of the Isthmus of Panama must have been a profound shock for any respectable daughter of Spain.

The English now withdrew towards the north coast and their ship – for *Swan* had been sunk deliberately by Drake as an unwanted encumbrance. At last, in the very outskirts of Nombre de Dios itself, fortune favoured them. He had been joined by a Huguenot captain, Le Testu, from Le Havre and his crew, burning for revenge on the Catholics for the massacre of St Bartholomew's Day in 1572. Now they made a joint attack on the mule-train as it approached Nombre de Dios on the last stage of its long journey from Panama. Great quantities of gold and silver fell into the hands of English and French, more than they could carry; some had to be buried. But meanwhile the Spaniards from the *flota* counter-attacked; Le Testu was wounded and had to be left behind with one of his crew to care for him. The Spaniards killed him where he lay and his faithful henchman was put to death with barbaric cruelty.

Meanwhile Oxenham had been attacking the coasters bringing treasure from other parts of the Spanish main to load aboard the *flota* so that *Pasco* already had a fair cargo. The three pinnaces carried in her now proved their worth, for their shallow draught enabled them to negotiate shoal water where larger ships could not go. Drake had used them to penetrate the little Rio San Francisco, twenty miles from Nombre de Dios, in support of his attack on the mule-train. Attacked by the Spaniards from the *flota*, however, they were forced to put to sea in heavy weather; they did not know where Drake was, nor what had happened to *Pasco*. Somehow he must rejoin them and direct them to the parent ship. He did so by superb seamanship, building a raft in great haste and sailing it along the coast aided by one of his crew and two Huguenots. When he eventually came aboard the pinnaces he showed his men a long face, so that they assumed that all their efforts had been in vain, but suddenly a smile lit up his rugged countenance and he pulled a piece of gold from his pocket, showing it to them all – and it was at this juncture that he made his now famous remark 'Thank God, our voyage is made'.

The rest of the treasure was loaded on board and Oxenham went ashore to collect the buried part and minister to Le Testu, only to meet a couple of Huguenot seamen who told him of their captain's death – they had stayed with him as long as they dared but fled before final massacre. With their help Oxenham dug up the buried treasure and returned with it to the ship. Drake, however, realized that *Pasco* was not seaworthy enough to attempt the long voyage back to England so deeply laden with King Philip's wealth. The enemy could supply his wants so he captured a Spanish frigate, sent her crew ashore, transferred his cargo and his flag and abandoned *Pasco*. He broke up the pinnace and gave her ironwork to the Cimaroons to make arrow-heads, as part of their reward for very valuable assistance. Before he did so, however, Drake, with that 'rakish gaiety' described by a modern author, decided to have one more impudent fling at the Spaniards. He sailed east along the Main and trailed his coat before the chief port and strongest castle, Cartagena, sailing past close in to the fort, silken pennants streaming, St George's flag at the topmast – and, cruellest shaft of all, not in *Pasco* but in a captured Spanish ship!

He returned to the Isthmus for a final share-out with the Huguenots. Spanish accounts estimate the booty taken as worth £40,000 and he gave half to his French allies who, well-pleased, set course for La Rochelle. Meanwhile Drake, leaving the Isthmus astern, sailed out via the Florida Channel west of Cuba and from there, with most favourable winds, made a very rapid passage, twenty-three days in all, to the Scillies. Then he had to tack up Channel against an easterly, but with his supreme sense of dramatic timing sailed into Plymouth Sound on Sunday morning, 9 August 1573, just at service time, when most of the population were listening to the sermon in St Andrew's. A watcher on the Hoe sped to the church and whispered the news – in a trice it was round like a flash – 'Drake is back!' – and the congregation unceremoniously ran out, so that 'few or none remained with the preacher'.

They hurried up on to the Hoe, as the unfamiliar looking ship with the foreign rig but with St George's flag at the main topmast and the pennants streaming in the east wind, came close-hauled up the Sound towards the Cattewater and cheer upon cheer echoed down upon her as she passed below, while the stocky figure on the poop deck waved in return and ordered his cannon to fire, so that they echoed back from the Hoe and Mount Batten and from the distant cliffs of Mount Edgcumbe. Drake was home, acclaimed at once as the popular hero throughout the westcountry and indeed through much of the rest of England as well; but to the queen's government in London, now bent on turning hot war with Spain into cold, his arrival just at this juncture, laden with Spanish booty, was an embarrassment in the extreme.

Fortunately for Drake he had plenty of friends to warn him of his danger. The Spanish ambassador was out for his blood. Those who wished him well warned him to disappear quickly. So the treasure was brought ashore for safe-keeping and somehow the captain quietly vanished. If he could appear and disappear at will in the Panamanian jungles, why not in his native westcountry? The great mystery was and is exactly where he went. He certainly left Plymouth; Saltash was too close, but there were plenty of places in his native part of west Devon, between Dartmoor and the Tamar, where the inquisitive were scarcely likely to penetrate. Four hundred years later it is still something of an unknown hinterland in metropolitan eyes; in Elizabethan times, when the Gubbins tribe held sway and Lydford Law prevailed, it was as remote as the moon. Did Mary Newman go with him? It seems likely that she did, as there is no record of her being molested by the agents of the Spanish ambassador in Drake's absence.

Certainly he turned up in Ireland in 1575 and saw service under Walter, Earl of Essex, both in Antrim and further south, when that turbulent country, as so often before and since, was

33

being used by a hostile continental power as a spring-board for an attack against England. Stow wrote in his *Annaels* 'immediately after his return [from Nombre de Dios] he furnished at his own propper charge three friggots with men, and munition, and served voluntarily in Ireland under Walter, Earl of Essex, where he did excellent service, both by sea and land, at the winning of divers strong forts.' It seems that when in the south Drake lay in wait in his ships in the creek still known as 'Drake's Pool', near Cork, ready to pounce upon any Spanish vessel trying to sneak into Irish waters. From this southern coast of Ireland, so similar in its indented fjords to the wooded estuaries of his home, he could conveniently keep in touch with Devon and thus learn what was stirring in international politics.

Philip II had his hands full in the Netherlands and did not yet want to go to war with England, though his long-term strategy never wavered – to restore all Europe to Catholicism and with it the kingdom that had once been his but had now utterly rejected him and all he stood for, espousing the outlook and beliefs of his wife's half-sister. As for Elizabeth, she wanted peace to establish herself more firmly. For the last few years she had had a tiresome guest on her hands in the shape of Mary, Queen of Scots, who, though driven from her own country and coming to England as a refugee, was yet the centre of a succession of Catholic plots. Philip of Spain was behind most if not all of these, which grew in intensity if not in sophistication as the years progressed; but for the time being these royal opponents played the game of international chess which a modern statue in the Tate Gallery, London, so well portrays.

English expeditions in the wake of Drake and Hawkins were for the time being few; those that did reach the Spanish Main found themselves summarily executed as pirates. Meanwhile the scientists and geographers were declaiming that there was another way to the riches of the orient which did not require Englishmen to brave the hazards of Spanish waters – by seeking a way round the north-east of Asia or the north-west of America, they said, for they were sure there were passages in both places if only they could be found. The astronomer, geographer and alchemist Dr John Dee was in the fore-front of these urgings. Navigators like John Davis of Devon and Martin Frobisher of Yorkshire listened eagerly to what he propounded.

So for a couple of years apparent stalemate reigned between England and Spain and Drake lay low, while the star of the queen's new favourite rose higher and higher. He was an almost exact contemporary of Drake, though a man of very different background and from a very different part of England; yet their fortunes were to be closely linked together for their own and their country's benefit and it was from the crest on this man's arms that Drake was to draw the inspiration which led him to name the world's most famous ship.

4

Hatton of Holdenby

In the rolling wooded country north-west of the city of Northampton stands Holdenby, crowning a hilltop from which ridges fall steeply, commanding a vista of wood and field. Here, in the year before Drake was born in Tavistock, Alice Hatton presented her husband with a son who was baptized Christopher in the lonely church which stands on the plateau west of the manor-house. The church contains the tombs of the Holdenbys including that of Elizabeth, who married Henry Hatton and so brought Holdenby to its most famous holders. On the wall of the Church is the pedigree, stretching back to Philip de Holdenby who died in 1211. Fuller, in his *Worthies of Northamptonshire* wrote 'Sir Christopher Hatton was born (I collect at Holdenby) in the county, of a family rather ancient than wealthy, yet of no mean estate.' Indeed the Hattons, if the heralds sent to trace Sir Christopher's ancestry are to be believed, were of equal if not greater antiquity than the Holdenbys. Fuller himself, in his *Worthies of Cheshire*, speaks of 'Hugh de Hatton. King William the Conqueror bestowed lands on one of his name and ancestors at Hatton in this county.' In Fuller's day the grant of these lands by the Conqueror was still in possession of Sir Christopher Hatton, KB, first Baron Hatton of Kirby, 'preserved in our civil wars, with great care and difficulty, by his virtuous lady'.

Certainly they could trace their descent from Piers Hatton

of Quisty Birches in Cheshire, whose son Henry Hatton married Elizabeth Holdenby, sister of William Holdenby, whose incised portrait may still be seen on a grave-slab in Holdenby Church. So the Hattons became the lords of Holdenby and Henry died in the ancient manor-house in 1511. The arms of the Hattons were three gold sheaves on a blue ground – azure, three garbs or – and their cognizance or crest a sprightly golden hind – a hind statant or, in the heralds' parlance. In a window in Long Stanton Church near Cambridge may be seen a memorial to 'Henry Hatton of Holdenby, d. 1511' surmounted by the golden hind. From the union of Henry and Elizabeth sprang three sons, the second of whom, John, only survived his father by about fifteen years; he married Joan Westby and they had two sons, William, father of Christopher, and John, from whom descended the long line of Hattons of Long Stanton. William Hatton married twice; there were no children of his first marriage to Mary Holdenby, but by his second, to Alice Saunders, he had three sons and a daughter. Francis, the eldest, died young, and Christopher, born in 1540, was to lead the family to its greatest fame. Through him too the name of the golden hind was to become the symbol of English seamanship and daring, familiar to posterity the world over. The remaining two children were Thomas Hatton and a sister, Dorothy.

Here in the Northamptonshire hills Christopher grew up as a typical country squire's son. His father, William Hatton, died when he was only seven and his education was largely entrusted to his mother's brother, William Saunders. When he was fifteen Christopher matriculated as a gentleman commoner of St Mary's Hall, Oxford, the principal of which was William Allen, later to become a cardinal and to earn the detestation of the Protestants, including Hatton himself. Initially however Christopher may have been brought up as a Catholic; he was always more tolerant of Catholics than many other great men at Elizabeth's court, though later events were to make him a strong upholder of the Protestant faith. Four years after he had entered Oxford, on 26 May 1560, when he was twenty, Hatton became a member of the Inner Temple. Fuller, with gentle humour, observed 'He rather took a *bait* than made a *meal* at the inns of court, whilst he studied the laws therein.'

Christopher Hatton was no dry pedantic student; he knew how to enjoy himself, taking part in dances and dramatic productions. So accomplished was he that he was appointed Master of the Game for the Christmas festival held in the Temple in 1561 and on Twelfth Night, 6 January 1562, he took part in the *Tragedy of Gorboduc* written by Thomas Sackville, which was presented at the Inner Temple. News of this highly successful production reached the ears of the queen herself, who immediately commanded that it be performed again before her, and this was duly done twelve days later, on 18 January, in the Palace of Whitehall, with Hatton again taking part. Fuller describes how, 'He came afterwards to court in a mask, where the queen first took notice of him, loving him well for his handsome dancing, better for his proper person and best of all for his great abilities.'

Elizabeth was then twenty-nine years of age, at the height of her splendidly mature young womanhood. She had been on the throne four years and was still basking in the adoration of her delighted subjects, released from fear after the years of Marian oppression, enjoying the greater security of her own position after her years of disregard and danger. Now her eye fell upon an attractive and accomplished young man, personable and physically fit, twenty-two years of age – 'one of the goodliest persons in England', as Nicholas Hilliard, the Exeter miniaturist, described him. Hatton's foot was on the first rung of the ladder to success and he was appointed a gentleman pensioner shortly after he first met the queen.

In the early summer of 1564 she ordered her master of armoury to make Christopher a complete suit of armour, prudently adding that it should be delivered to him when he paid for it. She may also have had an eye to the future, that the young man should appear at his best when on her service. In September of that year she entrusted him with the first of many duties connected with the Scottish crown, which were to involve tragedy as well as pageantry – on this occasion to welcome Sir James Melville, ambassador from Mary, Queen of Scots, on his arrival in England.

Hatton's accomplishments were by no means confined to dancing and acting, for he was as professional in the saddle as in the galliard. On 11 November 1565 he performed before the queen in the tilt-yard at Westminster to her great satisfaction. The occasion was the marriage of the Earl of Warwick, Ambrose Dudley, brother of the queen's favourite Robert, Earl of Leicester, to Lady Anne Russell. The queen noted Hatton's horsemanship with approval and decided to put it to good use ere long. Shortly before Christmas 1566 he was appointed to the second of his Scottish assignments. This was to go to Stirling as a member of the delegation representing Queen Elizabeth at the christening of Mary's infant son James, the future James I of England and Elizabeth's successor.

It might have been supposed that Hatton would be on his best behaviour – Melville had gone to meet him at Coldingham, near Berwick, and all honour had been shown him, but like many young Elizabethan hotheads he took offence at a fancied slight; soon after his arrival in Stirling he thought he detected an uncomplimentary allusion in a masque performed before Queen Mary. To smooth his ruffled plumage she made him a gift of a charm containing her picture.

After his return to England Hatton had the satisfaction of seeing the play *Tancred and Gismund*, of which he had written the fourth act, performed before Queen Elizabeth. His relations with his royal mistress were getting closer and signs of her favour were more frequently bestowed. In April 1568 she gave him the site of the former abbey and the demesne lands at Sulby in his own county of Northampton and leased Holdenby to him. In July came an appointment as keeper of the royal park at Eltham in Kent. Further grants followed in 1569, in which year he became a justice of the peace for Northamptonshire.

Shortly afterwards he became the Queen's Remembrancer of the Exchequer and was given an inn named 'The Ship' near Temple Bar – by an odd coincidence the same name as that of Drake's favourite inn in Exeter. Lands and wardships continued to come his way, as far apart as Yorkshire, Herefordshire and Dorset, the latter being a county with which he was to have particularly close associations. In April 1571 he was returned as member of parliament for Higham Ferrers, Northamptonshire and the next year as a knight of the shire for his native county. May 1572 was marked by further evidence of the royal confidence; he was appointed Captain of the Queen's Guard and secondly a Gentleman of the Privy Chamber. The same month he was sent to Sheffield to examine Mary, Queen of Scots, who four years before had taken refuge in England and it was while on this assignment that he met and apparently conceived a passion for Elizabeth Cavendish, daughter of the formidable 'Bess of Hardwick', Countess of Shrewsbury, but because of the queen's opposition nothing came of it. 1572 also saw the grant to him of the famous Corfe Castle in Dorset, 'the Key to the Isle of Purbeck'. In July he accompanied the queen on a 'progress' to Theobalds House in Hertfordshire.

Just as 1572 was an important year for Drake, so it was for Hatton. From that year dated the correspondence which began to flow between him and Elizabeth, growing more intimate as the months went by. Evidence of the queen's affection was often to be shown in her visits to those of her courtiers who were ill – Burghley and Walsingham were both honoured in this way – and when Hatton fell seriously ill with suspected kidney trouble, the queen came to visit him. So ill was he that his doctors ordered him to take the waters at Spa in the Low Countries; he took his leave of his royal mistress in person on 3 June 1573 and left England two days later. On the very day of his departure he wrote her a passionate epistle, using the cipher believed to denote her nickname for him – her 'Lids'. Elizabeth was fond of bestowing nicknames on her favourites – Leicester for example being her 'Eyes' and Hatton sometimes her 'Lids', sometimes her 'Mutton'.

> If I could express my feelings of your gracious letters [he wrote] I should utter unto you matter of strange effect. In reading of them, with my tears I blot them. In thinking of them I feel so great comfort that I find cause, as Lord knoweth, to thank you on my knees. The time of 2 days hath drawn me further from you than ten, when I return, can lead me towards you. Madam, I find the greatest lack

Within the print, at lower right:

Habes, Lector, candide, fortiff. ac inuictiff. Ducis Draech ad viuum Imaginem qui tote terrarum orbes, dicorum ambitum, et, menfium decem fpatio, Zephiro fauen: tibus, circumduxit, Angliam fedes proprias, 4. Cal Octobr: anno à partu Virgi: nit 1580 reuifit cum antea portu foluiffet ji. Decem: anni 1577.

A print attributed to J. Hondius showing Sir Francis Drake at about the age of forty-three

Hilliard's miniature of Queen Elizabeth I

Opposite The Hondius map showing the voyages of Drake and Cavendish round the world. Drake's voyage is marked by the line of smaller dots

Above left William Cecil, First Baron Burghley, Lord High Treasurer. The painting is attributed to Gheeraedts

Left Sir John Hawkins, painted by an unknown artist

Below The *Jesus of Lübeck* (left), one of the six ships commanded by Sir John Hawkins on the 1567 Caribbean voyage in which Drake participated

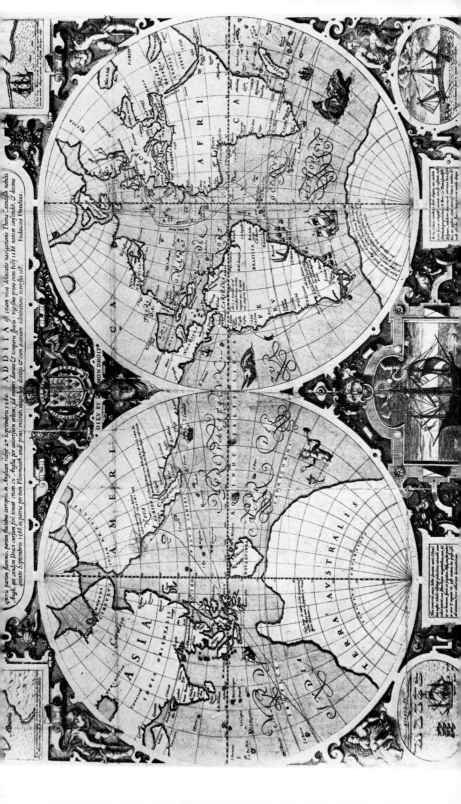

Sir Christopher Hatton, Drake's friend and patron, in honour of whom *Pelican* was renamed *Golden Hind*. This portrait was painted when he was Lord Chancellor in 1589

Details of the Hatton memorials in the church at Long Stanton, Cambridgeshire, showing the family crest, the hind, after which Drake named his ship

Henry Hatton
of
Holdenby d 1511

Right The silver model of the *Golden Hind* in Buckland Abbey

Below right The *Golden Hind* taking the *Cacafuego*, the Spanish treasure ship (shown as *Caca Plata* and *Caca Fogo* respectively in the picture), off Cape Francisco, South America

Bottom A modern watercolour (sepia) of the *Golden Hind* by Gregory Robinson as it must have looked during the circumnavigation

Opposite above Drake in California, from De Bry's *Grand Voyages*. The inscribed plaque is being set up in the background

Opposite below Drake in New Albion as pictured by De Bry

The inscribed plaque which Drake left in New Albion

The *Golden Hind* is towed into harbour by the ruler of Ternate's ships. Detail from a map of the circumnavigation by Nicola van Sype, *c* 1581

that ever poor wretch sustained. No death, no, not hell, no
fear of death shall ever win of me my consent so far to
wrong myself again as to be absent from you one day. . . .
Pardon (for God's sake) my tedious writing. It doth much
diminish (for the time) my great griefs. I will wash away the
faults of these letters with the drops from your poor Lydds
and so inclose them. Would God I were with you for but
one hour. My wits are overwrought with thoughts. I find
myself amazed. Bear with me, my most dear sweet lady.
Passion overcometh me. I can write no more. Love me; for
I love you. God, I beseech thee witness the same on the
behalf of thy poor servant. Live for ever. Shall I utter thus
familiar terms (farewell)? Yea, ten thousand thousand fare-
wells. He speaketh it that most dearly loveth you. I hold you
too long. I crave pardon, and so bid your own poor Lidds
farewell. 1573 June.

   Your bondman everlastingly tied, CH. HATTON.

Was this *amour courtois*, the infatuation of a younger man for
a mature, brilliant woman who was also his queen, or did it be-
token physical love? Mary, Queen of Scots and others of
Elizabeth's enemies thought and said the latter. But while not
many of Elizabeth's admirers wrote so openly and passionate-
ly, there is no proof whatever of any physical affair.

   Ten days later Hatton wrote from Antwerp:

This is the twelfth day since I saw the brightness of that
Sun that giveth light to my sense and soul. Madam, I have
received great honour in these Countries for the love they
bear you, or rather that fear of your greatness. . . . But
Madam, forget not your Lidds that are so often bathed with
tears for your sake. A more wise man may seek you, but a
more faithful and worthy can never have you.

and this was signed:

   'Yours all and ever yours, CH. HATTON.'

   After his arrival at Spa he wrote, referring to his other nickname:

   'Your Mutton is black; scarcely will you know your own,
so much hath this disease dashed me' and signed it again with

41

one of his ciphers. This was evidently written in the depths of physical depression but on 10 August there was some improvement for he wrote:

'My dear lady, I amend.... I find cause to think that much greater effects will flow ... upon the knees of my heart I most humbly commend my most faithful love and desire unto you' and signed it 'Your Lyddes'.

He was back in England in the autumn, where an unpleasant surprise awaited him and two of his friends. A fanatical Puritan student of the Middle Temple, named Peter Purchet, who described Hatton as 'a wilful Papist' who 'hindered the glory of God so much as in him lies' lay in wait near Temple Bar to murder him.

Sure enough along came two gentlemen on horseback and he dashed out with dagger raised, striking at the nearest one, thinking it was Hatton. But it was not Hatton who was severely, though not fatally, wounded, but none other than Drake's kinsman John Hawkins as he was riding towards Westminster with his fellow sea-captain Sir William Winter.

Next year Elizabeth Cavendish, whom Hatton had coveted, was married to the Earl of Lennox, Darnley's younger brother. Hatton, together with Leicester and the other members of the royal household, attended the queen on her lengthy progress westwards to the city of Bristol. Her favour was now shown very clearly. Christopher needed a town house and cast his eyes on Ely Place, near Holborn; it occupied a pleasant site on a gentle slope overlooking a stream and was noted for its gardens and strawberry beds. The latter indeed figure in Shakespeare's *Richard III* in which the Bishop of Ely is sent to procure more strawberries while the King disposes of Hastings. The Bishop of Ely's town house remained part of Cambridgeshire; the incumbent in Hatton's time was Bishop Cox and when he objected to granting him part of the lease the queen settled the matter in her typically forthright manner, writing: 'Proud Prelate! I understand you are backward in complying with your agreement, but I would have you know that I who made you what you are can unmake you; and if you do not forthwith fulfil your engagement, by God I will immediately unfrock you. Elizabeth.'

So Hatton acquired half the lands of Ely Place and his name is perpetuated there still in Hatton Wall and Hatton Garden; where his part of the garden met that of the bishop stood a cherry tree. Close to it arose the tavern called 'The.Mitre', built chiefly for the benefit of Hatton's servants and in it to this day may be seen the preserved trunk of the cherry tree.

He also had his eyes on a fitting house in his native county in which to entertain his royal mistress, as he fondly hoped. In 1575 he acquired from Sir Humphrey Stafford the fine Kirby Hall, standing in the gentle undulating country near Gretton, for £400, and promptly set about enlarging and embellishing it. Other Northamptonshire manors came his way; while in Dorset in addition to his holding of Corfe Castle and the Isle of Purbeck, he acquired the castle of Brownsea at the seaward end of the island commanding the entrance to Poole Harbour from which he could and did levy a lucrative toll on shipping.

Early the following year Hatton was appointed a member of a parliamentary committee investigating a speech made in the Commons by a Cornish member, the Puritan Peter Wentworth, sitting for Tregony near Truro, who as a result was committed to the Tower. Hatton, however, was employed on the first of those errands of mercy and kindness for which he was to become famous, when the queen sent him to Wentworth as bearer of a gracious message from her 'remitting her justly occasioned displeasure'. Over the years numerous supplicants for Hatton's favours and intercession bear witness to his unfailing kindness and readiness to listen to and help those in misfortune, even those whom his own eloquent advocacy had brought to book.

The same year Drake returned from his self-imposed exile in Ireland; the climate was healthier now for him and the Nombre de Dios expedition was no longer held against him. While in Ireland he had formed a close friendship with Thomas Doughty, a gentleman of some influence with the Earl of Essex who had also at one stage been employed by Hatton as his secretary.

A more dissimilar pair than Drake and Doughty it would be hard to find – the one a ruddy-cheeked farmer's son, the other a polished, well-read, university-educated, Italianate man of the world. For some time Drake had been toying with the idea of an expedition to enter the 'closed ocean', the Pacific, which he had seen from the tree-top in Panama, and trounce the Spaniards really hard, but he needed the queen's approval and far greater financial backing than he could command. He confided his ideas to Doughty who saw in them a chance of personal advancement, particularly if people of great consequence, not excluding the queen, could be made to back the project. The trouble was that basically Doughty was Lord Burghley's man and the lord treasurer had no stomach for Drake's activities. He was at pains not to go to war with Spain and not to undermine the prospects of England's trade by privateering. Even if higher authority decreed that the expedition should go forward he would need his agents to prevent it being too successful; Doughty saw all this and realized that he fitted the role perfectly, but meanwhile it was in his interests to get the voyage approved. He therefore sought out Christopher Hatton and introduced Francis Drake to him.

This was a momentous occasion. From it stemmed a circumnavigation and the naming of the most famous ship in the world. The two men, so different in their backgrounds, took an immediate liking to each other. Their chief interest in common lay in the fortune of England and in the queen they both served; apprehension of the designs of the king of Spain also bound them together and they shared a directness of purpose and clarity of vision. The upshot of the interview was that Hatton mentioned Drake's presence and ideas to the queen and it was arranged that he should be ushered into the royal presence. So the Devon sea-captain knelt before Queen Elizabeth; her firm, blue-eyed gaze encountered his. She liked his sturdy, bluff build, his red cheeks, his burr. Here was the uncomplicated man of action she sought.

'Drake,' she said immediately, 'I would fain be revenged upon the King of Spain for divers injuries he has done me' and went on to enlarge upon the theme. 'Your Grace,' Drake rejoined, 'it is not possible to attack him in Spain; he must be annoyed in his Indies.' It did not take long to convince Elizabeth that here was the man to do the annoying but she made it clear to him that in the present state of politics and national unpreparedness he was on his own and that she must if needs be disown him. He accepted this without a flicker. So a plan for his voyage was drawn up 'but of all men my Lord Treasurer must not learn of this', said the queen, with her clear insight into the characters and ways of man. She herself would supply a ship for the venture and the rest of the small syndicate which stood to gain heavily if the voyage were a success consisted of Drake himself, Christopher Hatton, Leicester, the Winter brothers, the Earl of Lincoln, Lord Admiral, Walsingham and Hawkins. It might indeed have been Hatton himself instead of Drake who led the expedition. In 1575 the then Spanish ambassador, De Gueras de Spes, had reported to King Philip preparations for just such a venture, led by none other than Christopher Hatton, but he drew consolation from his personality – 'Hatton was such a good gentleman that they would certainly do no harm with his consent' – and he was sure that the sole intention of the voyage would be to trade with the Indies. Unfortunately for the king of Spain the proposals came to nothing and of the two friends who might have led the expedition it was Drake not Hatton who was to present himself on an unsuspecting Pacific coast.

In the interim another colourful figure had offered himself as the potential leader of an expedition to discover the supposed continent which geographers called *Terra Australis* that was thought to lie not where Australia in fact does but to extend from the Antarctic right up to the southernmost tip of South America. This was none other than Sir Richard Grenville, one of the richest men in the westcountry, member of an ancient aristocratic family of north Cornwall and north Devon; his ancestral home was at Stowe, in a combe leading inland from the fearsome Atlantic coast, not far from the Cornish-Devon border near the village of Kilkhampton, in whose church his family tombs lay. The family also had a house at Bideford, while Sir Richard was married to an acknowledged beauty of the St Leger family from Annery House beside the Torridge, between Bideford and Torrington.

After the Dissolution of the Monasteries the famous and

formerly rich abbey of Buckland had been granted to Sir Richard's father, another Sir Richard, by King Henry VIII. Buckland Abbey lay in a lateral combe and bowl of the hills on the east bank of the Tavy, some three miles downstream from Drake's birthplace. It had been founded in 1273 by Amicia de Clare, Countess of Devon, for the Cistercian Order and during the Middle Ages it vied with Tavistock as a centre both of religious life and mercantile activity. To this abbey, across the wastes of southern Dartmoor, ran the Abbot's Way, a faint and at times indecipherable track marked here and there by granite crosses to guide the befogged and benighted, by which churchmen and merchants found their way from Buckfast Abbey on the east of the moor to Buckland and Tavistock on the opposite side. There it stood, its great square transeptal tower dominating the church set against the hillside, and behind it the splendid tithe barn into which the monks carefully garnered the produce of west Devon. In 1576 Grenville set about converting it into a mansion, as he needed a country seat nearer Plymouth as a base for his operations. He filled the former church right up to the chancel arch with two floors and in the hall on the ground floor caused a splendid plaster ceiling and frieze to be installed. But his restless spirit was craving for something more exciting than the business of a Devon squire and so he went to the queen with his plea for a licence to discover *Terra Australis* and colonize it. Elizabeth granted him his licence and full of hope he returned to Buckland and started to fit out his ships in Plymouth, but the unpredictable queen, for reasons of her own, as suddenly withdrew the licence. The mortified Grenville was forced to sell his ships again and caused his decorator to embellish the west wall of the hall at Buckland with a motif of the warrior with his arms at peace.

Grenville was then some forty-three years of age, tall, handsome, hot-tempered, with a fierce look in his eyes; as the scion of an old west country family he regarded Drake as a bumptious upstart. The latter, now thirty-six, was 'low of stature, thick-set and very robust; he has a fine countenance, is ruddy of complexion and has a fair beard.' These two, both good westcountry men, were each representative of their social class; they might not get on personally, but they were both devoted servants of the queen. It was on Drake that her favour now shone and preparations for his voyage went ahead all through the spring and summer of 1577. The flagship should be no cumbersome, lumbering galleon like the *Jesus of Lübeck*, which had proved herself unwieldy in the supreme moment of danger, but a lean, fast ship of the new design which Hawkins had learnt from the French and the Portuguese and was even then using every effort to get the Navy Board to accept as the backbone of the queen's navy. Drake's flagship must be a vessel which would handle well, outsail the Spaniards and be well armed so as to inflict maximum damage in a swift, glancing attack.

An inspiration to the voyage itself and indeed to all those of Elizabethan navigators venturing into unknown seas came from the 'Welsh wizard', the scientist, astronomer and geographer Dr John Dee. At his house in Mortlake he delighted to receive the great seamen of the age, Drake included, and fill them with his ideas of *Terra Australis*, the North-East Passage round the coast of Russia to China and the North-West Passage between Greenland and the Americas which led to Asia the other way. He looked for a golden future when a British empire ('British' not 'English', he fiercely insisted as a good Welshman) would cover as much of the globe as did those of Spain and Portugal. Among those who followed the teachings of Dee and went in search of the North-West Passage was a navigator who was no Devonian indeed but an obstinate, cantankerous Yorkshireman – Martin Frobisher – and on 8 June 1576 he sailed off in an attempt to discover it. His voyage took him into the bays and sounds round Baffin Island and in honour of his friend Christopher he bestowed the name 'Hatton Headland' on one of its capes. Even more personal satisfaction for Hatton was now at hand.

As Drake's final preparations were being made, a few days before his fleet sailed from Plymouth, Elizabeth and her court were at Windsor Castle where, on 11 November 1577, 'this day Chr. Hatton Esquire Captain of her Majesty's Guard was

5

To the coast of Barbary

Drake's expedition had been delayed till the autumn. The weather in the Western Approaches was often bad at that season, but he reasoned that they would soon be out of it, sailing into blue water further south. At last all the months of preparation were complete and his fleet was ready.

The said Capitaine *Francis Drake* having in a former voyage in the yeares 72 and 73 having had a sight, and onely a sight, of the South *Atlantic* [sic – the Pacific is meant] and thereupon either conceiving a new, or renewing a former desire, of sailing on the same in an English bottom, and with the help of divers friends adventurers, he had fitted himself with five ships.

These were:

the *Pellican*, admirall, burthen 100 tonnes, Captaine-generall *Francis Drake*
the *Elizabeth*, vise-admirall, burthen 80 tonnes, Captain *John Winter*
the *Marigold*, a bark of 30 tonnes, Captain *John Thomas*
the *Swanne*, a fliboat of 50 tonnes, Captain *John Chester*
the *Christopher*, a pinnace of 15 tonnes, Captain *Thomas Moone.*

In Tudor fashion the name 'admiral' was applied to the ship

whereas nowadays we would say 'flagship' and apply the title to the officer. The dimensions, albeit their modern equivalents would be higher – the *Pellican/Golden Hind* is now estimated at about one hundred and fifty tons – yet show what cockleshells they were thus to venture into the unknown. Not that Drake's officers and men yet had an inkling of what was his intended destination. John Cooke of the *Marigold*, whose narrative displays a strong anti-Drake bias, wrote 'the xx of novembre in the year above written Francys Drake, John Winter, Thomas Doughty and several companions and friendly gentlemen in a fleet of five ships ... departed Plimouth onto his pretended voyage for Alexandria and had for that place made wages with his men.' Francis Fletcher, the flagship's chaplain spoke of 'setting our course for the frette of Jubolter under pretence to travel to Alexandria'. In modern parlance, Drake's sailing orders were secret and he did not intend to disclose them to his crews – and even less to his enemies or the king of Spain's spies. Whether any of those spies were present in the fleet is a subject on which controversy has raged ever since.

The five ships, ensigns and pennants flying, made a brave sight as they sailed out of the Sound 'about 5 of the clocke in the afternoone, November 15 of the same yeare' but Drake and the older seamen sniffed the wind and knew it was banking up for a real blow. However, 'running all that night Southwest, by the morning came as farre as the Lyzzard', but then the experts' predictions were all too drastically fulfilled. 'Meeting the wind at southwest, quite contrarie to our intended course, we were forced, with our whole fleet, to put into Falmouth,' wrote the chaplain – forced to turn in fact and run before the wind. But even the shelter of Pendennis and the Anchorage of Carrick Roads were not sufficient protection.

The next day [November 17th] towards evening, there arose a storme, continuing all that night and the day following (especially between 10 of the clocke in the forenoone and 5 in the afternoone) with such violence, that though it were in a very good harbour, yet two of our ships (viz. the admirall in which our generall himself went) and the Marigold were faine to cut their main masts by board, and for the repairing of them and many other damages in the tempest sustained (as soone as the weather would give leave), to beare back to Pimmouth againe, where we all arrived the thirteenth day [November 28th] after our first departure thence.

This was certainly an inauspicious start and the inhabitants of Plymouth shook their heads to see the fleet come trailing back into Sutton Harbour. Repairs took a fortnight; then, as the chaplain picturesquely put it, 'with happier sayles we once more put to sea, December 13th 1577'. It was exactly a month since their false start. The fleet was now in good shape, however; the total complement was 164 'able and sufficient men' and the equipment and stores were of the highest order. Drake 'furnished them also with such plentiful provisions of all things necessary as so long and dangerous a voyage did seeme to require; and amongst the rest, with certain pinnaces ready framed, but carried aboard in pieces, to be set up in smoother water, when occasion served.' This was the system which had proved so efficacious at Nombre de Dios.

Drake certainly did not intend to make it a Spartan voyage devoid of comforts.

Neither had he omitted to make provision also for ornament and delight, carrying to this purpose with him, expert musicians, rich furniture (all the vessels for his table, yea, many belonging even to the Cooke-roome being of pure silver) and divers shares of all sorts of workmanship, whereby the civilitie and magnificence of his native contrie might, amongst all nations whithersoever he should come, be the more admired.

The weather seemed to have got over its bad temper and they went ahead steadily, 'holding our way with a prosperous wind and good success in all things (one boy only, lost out of the bark Canter in the Bay of Portugal, excepted)'. John Cooke does not say who was the boy lost overboard from the 'caunter', another name for the 'pinnace' *Christopher*, but his was the first and youngest life sacrificed on the voyage.

Once out of sight of those tiresome landsmen who were likely to betray his plans Drake let fall at least a hint that their destination was not Alexandria. 'Our generall gave us reason to conjecture in part whither he intended, both by the directing of his course and appointing the *Rendezvous* (if any should be severed from the fleet) to be the iland *Mogadore*.' Mogador is in Morocco, south-west of Fez, off the mainland of Africa and therefore it was abundantly clear that they were not bound through the 'frette of Jubolter' into the Mediterranean. Rumour ran rife as to what Drake had in mind; the possibilities were limitless, but as yet no one dreamed of the true magic which lay ahead.

And so sailing with favourable winds, the first land that we had sight of was *Cape Cantine* in *Barbarie* December 25th, Christmas Day in the morning. The shore is fair white sand, and the inland contrie very high and mountainous; it lieth in 32 degrees 30 minutes north latitude, and so counting from hence southward about eighteen leagues we arrived the same day at *Mogadore*, the Iland before named.

This *Mogador* lies under the dominion of the King of *Fesse*, in 31 degrees 40 minutes, about a mile from the shoare, by this meanes making a good harbour between the land and it.

The Moorish king of Fez, seeing the fleet enter the sound between the island and the mainland, assumed it was Portuguese. 'Continuing along the coast of Barbarie, we sailed neere to the citty of *Lions*, which is sometimes said to have been a city of great fame' the legend being, the chaplain explained, that because of its great wickedness 'the Lord sent an army of Lyons upon it'. They sailed on and 'the next morning came in sight of Sophia, the chief port on that side of the land, from whence being discovered by the inhabitants afar off they sent out two shippes against us in all fast, if happily we had been whom they hoped for' – to wit the Portuguese, whom the king was expecting to come to his aid against his uncle, who had usurped his throne.

A westcountryman named John Fry, who had been to Morocco on an earlier trading voyage, 'had attayned to some use of the tongue' and now 'did sodainly but unadvisedly leap out of the boat on to the shoare' – 'unadvisedly' because the Moors seized him, 'inforcing him with a dagger sett to his breaste either to go with them or presentlye to dye'. Drake went ashore with a party of armed men to rescue him but the Moors hid from him and he decided to wait no longer.

Wherefore having made provision of wood, as also visited an old fort, built sometime by the king of *Portugall*, but was ruined by the king of *Fesse*, we departed, December 31st, towards Cape *Blanck*, in such sort that when Fry returned he found to his great grief that the fleet was gone; but yet, by the king's favour, he was sent home into *England* not long after in an English merchant ship.

The 'old fort' of the king of Portugal was a relic of those voyages, less than a century before, that Prince Henry the Navigator's pioneers had made down this perilous coast, then totally unknown to Europeans, as bit by bit they blazed the trail to the orient. Traditionally the point of no return had been Cape Boyador, beyond which the waters were said to bubble over the precipice at the end of the world and men walked with their heads beneath their shoulders. The Portuguese discoverers had given the lie to all that, but the coast remained inhospitable and little known to the white man.

Chaplain Fletcher remarked, as they sailed on southwards, that despite the heat a snow mountain was visible inland.

In the way sayling from Mogador to this place, upp in the countrye, did appeare a high and mighty spire, covered at topp with aboundance of snow as white as Salmon, which notwithstanding the country be exceeding hott, yet it seemeth never to be dissolved, because it reacheth so high into the cold and frozen region that the reflection of the sonn can never come to it from the face of the earth.

There followed a period of 'foulle weather' with adverse winds until 7 January 1578, when the ships passed Cape Guir or Rhir (which Fletcher rendered 'De Guerre') in 30 degrees 'where we lighted on three Spanish fishermen called *Caunters*, whom we took with our new pinnace and carried along with us till we came to *Rio del Oro* on January 13, just under the tropic of Cancer where with our pinnace also we took a cara-vell'. Two days later the *Marygold* captured another caravel off Cape Barbas. By this time the weather had improved and the chaplain was able to observe exultantly 'Now we coasting along for Cape Blank or White Cape had every sale at com-mand as if Neptune had been present, without any resistance or refusall or resisting'.

They were off the great cape on 16 January and it impressed them as it had the Portuguese before them. One version des-cribes it as 'showing itself upright like the corner of a wall, to them that come towards it from the North', this being the more remarkable since the land between Cape Barbas and Cape Blanc is low, flat and sandy. The chaplain's description is as usual more colourful: 'We found it so fair and stately, and the onely ornament of that land.' In the lee of the cape, where the ships anchored, they 'found certain Portugall ships, who continually, as in like case other nations divers, do frequent that place, abounding with infinite store and great variety of good fishe'. The Arabs called the cape *Aldjebel-allames*, or 'the Glittering Mountain'.

Drake decided to make a six days' stop here, to rest his crews and take aboard fresh provisions 'for their future supply at sea'. They then cleaned and trimmed all the ships and let their Spanish prizes go, 'excepting one *Caunter* (for which we gave the owner one of our own ships, viz the *Christopher*)'. Fair exchange is no robbery and as Drake transferred the name *Christopher* to the Spanish prize he kept he was no doubt satisfied with the exchange and also that his friend Hatton, after whom *Christopher* had been named, would approve. They also kept one of their Portuguese caravels, 'which was formerly bound to Saint *Iago*, which we caused to accompany us hither – that being Sao Tiago in the Cape Verde Islands, for which the English fleet set course from Cape Blanc on 21 January.

The Cape Verde Islands, lying west and south-west of Cape Verde on the African mainland near the River Gambia, were discovered by the Portuguese about 1460. That was the year of the death of Prince Henry the Navigator and the islands were donated to his adopted son and heir, Prince Fernando, by King Alfonso in 1462. The actual palm for discovery is disputed between the navigators Cadamosto and Diogo Gomez, the former claiming to have discovered the island of Sao Tiago or Santiago on St James's Day and to have given it his name. The first island they reached was Boa Vista, 'good to look upon', lying some three hundred miles out into the Atlantic from the Cape; Sao Tiago lies about eighty miles south-west of Boa Vista and the third major island of the extensive group, Sao Nicolau, about the same distance to the west. Sao Tiago was the first major one to be colonized by the Portuguese; the other principal ones are Maio and Fogo. The Portuguese had thus been there for just over a century when Drake's expedition came their way.

England and Portugal had been allied for two hundred years officially from 1373 but more effectively from the Treaty of Windsor in 1386 when Philippa of Lancaster, daughter of John of Gaunt, married Joao I of the House of Aviz. The 'ancient alliance' still exists, although it has undergone strains from time to time, and from the mid-sixteenth century to 1640 was one of the worst of these periods. Not only was English maritime expansion baulked by Portuguese dominion of much of the globe but Pope Alexander VI had ostensibly put a complete veto on colonization by other powers when he arrogantly declared in 1493 the known world to be divided between Spain and Portugal, the former to the west and the latter to the east of an imaginary line drawn some three hundred leagues to the west of Africa – an eleventh hour stipulation by Portugal having saved her from losing Brazil, discovered in 1500 by Pedro Alvares Cabral, to Spain. Spain was of course the main enemy in English eyes; the English saw however that the House of Aviz, which had ruled Portugal for two hundred years, was decaying, for its final representative was a celibate cardinal-king and on his death Philip II intended to snap up the Portuguese crown and its rich empire and fleet.

Drake therefore regarded himself as at liberty to capture Portuguese ships as well as Spanish, though he did not in fact make attacks on as many Portuguese towns as Spanish and left Brazil severely alone. How prescient he was can be seen by the fact that Philip had annexed Portugal before Drake's return to England. In 1589 Drake was to support Portuguese aspirations against Spain by his campaign at Peniche and Lisbon in aid of the claimant, Don Antonio. But now, six days after leaving Cape Blanc, the English ships coasted along Boa Vista and 'the next day after we came to anchor under the west part of the island *Maio*, it lyeth in 15 degrees'. They stayed there three days 'and passed by the Iland of *St Iago*, ten leagues west of *Maio* in the same latitude. . . . On the south-west of the Iland we took a Portugall, laden the best part with wine, and much good cloth, both linnen and woollen, besides other necessities, bound for Brazill.' This capture was of immense importance for Drake's voyage, for the pilot was Nuño da Silva, an expert on the route from Portugal to Brazil and well provided with nautical instruments and charts. Drake seized his person and his belongings, kept him on board for over a year, making him eat at his table so that the Spaniards described him as 'the English captain's all in all'. Nuño da Silva's log-book, which he kept throughout his voyage with Drake, succinct in the best seamanlike way, is a prime source of information and from his depositions in later years, when he had the misfortune to fall into the hands of the Inquisition, who suspected him of having turned heretic under English influence, we learn a great deal about life on board *Golden Hind* and about Drake and his crew.

Nuño da Silva had been a seaman all his life. He was a native of Lisbon, the son of a seaman, Alvaro Joannes, and of Joanna da Silva; his mother brought him up till he was eight when he shipped along with his uncle, Adam Fernandez, a pilot who took him to Brazil. Nuño later married in Portugal, making his home in Gaia, on the south bank of the Douro, facing Oporto, raising a family there and sailing regularly in the service of the king of Portugal on the run to Brazil. He was now in his fifties, described as of medium stature, of olive complexion and slightly greying hair. He wasted few words on his capture in his log-book: 'The nineteenth day of the month of January. The English took us, opposite Santiago, by force of gunfire. Our ship discharged four shots at them.'

This conceals the fact that his capture was not effected

without some difficulty. Chaplain Fletcher gave one of his typically graphic descriptions of what really befell at Sao Tiago:

> We coming to the southerly cape of this Iland, we discovered neare to the seasyde the towne of St James, with a castel and blockhouse, as it should seeme well mounted with ordinance; for two ships of Portugall being lately come forth of the harbour, bound for Brasilia in a merchant voyage, we sent our pinnis over to command them to repair to our fleet, and our pinnis recovering the one which was further off at the sea than the other, the castel applyed to the pinnis with great shott to defend the shipp that was next them till shee might gett into harborow, and reserve the other which was in our power; but wee brought it away without any harm don to our pinnis or men, being a shipp of Portugall laden with singular wines, solles and canaryes, with wollens and linen cloths, silken and velvetts, and many other good commodities which stood us in their stead, that shee was the life of the voyage, the neck whereof otherwise had been broken for the shortness of our provisions.

There were a great number of gentlemen and merchants in Da Silva's ship, according to the English reports, and Drake took them along with him as he sailed through the archipelago, transhipping cargo. Chaplain Fletcher noted that

> ... the southernmost Iland of Cape Verde is called Brava, because it exceedeth all the rest in greeness and flourishing.... This Iland being without inhabitants, (one only hermit excepted, who had vowed in that place all the days of his life to lead a solitary life, and upon his beads to serve our Lady and Saint James) is full of nutt trees, yielding fruit in that wonderful sort.

For once in a way he had no scathing remarks to make about the hermit, for as a good Protestant Fletcher devoted pages of his narrative to deploring the idolatrous practices of the Portuguese. There were even worse things, however; he had noted, for example, a ruined oratory on the island of Maio

... the reason of this ruin being, we considered to be, not the want of idolatrous affections in the Portugalls, which possessed the island, but the generations of drorydes, I mean pyrotts, who being a speciall greedy and hatred against the Portugalls, in the hope of purchase, take the opportunity of this place to lay in wait for such shipps and goods as come eyther out of Portugall outward or from Brasilia whomward bound, makeing their stay for provision at the island of Saint Jago, another of the ilands of Cape Verde.

Drake's treatment of the Portuguese was certainly not the same as that meted out by the 'pyrotts' who so disgusted his chaplain: 'such caterpillars of every kingdom and nation as are pirates and hyaenas of the sea,' he called them. Fletcher went on

South west from Sant Iago in 14 degrees 30 minutes about twelve leagues distant, yet by reason of the height seeming not above three leagues, lyeth another Iland, called of the Portugalls Fogo, viz. the burning Iland of fierie furnace. . . . Here we landed the portugalls taken neere Saint Iago and gave them in exchange of there old ship, our new pinnace built at *Mogadore*, with wine, bread and fish for their provision, and sent them away, February 1st.

So the gentlemen and merchants did not fare too badly at the hands of the English but

. . . now the Portugalls of the shipp having been discharged and set freely at liberty, as hath been said, we reserved to our service only one of their company, one Sylvester, their pilot, a man well travelled both in Brasilia and most partes of India on this side of the land who, when he had heard that our travel was into the Mare del Zur, that is, the South Seas, was most willing to go with us.

If the chaplain is to be believed – and it seems unlikely that such a sincere man of God should lie, even if others of lower rank were not told – this means that between Mogador and the Cape Verde Islands Drake had disclosed to his officers at least that he meant to press on into the Pacific. The excitement must have been terrific and no wonder that Nuño da Silva eagerly accepted the chance to join in this voyage of exploration, even if his inclusion was not voluntary. 'And so,' wrote the chaplain, 'we take our farewell from the contiente knowne parts of the world, or earth, to travill into the new discovered parts of the world, by the Gracious Providence of God.'

6

Across the South Atlantic

So far all had gone well for the English fleet. The chaplain sang the praises of the equatorial regions and demolished some of the cherished theories of the great masters of the past who had written about those waters without ever having visited them.

> For whereas Aristotle, Pythagoras, Thales and many others, both Greekes and Latins, have taught that *torrida zona* was not habitable ... we proved the same to be altogether false, and the same zone to be earthly Paradise in the world, both at sea and lande, yea the increase of things and the excellency of all God's creatures in that zone is seven degrees above all other parts of the earth, as partly may be understood of what is spoken allway of the Ilands of Cape Verde.

From the islands they had set course south-west and at first had the advantage of the north-east trade winds, which blew them merrily onward.

Fletcher described the abundance of fish encountered and caught

> ... dolphin, *bonetta*, flying fishes and many others, neither did we want even to the fall of flesh continually sent us by God, beyond the expectation or reason of man; for being (by conjecture) 500 leagues from any land, the fowles which naturally lodged and bred at land did come so infinitely to

60

our shipps so far off at the sea, a thing most rare, that our labour and timely exercise was to kill and eat and save the overplus.

He gave one of his graphic descriptions of Drake's men gleefully creeping up on exhausted birds.

That which is stranger, they fell upon all parts of our shipps to rest themselves, taking them as it seemed for mooring rocks, without any feare or doubt of harme or danger, in so much that they suffered themselves to be strucken dead with cudgells one by one, to be snared with lines put about their neckes with poles and to be taken with hands without motion or remooving away, as if they had been commanded of God to yield themselves to be meat for us.

Some seventy years later his fellow-clergyman Thomas Fuller was to give similar praise for the flights of larks which suddenly landed in besieged Exeter at the height of the Civil War.

Fletcher's narrative reflects the novelty which sailing in these waters gave Englishmen. They were not so unfamiliar to the Portuese and Nuño da Silva was able to tell his captors stories about the birds, some at least of which seem to have been albatrosses. 'The fowles are in bignes eagles' fellows, whereof we had strange reports from our Portugall pilot, who professes to have experience of their nature and quallityes, that is, that they cannot abyde to touch the water with their feet.'

Before long however the equatorial counter-current manifested itself and where Fletcher had written 'we drave toward the lyne', we now have his and John Cooke's descriptions of some of the misfortunes which befell them as the ships reached the dreaded doldrums, that area of flat calms, baffling sudden storms and great heat where men cooped up in small ships found tempers fraying. Odd climatic phenomena manifested themselves. The chaplain observed that 'sometymes the water which fell out of the ayer when we came neare the Equator was so quallified of the heat of the sonn, that it falling upon the cloathes of our men, which laye in heapes or folded upp, if they were not within short tyme washed or hanged abroad, they were so burned they would moulder to pieces as a piece of loose earth.' One torment was, however, lessened by their being in the tropics. 'In passing from our country, being winter, lice increased infinitely on the cloathes of our men, and were a great plague to many; but no sooner were we come within the burning zone, but they all dyed and consumed away of themselves, so that till we came beyond the southerly tropick to Brasilia, there was not any to be found among us.'

Thomas Doughty had been placed in command of the Portuguese prize ship *Maria* (anglicised into *Mary*) at the Cape Verde Islands, but there had been trouble between him and Drake almost at once because one of the chests of silver carried in her had been broken open. One thing Drake would not stand was tampering with cargo and he accused Doughty, who made a counter-accusation against Drake's younger brother Thomas, fifteen years the captain's junior. This young man of course served as a seaman like any ordinary member of the crew, as Nuño da Silva did not fail to observe. John Cooke, that unswerving member of the pro-Doughty faction, wrote that 'first mester Doughty called Thomas Drake unto hym and shewed hims his great follye in this behalf . . . to be briefe he told him he could not open it but he would declare it with what favour he might, so at the generall's next coming aboard the pellycane [for Drake and Doughty had changed places and Drake was now sailing in the prize, Doughty in the flagship] master Doughty opened the same unto him, who presently falling into some rages and not without some great othes [one may imagine Drake's colourful nautical language flowing at the smooth, cool accuser] demanded to know how Doughty dare accuse his brother of theft.' The matter blew over for the time being, but misdemeanours on Doughty's part 'found in the end an opertunytye to dysgrade him'.

The next trouble befell when the ships lay becalmed in the doldrums. One of Drake's confidants and one of Hatton's men in the expedition was John Brewer, the trumpeter, whom Drake entrusted with such errands as going round the fleet with messages and one Sunday morning before service time he was duly despatched from the *Mary* to the *Pelican*. 'It chanced

John Bruer, the trumpet, to go aborde the Pelycane, where, for that he had been long absent, the company offered hym a Cobbey.' A 'cobbey' was a bit of rough seamen's horseplay whereby the recipient was firmly held, his trunk-hose or breeches pulled down and every man gave him a smack on his bare buttocks.

> Among the whiche Master Dowghty puttyng in his hand, said fellowe John, you shall have in my hand, although it be but lyght among the rest, and so laynge his hand on his buttocke, which perceyved of John trumpet, he began to sware wounds and blud to ye companye to let him lose for they are not all (qd he) the Generales friends that he here, and with that he turned hym to Master Doughty and sayde unto him (as hymself presently after told me in the price) God wounds, Dowghty what doest thou meane to use this familiaritie with me, considering thou art not the Generals friend? who answered him 'What, fellow John, what mean you to use these words to me, that am as good and sure a friend to my good Generall as any in this flete, and I defye hym that shall saye the contrary?'

The damage however was done. John Brewer may have gone aboard the flagship as a kind of *agent provocateur*, or he may not have minded getting a cobbey from his fellow-seamen but objected to what he regarded as a slight from an officer. Certain it is that he returned to the 'price', as Cooke termed the prize ship, in haste and went immediately to Drake complaining about Doughty.

> Thus John Bruer, comynge agayne presently aboarde the price, had not talkt any longe tyme with the Generall but the boate went aboarde and rested not, but presently brought Master Doughty to the prises syde, Master Drake being in the midst of service, who herynge the boat at the ships syde stode up, and Master Doughty offering to take holde of the ship to have entered, qd the Generall, Staye there, Thomas Doughty, for I must send you to another place; and with that commanded the maryners to rowe him aboard the fleeboate, sayenge unto hym it was a place more

fit for hym than that from whence he came. But Master Doughty, although he craved to speke unto the Generall, could not be permitted, neyther would he here hym.

So Doughty, from being captain of the flagship, found himself conveyed a prisoner to the fly-boat *Swan* and ugly rumours began to circulate round the fleet. Was he Burghley's spy, sent aboard by the lord treasurer who suspected Drake's true intentions, or, worse still, was he an enemy agent, in the pay of Philip of Spain? He was a cultured, Renaissance-type Englishman, a skilled courtier, whom the simple seafaring man tended to regard with suspicion as 'smooth'. Drake himself, with his yeoman's background, although formerly very friendly towards him, had evidently convinced himself that this softly spoken, articulate man was not to be trusted. Something had happened in his garden in Plymouth before sailing, which was to clinch the matter tragically, as we shall see.

On the thirty-fifth day out they did sight land, albeit briefly, for Nuño da Silva wrote in his log for February: '20th. Crossed the line the twentieth of this month. At the end of this month were in with the island of *Fernam de Llonha,*' by which he meant the volcanic archipelago of Fernando de Noronha, which lies just over a hundred miles off the northeastern tip of Brazil and bears the name of the Portuguese navigator who discovered it seventy-five years before Drake passed that way. Da Silva's dates and the chaplain's do not quite agree and the discrepancy is not entirely explained by the Portuguese using the 'new style' calendar and the English the old. Fletcher wrote 'we sayled sixty three days without sight of land passing the line equinoctiall the 17th day of the same month till we fell with the coast of *Brazill*, the fifth of *April* following, in 31 degrees 30 minutes.'

He exulted to see the coast of South America 'After so long but a sweet pleasant travaile,' he wrote 'by the Providence of God we chanced and fell in the sight of Brasilia, where at the first the land seemed to make us a faire offer of opportunity to do that we had long desyred and now was most necessary for us, that is, to trim our shippes, being very fowle.' It was now three months since they had left Plymouth and careening was essential, the hulls being covered with barnacles and marine growth; but they were due for an unpleasant surprise and only the presence of Nuño da Silva on board the flagship was to save the fleet from disaster.

The pilot wrote tersely in his log 'on the tenth day of the month of March we were in a bay in 13 degrees' (which must have been about the site of modern Bahia) and the chaplain described it as

> ... very pleasant, a fare bay and a sandy ground, fitt for our purpose ... but the case was quickly altered, sweet meates would have sower sawce for we had no longer held our way inward but the sight of land was taken from us, and that sodainly, with such a hasynes as if it had been a most deadly fogg, with the palpabel darkness of Egypt, that never a shipp could see another.

This was followed by terrible storms fit to lay bare the sea-bed

> ... and we were upon a lee shore and the shoales increased upon us. So that if the Portugall pilot had not been appointed of God to do us good, we had perished without remembrance ... knowing the present danger, he presently cryed a returne as we colde, or els no way but imminent death, wherein, though we made all possible speed, yet one of our shipps touched with the shoales, but by God's Providence came cleere away.

Another account described a violent storm, lasting about three hours, 'with thunder, lightning and rain in great abundance accompanied by a vehement south winde directly against us, which caused a separation of the *Christopher* (viz. the Caunter which we took at Cape *Blanck*, in exchange for the *Christopher*, whose name she henceforward bore) from the rest of the fleet.'

Evidently Drake was so grateful to Nuño da Silva for his timely warning that he held a council with his officers to decide whether they should let him go and give him back his own ship again, but as he was now the sole member of his company left and his knowledge was too useful to forgo, they decided against it. He himself wrote in his log 'All this month he ran along the coast of Brazil for to go to *Spirito Santo*, to put me on land and give me my ship and for this they held council.

Thomas Doughty meanwhile was stirring matters up by his behaviour in the *Swan*. The fly-boat's master, John Saracold, had a strong antipathy to Doughty and the latter tried to show dissension between him, the captain, John Chester and Drake. No sooner had he come aboard than he let it be known that he was a prisoner, suspected of witchcraft and being 'a traitor to the generall, of the which he sayd he would purge himself in England before their betters ... to their great shame'. He boasted openly that Drake owed the furtherance of his voyage to him and to his influence with important people in London and prior to that to his good standing with the Earl of Essex in Ireland.

One day after dinner talk turned to 'ennemyes or tretors with the general on ye viage' and Saracold said that Drake 'might do well to deale with them as Magellanes dyd; which was to hange them up to be a sample to the rest.' Doughty instantly retorted 'Nay, softe; his authority is none such as Magellanes was; for, sayth he, I know his authoritye so well as he himself doth. And for hanging, it is for doggs and not ffor men.' Saracold was clearly not to be influenced by Doughty, but differences between him and Chester might be exploited. Doughty put it to him that 'whereas Mr Chester's authorytye seemed to have been taken away by the Master, if he would be ruled by him, he would give him authorytye againe, and would put the sworde into his hands, to rule as he thought good, and that if Mr Chester would be ruled, he would make the company to cutt anothers throte.' This was pure mutiny; Smith, in his evidence later, described Doughty and Chester as sworn enemies, so it was foolish to sound off thus before the captain of the *Swan*. Smith quoted Doughty as saying that 'though Mr Chester was his enemye, whom he would never forgive, yett had he friends which had and would work for hym; and that he had promised to be Master in another and better shipp.'

Thus Doughty, using his smooth tongue, was doing his best to stir up mutiny against Drake, to undermine Drake's authority and even to suborn ships' companies to follow him away from the chosen course. But he evidently overplayed his hand and his activities did not pass unnoticed, for the day of reckoning was soon to come.

7

The Isle of Blood

Spirito Santo, to which Nuño referred, now called Espirito Santo, lies some two hundred miles south of Bahia, between 18 and 20 degrees south. Drake continued his course southward, however, until the morning of 14 April when the ships passed

> ... by Cape Saint *Mary*, which lies in 35 degrees, neare the mouth of the River Plate; and running within about six or seven leagues along by the maine, we came to anchor in a bay under another cape, which our Generall afterwards called Cape *Joy*, by reason that the second day after our anchoring there, the Christopher (which we had lost in the former storme) came to us again.

Drake had in fact named the River Plate as a rendezvous when leaving Cape Verde should any ship lose contact and so the *Christopher* knew where to look for him. But from now on it would not be so easy; he was in fact forced to spend much of his time sailing up and down the east coast of South America looking for dispersed members of his fleet.

> The same day [the narrative continues] after the arrival of the Caunter, we removed some twelve leagues further up into another, where we found a long rocke, or rather Iland of rockes, not far from the main, making a commodious

harbour, especially against a Southerly wind; under them we anchored and rode till the twentieth day at night, in which meane spell we killed divers seales or sea-wolves (as the Spaniard calls them), which resorted to these rockes in great abundance. Hence, April 20, we weighed againe and sayled yet further up the river, even till we found but three fadome deep, and that we rode with our ships in fresh water.

The fleet put to sea again a week later and now the fly-boat *Swan* promptly lost contact with the rest. Drake was certain she would turn up again, but came to the conclusion that it would be too risky, in view of the hazardous waters which he knew lay ahead, to keep so many ships together. He therefore decided to find another harbour and reduce their numbers by abandoning at least one after transhipping her cargo. This was easier said than done; the coastline of Argentina and Patagonia was not hospitable and they remarked that its inhabitants were a race of giants. They searched 'all that coast from 36 to 47 degrees (as diligently as contrary winds and sundry storms would permit) and yet found none for that purpose. And in the mean time, viz. *May* 8, by another storme the Caunter also was once more severed from us.'

They had now reached well south in Patagonia and very nearly lost Drake himself.

May 12 we had sight of land in 47 degrees where we were forced to come to anchor in such roade as we could find for for the time. Nevertheless our Generall named the place Cape *Hope*, by reason of a bay discovered within the headland, which seemed to promise a good and commodious harbour. But by reason of many rockes lying off from the place, we durst not adventure with our ships into it without good and perfect discovery made beforehand.

Such 'good and perfect discovery' Drake would leave to nobody but himself for:

Our General especially in matters of moment, was never wont to relye onely on other mens care, how trusty or skilful soever they might seem to be; but always contemning danger, and refusing no toyle ... neither would hee at this time intrust the discovery of these dangers to another's pains, but rather to his own experience in searching and sounding of them. A boat being therefore hoisted forth, himself with some others the next morning, *May* 13, rowed into the bay; . . . but there was suddenly so great an alteration in the weather, into a thick and misty fogge, together with an extreme storm and tempest, that our Generall, being now three leagues from his ship, thought it better to returne, than either to land or make another stay; and yet the fogge thickened so mightily, that the sight of the ships was bereft them, and if Captain Thomas (upon the abundance of his love and service to his generall) had not adventured with his shipp to enter that bay in this perplexitie, our Generall had been further endangered, which was now quickly received into his ship.

The weather improved next day and Drake went ashore to light beacon fires in the hopes of signalling to the missing ships; he eventually got them all together save *Swan*, still missing since their departure from the River Plate and the Portuguese prize *Maria* 'Which waighing in the last storme the night before, had now lost company, and was not found again in a long time after. . . . In this place we found great store of Ostriches, at best to the number of fifty.'

They sailed next day, setting course south by west but only 'made about nine leagues in 24 houres, bearing very little sayle, that our fleet might the easier gett up unto us, which by reason of contrary windes were cast astern of us.' This was another example of the flagship's quick sailing propensities into the wind, at which she outclassed all the rest of the fleet. In 47 degrees 30 minutes they found a bay which was 'faire, safe and beneficiall to us' in which they anchored, moving further into the bay next day and staying there a fortnight in all. This was in all probability the Golfo San Jorge. But Drake would not rest until he had recovered the rest of the fleet. Next day he despatched his vice-admiral, Winter, southward in the *Elizabeth* while he set off northward in *Pelican* to search and had the good fortune to encounter the *Swan* which he led into the bay. However he decided that she was too much of a liabil-

ity and so 'being afterward unloaden and discharged of her
fraught, shee was cast off, her iron-worke and other necessities
being saved for the better provision of the rest.' They called
this place 'Seale Bay' because the seals were so numerous – 'we
netted two hundred in the space of one houre' – and having
revictualled 'and happily furnished all our businesses' they
sailed on 3 June southwards and nine days later came to a
little bay where they anchored for a further couple of days
'spent in the discharging of our Caunter, the *Christopher*,
which we here layed up'. The fleet was now two light and,
further, none of the remaining ships bore a name honouring
Drake's patron, a fact which evidently had not escaped him.

They weighed anchor again on 14 June and held on a southerly course until the seventeenth when they anchored again in
another bay 'in 50 degrees 20 minutes, lacking but little more
than one degree of the mouth of the Straits through which lay
our so much desired passage into the South Sea'. But Drake
would not enter the formidable Magellan Straits without one
more attempt to find the missing *Maria*. As the narrative says,
somewhat inaccurately 'Here our Generall on good advice determined to alter his course, and turn his sterne to the northward againe [this must mean his 'stemme'] if happily God
would grant we might find our ship and friends whom we lost
in the great storme.'

So they turned back again on 18 June in the morning and set
a course northwards, and the following evening, being a few
leagues from Port St Julian, they sighted the *Maria*. The location of the meeting was to have a profound effect on the fortunes of Thomas Doughty, for if the fleet had not returned
to seek the Portuguese prize it would probably not have gone
to Port St Julian at all.

And forasmuch as the ship was farre out of order, and very
leake, by reason of extremity of weather which she had
endured, as well before her loosing company as in her
absence, our Generall thought good to beare into Port St
Julian with his fleet, because it was so nigh at hand, and so
convenient a place; intending there to refresh his wearied
men, and cherish them which in their absence had tasted

such bitternesse of discomfort, besides the want of many things which they sustained.

The decision was taken; 'this the next day, the 20th June, we entered Port St *Julian*, which standeth in 49 degrees 30 minutes and hath on the South side of the harbour picked rockes like towers, and within the harbour many Ilands, which you may ride hard aboard off, but in going in you must borrow of the North shoare.'

Port St Julian was a grim and sinister place. 'On the maine our men found a gibbet, fallen down, made of a spruce mast, with mens bones underneath it, which they computed to be the same gibbet which *Magellane* caused to be erected, in the year 1520, for the execution of *John Cartagene*, the Bishop of Burgos cousin, who by the kings order was ioyned with *Magellane* in commission and under him vice-admiral.' It was an unhappy omen, particularly since Doughty had been one of Drake's commanders and had disputed his commission with him, a coincidence which Francis Fletcher did not fail to notice. Moreover the *Pelican*'s cooper took macabre pleasure in making 'tankards and canns for such of the company as would drink in them' out of the wood of the gibbet which 'being of firwood we found here sound and whole albeit 50 years at the least before our tyme'. The chaplain himself had no stomach for such a gruesome memento 'whereof for my owne part I had no great likeing, seeing there was no such necessity'. He described Port St Julian thus:

No other thing in this place we found worthy remembrance, save onely that whereas Magellanes performing the first voyage about the world, falling with this port, as wee did, did first name it Port St Julian and som aboard here had a mutiny against him by some of his company, for which he executed divers of them upon a gibbet, close by the sea upon the maine land, over against the Iland.

From the moment the English fleet anchored in the bay, trouble was in store.

On 22 June Drake decided to go ashore to see what the port provided. He took a small party in the ship's boat, consisting of Robert Winterhey, one of his gentlemen, his own brother Thomas Drake, John Thomas, Oliver the master gunner of the *Pelican*, John Brewer the trumpeter and Thomas Hood. The weather was a 'misling rain' but nevertheless Winterhey, who was a keen shot, took his bow and arrows and Oliver a 'fowling piece' in the hopes of shooting some game, while the whole party took targets to set up on shore for archery. As soon as they landed they were spotted by the Patagonians and 'two young giants repaired to them' with every sign of pleasure. When Winterhey arranged a shooting match they were delighted. The targets were set up and all the party began firing arrows; they invited the two young Patagonians to join the sport. Winterhey took on the rest with a wager that he could shoot as far with one arrow as the rest with two when 'suddenly there came two other giants (old and grim weather beaten villains)' who did not take at all kindly to being invited to join in. They sent the two young giants packing, making it evident that they disapproved of their association with the English and when 'letting goe' poor Winterhey's 'string brake ... the giants seeing and supposing there were no other engine of warr in the world but bowe and arrows (because they were acquainted with none other) and seeing our man to go about to put to another string, tooke present advantage, and chargeing his bowe clapt an arrowe into the body of him and through his lunges.' Winterhey was not killed outright and lay in agony while the fight continued.

The master gunner immediately tried to fire his 'fowling piece' which was the only fire-arm the party had with them, 'bent it at the giant, but the touch being dankish would not later fyer' and while he was struggling to light it in the drizzle the giant shot another arrow at him, 'and struck him in the breast, and through the hart and out at the back of a ribb, a quarter of a yard at least' and so he 'presently dyed'.

Things were going badly for the little landing party but Drake took command, realizing that their only defence lay in shielding themselves with the targets, so that the Patagonians should waste their arrows on them and 'if anny went by, those which stood behind should take them upp and brake them and so drive the enemy out of his arrows'. This is exactly what happened and the Patagonians soon had only one arrow left, while none of Drake's men was hurt.

Which the General perceiving, he then took the fowleing piece in hand, and primeing it anew, made a shot at him that began the quarrel, and striking him in the panch with hale shott sent his gutts abroad; it seemed by his crye, which was so hideous and horrible a roar, as if ten bulls had ioyned together in roaring whereat the courage of his partners was so abated they were glad by flying away to save themselves.

Drake's men now hastened to the help of Winterhey, found him still alive and conveyed him out to the *Pelican* 'if happely they might have any hope of recovery; but he died within few houres'. The master gunner's body had been left ashore in their haste.

With all speed therefore, our boat being well manned, we sent for our other dead man. When our man came to him, the enemy had thrust into one of his eyes one of our arrows, as deep as they could, had taken away his capp, one of his stockens and one of his shooes and so left him. Who, being brought to the Island the next day, after a sermon to put us in remembrance of our death ... we buried him with such honnor as in such cases marshall men used to have when they are dead, being both layd in one grave, as they both were partakers of one manner of death and ended their lives together by one and the same kind of accident.

This incident was not calculated to improve Drake's humour; of seven who went ashore, five had returned. Parson Fletcher mused on the reason why the Patagonians here were so hostile whereas they were 'so kind, loveing and harmless in other partes' and deduced that it was because Magellan had forcibly kidnapped two of their number 'to the shedding of blood and murder of both sydes' and for this reason those at Port St Julian had conceived a burning dislike of Europeans; it may be that the 'old grim weather beaten villains' had been alive at the time of Magellan's visit fifty years before.

'Our diet began to wax short,' the chaplain continued 'and small mussels were good meat, yea, the sea-weeds were dainty dishes; by reason whereof we were driven to search corners very narrowly for some refreshing but the best we could find were shells instead of meat.' He was astonished at the size of the shells, which the Patagonian giants left lying about empty after their feasts – 'a paire of shells could weigh five poundes'.

It was perhaps due to the general misfortune of Port St Julian that the Doughty affair came to a head and the rumours circulating about him round the fleet crystallized into something which Drake dared no longer ignore. Fletcher, who was a distinct Doughty partisan, wrote:

> ... but now more dangerous matter and of greater weight is layd to his charge, and that by the same persons, namely for words spoken by him to them, being in England, in the Generall's garden in Plimouth, long before our departure thence; which had been their parts and duties to have disclosed them at that tyme, and not to have concealed them for a tyme and place not so fitting.

Drake's drum summoned the companies of all ships ashore to the island and there they held a trial. A jury of forty, 'the chiefest of place and judgement in the fleet', was appointed and one by one the witnesses against Doughty spoke up, not excluding Fletcher and John Cooke, for all that they afterwards represented themselves as his sympathizers. Drake, it was said, had refused to believe what was said to have befallen in his garden in Plymouth, being unwilling to believe such things of a man he regarded as his friend. Now, however, the evidence came out. Doughty had sworn that the present voyage would never have come to fruition had it not been for him, that it was he who first brought Drake to the notice of the Earl of Essex and 'that they sayd Thomas Doughty did help our captayne to the queens pay in Iarland, when our captayn was glad to come into Iarland ffor feare of my Lord Admiral and the rest of the Counsayle, because of his Indies voyage'. Doughty had further claimed that, on the death of Essex he had 'preffered our captayne to His Mr Master Hatton' and that he and Drake had conferred together in Ireland as to the possibility of fitting out an expedition themselves for which Doughty claimed he had been prepared to venture a thousand pounds – a very large sum of money for those days. 'And that afterwards our Captayne came to London and sought hym the sayd Thomas Doughty at the Temple, and challenged him for his promise as touching this viage.' Doughty said he considered it 'more meate for a prince than a subject' and went straight off to 'Mr Secretary Wallsingham and Mr Hatton, and lyke a true subject brake the matter to them, and they brake it to the queene's majestye, who had a great good lykynge of it.' She summoned Drake, said Doughty, and commanded the voyage to go forward, giving Drake and himself equal authority and 'as large a commission as ever went out of England, and that the whole adventure passed under the hand of the said Thomas Doughty, which was no small matter'. Indeed he boasted that he had done so well by them in Ireland, and discharged his duty and service so honestly under the Earl of Essex that 'the queene and the counsayle had layd a great charge upon him'.

In short, he was the prime mover in the expedition and the real power behind it, sharing absolute authority with Drake, for now came the crunch 'that our captayne was not to do anything without the assent of the said Thomas Doughty, swearing with great othes, that he the sayd Thomas Doughty was to do a great many of men good'. The witness went on that Doughty had sworn that he 'would make me the richest man of all my kyn if I would by ruled by him, and that the said Thomas Doughty would not give this adventure for 11000 pounds. These words he spake at Plymouth, and aboard the Pellican and at the Isle of Maio.' This certainly smacked of mutiny and there was more in the same vein.

In my cabbyn aboard the Pellycan, he the said Thomas Doughty came to me, when their had certayne words passed betwixt Wm Leage and me, which Thomas Doughty sayd that the captayne was very much offended with me, and that our captayne would set me in the Bylbos; but that he the said Thomas Doughty sayd he would not suffer it and that our captayne should not offer it me; ffor I was one of those whom the sayd Thomas Doughty loved and made account of, and bade me kepe my cabbyn two or three dayes, and that the captayne and I should be ffrendes again.

The overtone was the same, undermining Drake's authority.

Another witness spoke of what Doughty had said when in the Portuguese prize *Maria* – that he was sorry he had not undertaken the voyage by himself which he could have managed well enough, without other adventurers being a party to it 'and the sayd Thomas Doughty sayd that their woll counsayle would be corrupted with money, yea the queenes maiestie her selff'. This was treasonable stuff indeed, moreover in a credulous and ignorant age it was equally dangerous to brag of skills in the occult arts, which Doughty had done. 'Book learning' anyway was suspect among Elizabethan seamen but 'John Doughty told me and John Deane that he and his brother could counger as well as any man in the lykeness of a beare, or a lyon, or a man in harnis. . . . More, John Doughty told me and John Deane that he the said John Doughty could poyson as well as any man, and that he could poyson a man with a dyamond.'

Next all the quarrels and machinations of Thomas Doughty aboard the various ships came out. Of these the most serious was to suborn the crew of the *Pelican* and desert the expedition for a privateering venture of his own on the Spanish Main.

> Thomas Doughtye, being requested that he woulde tell the captayne that ther wear some whiche made motion to sell one shippe against another, and so to carry away the Pellycane, the said Thomas Doughtie refused to give the captayne to understand of yt. And when that was sayd by Francis Fletcher, that he would tell the captayne of yt, the said Thomas Doughtie desired hym very earnestlie he would not. For, sayeth he, I shall be despatched.

In this again the chaplain played something of an equivocal role; he had evidence of intended mutiny, knew he should have warned Drake, but listened to Doughty and did not do so – yet later professed that the latter had been unfairly treated by Drake.

Doughty was also said to have been frequently in secret conclave with one Thomas Cuttill, to have promised him £100 and, more significantly, that he 'would kepe the said Cuttill in the Temple from my lord admyrall and all offycers, to goe and come whatsoever the matter was'. Finally Doughty claimed that 'he knew sertayne secretts of our generall, which, sayeth he, I will never utter, although he should use me very hardlye; and yet, sayd he, the utterynge of them would touch him muche.'

The four who swore to all this were Francis Fletcher, John Saracold, John Chester and Emmanuel Watkins. Another from the *Swan* who deposed against him was Gregory Cary, who declared with Saracold and Fletcher that Doughty 'dyd know that the generall could not cast hym off, from being equale with him, ffor that he sayd Thomas Dowghtie is a gentleman, and had been his equal both at home and abrorde in Iarland and now at the sea, especially as ffor that the sayd Thomas had bene the special help of the sayd generall to prefferment'. Doughty had promised Henry Spindelay, the gunner of the *Swan*, that he would lend him £40 when they returned to England (without Drake, the inference was) 'and much promyses he made to dyvers others, and affirmed that he would make one of them cut anothers throte'. Finally no less than twenty-nine witnesses, including John Cooke himself, affirmed that 'the said Thomas Doughty was not to be charged with the least parynge of a nayle, and that the Captayne knew it well; but that he disembled to please a sort of cogginge and lyinge knaves which are about him.' A friend of Doughty, Thomas Vicary, spoke up for him but Cooke said Drake cut him short, calling him a 'cunning lawyer'.

The long catalogue was eventually ended. There was clear evidence of attempted subversion, though it is questionable whether there was much more than that; nevertheless in Tudor eyes subversion was treason. Drake had observed significantly during the trial that 'her Majesty, before his departure, had committed her sword to him, to use for his safety, with this word; *We doe account that he which striketh at thee, Drake, striketh at us.*' Drake then asked the jury of forty whether they found Doughty guilty and deserving death, to which they unanimously agreed; 'it stoode by no means with their safety' they said 'to let him live.' It then remained for Drake to offer Doughty the choice either to be marooned ashore or to return to England 'to answer his deeds before the Lords of her Majesties Counsel' or to be executed forthwith; if the latter, to choose the means, with the grim gallows of Magellan pointing significantly skywards on the shoreline. After a night's reflection Doughty answered that, as a gentleman he would choose death by beheading.

His reasons for refusing the alternative of return to England to face the Privy Council may seem so implausible as to suggest he had no hopes of acquittal and therefore the certainty of a horrible death.

> If he should return to England, he must first have a ship, and men to sail her, with sufficient victuals; two of which they had, yet for the third he thought no man would accompany him in so bad a message to so vile an issue, from so honourable a service. Therefore he professed that with all his heart he did embrace the first branch of the generalls proffer, desiring only this favour, that they might receive the holy communion once agayne together before his death.

Fletcher in his narrative, despite his evidence against Doughty at the trial, declared that when receiving holy communion at his hands Doughty had protested his innocence. It hardly seems right that a priest should disclose what a communicant said to him at such a moment, but Fletcher declared that he must tell the truth and certainly the circumstances were exceptional.

It seemed that the strain was at last lifted from Doughty; no hope now intervened to disturb him and he behaved with consummate dignity to the end. As John Cooke put it 'Master Thomas Dowghtye with a more cheerful countenance then than he had in all his life to then shown, as one that dyd altogether contemne lyfe, prayed hym that ere he dyed he might receyve the sacrament which was not only granted him, but Drake himself offered to accompany hym to the Lordes table, for the which master Doughtye gave hem hearty thanks.' Thus the curious situation arose of judge and condemned man receiving communion together at the hands of the chaplain and dining afterwards together as they had in happier days:

> . . . havyng thus receyved the sacrament there was a banquett made [wrote John Cooke] In which tyme the place of execution being made ready after dynnar, as one not willing anny

longer to delaye the tyme, tolde the generall that he was readye as soone as it pleased hym, but prayd hem that he might speake aloane with hem a fewe words with him. The ii talked a parte the space of half quarter of an houre.

What they said to one another is nowhere recorded but the inference is that Doughty made some kind of confession and the two were reconciled.

Then he was brought to the place of execution [on the island, not on board ship] where he shewed himself no less valient than before; he first prayde for the queenes majestie of England he then, prayed for the happy successe of this voyage ... master doughtye embrasynge the generalle namynge hym his good capitayne bat hym farewell and so byddinge the whole companye farewell he layde his head to the blocke, the whiche being stricken off [wrote John Cooke] Drake moaste despightfully made the head to be taken up and shoewed the whole company hymself sayinge – look, this is the end of traytors.

Fletcher grieved for him – 'his gifts very excellent for his age, a sweet orator, a pregnant philosopher ... he delighted in the study, hearing and practice of the word of God, daily exercising himselfe herein by reading, meditating to himselfe ... as if he had been a minister of Christ.' Perhaps the chaplain was hoodwinked by apparent piety, but perhaps not, for as we shall see he later summed up the Doughty affair succinctly.

They buried Doughty with Winterhey and the master gunner under 'a great grinding stone, broken in two parts ... which we took and set first in the ground, the one part at the head, the other at the feet, building up the middle part with the stones and turfs of earth and engraved in the stones the names of the parties buried there with the time of their departure.' Then they returned to the ships but the shock of this event permeated the fleet so deeply that Drake realized some drastic action on his part was needed to reunite the discordant factions before the most hazardous part of their voyage. So once again his drum rolled and the ships' companies were lined up, rank upon rank. Drake stood in the doorway to the tent set up ashore with Captain Thomas of the *Marigold* on one side and Captain Winter of the *Elizabeth* on the other. In his hand he carried a great sheaf of papers brought from his private cabin and addressed the whole gathering in ringing tones, telling them of the dangers before them and the calumnies which had threatened to disunite them at a vital time.

Here is some again, my masters, not knowing how else to discredit me, say and affirm that I was set forth on this voyage by Master Hatton, some by Sir William Winter, some by Master Hawkins but this is a company of idle heads that have nothing else to talk of. But my masters I must tell you I do honour them as my very good friends, but to say that they were the setters forth of this voyage, or that it was by their means, I tell you it was nothing so.

It was from the queen herself that the impetus and inspiration came, as he now proceeded to show.

Indeed thus it was; my Lord of Essex wrote in my commendations unto secretary Walsingham more than I was worthy, but belike I had deserved somewhat at his hands, and he thought me in his letters to be a fit man to serve against the Spaniards, for my practice and experience that I had in that trade. Whereupon indeed secretary Walsingham did come to confer with me, and declared that her Majesty had received divers injuries of the king of Spain, for the which she desired to have some revenge; and withal he shewed me a plot willing me to set my hand and to note down where I thought he might most be annoyed. But I told him some part of my mind, but refused to set my hand to anything, affirming that her Majesty was mortal and that if it should please God to take her Majesty away, it might be that some prince might reign that might be in league with the King of Spain, and then will mine own hand be a witness against myself.

How wise was Drake is shown by the fate of his fellow-Devonian, Sir Walter Raleigh, at the hands of James I to placate the Spanish ambassador. Drake's prudence also explains why, though the draft plan of his voyage has been discovered in recent years among the manuscripts in the British Museum, nothing is signed by him.

He continued:

> Then was I very shortly after and in an evening sent for unto her Majesty by secretary Walsingham, but came not to her Majesty that night, for that it was late. But the next day coming to her presence, these or the like words she said; 'Drake, so it is that I would gladly be revenged on the king of Spain for divers injuries that I have received' and said further that I was the only man might do the exploit and withal craved my advice therein. I told her Majesty of the small good that was to be done in Spain, but the only way was to annoy him by the Indies.

These words made a deep impression on his hearers but John Cooke wrote spitefully as usual: 'Then with many more words he showed forth a bill of her Majesty's adventure of a thousand crowns, which he said that at some time before her Majesty did give him towards his charges.

'He also showed a bill of Master Hatton's adventure and divers letters of credit that had passed on his behalf, but he never let them come out of his own hands.' In view of the suspicions Drake entertained about some of the pro-Doughty faction it is hardly likely that he would! 'He also said that her Majesty did swear by her crown that if any within her realm did give the King of Spain hereof to understand (as she suspected but two) they should lose their heads therefore.' Doughty had so suffered; there were others whom Drake now named, who he said were also guilty, 'but there shall be no more deaths'. They knelt before him and admitted their guilt.

Then, suddenly, Drake dismissed all his officers from their posts, refusing to listen to their astonished protests. He explained why, in an outburst against the class distinction which so bedevilled the navy of Spain and which he meant to eradicate from the English tradition. In what he now demanded lay the seeds of the future navy – indeed his change of emphasis, his insistence on absolute discipline, laid the foundations of traditions which exist today. He would preach the sermon that day, he told chaplain Fletcher. 'My masters, I must have it left,' he roared, 'I must have the gentleman to haul and draw with the mariner, and the mariner with the gentleman. I would know him that would refuse to set his hand to a rope.'

This shaft went home; the gentlemen adventurers had thought it beneath them to help in the working of the ship, and he continued by describing the immense difficulties that lay before them and that complete unison only could overcome. If any man's heart failed him, he would give him a passage home – but let them not cross his course, or he would send them to the bottom. 'You come of your own free will, then,' he concluded as silence reigned and told them that it rested with them to make the renowned voyage round the world or end as a reproach to England and a laughing-stock to Spain. He then reinstated his faithful and disconcerted officers.

'These things ended our generall discharged the *Mary* viz, our Portugall prize, because she was leake and troublesome, despoiled her and then left her ribs and keel upon the Iland.' No doubt Nuño da Silva was grieved to witness the death of his former ship, in which he had hoped Drake might send him home; evidently Drake had intended to do so, but when the whisper of treachery reached him he had kept the *Mary* as a possible vehicle to transport the mutineers home.

So the rest of the fleet made ready to sail. 'These thinges,' wrote Fletcher in his colourful way 'with dropps of blood from the harts of some, thus ended we went about our other businesses and necessary affairs.' Doughty, for him, had

> ... left unto our fleete a lamentable example of a goodly gentleman who, in seeking advancement unfit for him, cast away himselfe; and unto posteritie a monument of, I know not what, fatall calamitie, as incident to that Port, and such like actions which might happilie afford a new paire of parallels to be added to Plutarchs; in that the same place, neere about the same time of the yeare, witnessed the execution of two gentlemen, suffering both for the like cause, employed both in like service, entertained both in great place, endued both with excellent qualities, the one fifty-eight years after the other.

8

Golden Hind

On 17 August 1578, the reduced fleet sailed out of the ill-fated Port St Julian, where Doughty's bones now mingled with those of Magellan's victims. No doubt there was no one on board the remaining ships – *Pelican, Marigold* and *Elizabeth* – who was not glad to see it fade astern. The discord and distrust engendered by the Doughty episode was astern too and Drake, by his forthright address, had encouraged the gentlemen to haul with the mariners and the mariners with the gentlemen. But Drake, with his uncanny genius for getting the best out of any situation, still had another card to play.

> On August 20 we fel with the cape, neere which lies the entrance into the straight, called by the Spaniards *Cape Virgin Maria*, appearing five leagues before you come to it, with high and steepe gray cliffs, full of black starres, against which the sea beating, sheweth as it were the spoutings of whales, having the highest of the cape like cape Saint Vincent in Portugall.

Thus the English described the awesome headland now called Cape Virgins which marks the eastern entrance to the Magellan Straits. Here at the start of the voyage into the unknown, through a wild and perilous waterway only one European navigator had negotiated before, Drake staged a spectacle to give his men new heart and his voyage new purpose.

At this the generall caused his fleet, in homage to our sovereign lady the Queenes maiesty, to strike their topsails upon the bunt as a token of his willing and glad minde, to shewe his dutiful obedience to her highnes, whom he acknowledged to have full interest and right in that discovery withall, in remembrance of his honourable friend and favourer *Sir Christopher Hatton*, he changed the name of the shippe which himselfe went in from the *Pelican* to be called the *golden Hinde*. Which ceremonies being ended, together with a sermon, teaching true obedience, we continued on our course into the said frete.

Young John Drake, the captain's artistic nephew, was set to work as the ship wallowed into the formidable strait to embellish the stern and topsides with the red and yellow of Hatton's livery colours, a piquant change from the green and white favoured at the time; he adorned the stern with the splendid fourteen quarterings of Sir Christopher's arms and with the aid of the ship's carpenter replaced the pelican figurehead by a spirited golden hind. The old Portuguese pilot, Nuño da Silva, looked on and murmured that young Drake had the skill of a Leonardo da Vinci. Thus the gratitude of Drake to Hatton for first sponsoring his venture and for becoming its prime supporter after the queen was shown to all men, so that the man who with her financed the great venture was immortalized through his crest or cognizance, the 'hind statant or'.

No more felicitous name could it seems have been chosen; under it she sailed round the world safely through all dangers and vicissitudes. And before we sail further with her through that perilous strait we may do well to consider what manner of ship was she.

Well-found and happy, a good and efficient sea-boat, this much is confirmed in all the contemporary documents, of all of which the chaplain's narrative speaks perhaps the loudest when it describes how she spoke to them all when she lay in her greatest danger.

Lady Elliott-Drake has written that she was built at Deptford. In the words of Nuño da Silva, who saw the ship through a sailor's eye, 'The flagship is in great measure stout and strong. She has a double hull, one as perfectly fashioned as the other. She is fit for warfare and is a ship of the French pattern.' Probably he meant by this that the *Golden Hind* had the lean, low lines which had been perfected to replace such ungainly bulks as that of the *Jesus of Lübeck* and to out-manoeuvre the great Spanish galleons.

She sails well and answers her helm well. She is not new and she is neither coppered nor ballasted. She has seven gun-ports on each side and inside she carries eighteen pieces of artillery, thirteen being of bronze and the rest of cast iron, as well as an abundance of all kinds of munitions of war. She also carried workmen and a forge for making nails, spikes and bolts. She is watertight when navigated with a moderate stern wind, but in a high sea she labours and leakes not a little, whether sailing before the wind or with the bowlines hauled out.

Her crew knew these leaks and that knowledge was to stand them in good stead when she ran aground on a reef in the East Indies.

Golden Hind was exceptional for such a comparatively small ship in that topgallants could be hoisted above her fore- and main-topsails when occasion demanded, for instance when full speed was required to elude Spanish pursuers, as no less an authority than Pedro Sarmiento de Gamboa testifies. She was square-rigged on fore- and main-masts, with a lateen on her mizzen sheeted to an outlicker. She carried a spritsail but no spritsail topmast. Bowlines were fitted to all square sails and bonnets for reducing sail, with martlets for brailing the sails to the yard – a rather cumbersome arrangement which was in vogue for about three centuries from 1340 onwards.

Her cables in general were made of eight-inch rope, but her forestay was an inch less and her mainstay an inch more. She had no bobstays for the bowsprit and no double blocks except for the fiddle blocks. Her total sail area was 4,150 square feet; she carried three anchors of five hundredweight each and one kedge. As to the dimensions of her hull, these have been the subject of endless research and controversy that still rages today, but it is fair to say that her length between perpendiculars was about 74 feet (the dock built to contain her at Greenwich was 75 feet long and her upperworks projected above it) and length overall between 100 and 105 feet – a tenth that of the modern *Queen Mary*. Beam was 19 or 20 feet, depth 9 feet and in the gun deck aft 8 feet. When deeply laden with Spanish silver she drew 13 feet of water. Her keel, 47 feet long, was of elm and her beak, from which the golden hind figurehead projected, of best English oak, weighing 9 tons in all.

Golden Hind's tonnage has been the subject of wild speculation and earnest research. Among the former may be numbered Don Francisco de Zarate's estimate of four hundred tons; even allowing for differences between English and Spanish systems of measurement one must conclude that this figure was set in order to convince the viceroy of the inevitability of surrender to this leviathan. Fletcher's account described the ship as 'of 100 tons'; by modern calculations one hundred and fifty would probably be nearer. She had two main decks, with a forecastle deck, a half deck and upper deck aft. The height between decks was only 5 ft 6 in and in the forecastle was down to 5 ft; even in the great cabin it did not exceed 6 ft so she was no ship for tall men, though tailored admirably to Drake himself.

Examining her deck by deck we should have seen, above the all-important ballast – 'vallesta' as the Inquisition's scribes rendered it, for it was later to be filled with Spanish silver and gold – the stores for bo'sun, carpenter and sailmaker and on the same deck, but further for'ard, the cable locker. The galley or 'cook room' with its silver utensils lay just abaft the stores, with a ventilating shaft leading upwards to the gun deck. Next abaft the galley were stored the water-casks, an all-important feature of the Elizabethan ship and one which dictated the need for periodic landings, even in enemy territory, to replenish.

For'ard of the mainmast, which was stepped through both decks, stood an ammunition locker and then came the steward's stores. Salt meat was stored in casks on this deck, with dry stores and chests of bread stacked above it. Abaft

Fish with an inset map of West Africa

Fogo, the 'burning island'

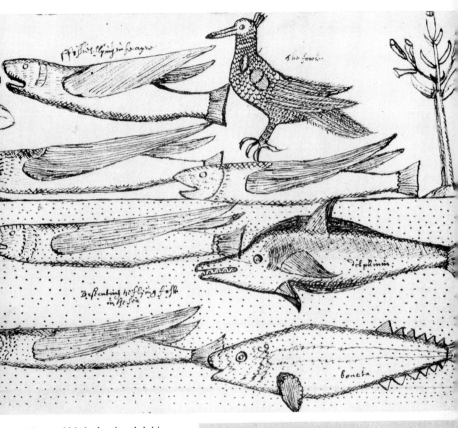

Fishes and birds: bonita, dolphin, albatross

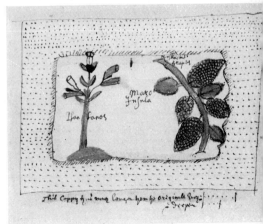

Maio, Cape Verde Islands – with fruits

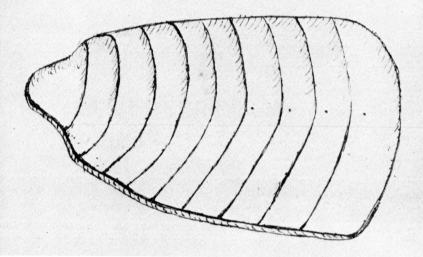

'The Ducklike foule' and 'the mussel shell'

'The manner of ye Boats in all ye islands
Southward of America in ye South Sea'

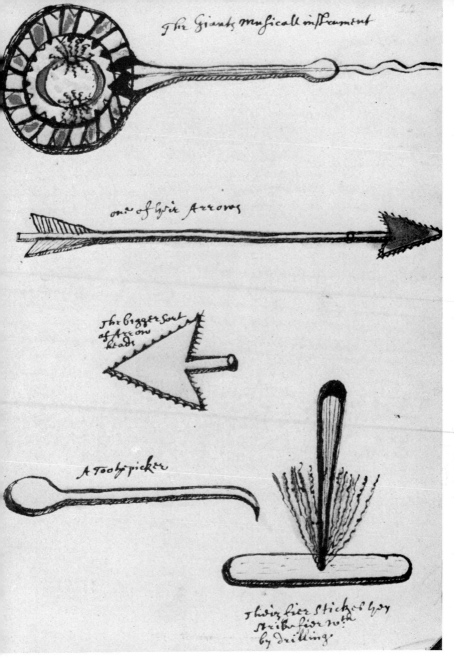

The Giants musicall instrument

one of theire Arrowes

The bigger sort of Arrow heads

A Toothpicker

theire fier stickes they strike fier with by drilling

'The Giants' musical instruments', an arrow and arrowhead, equipment for making fire and a 'toothpicker'

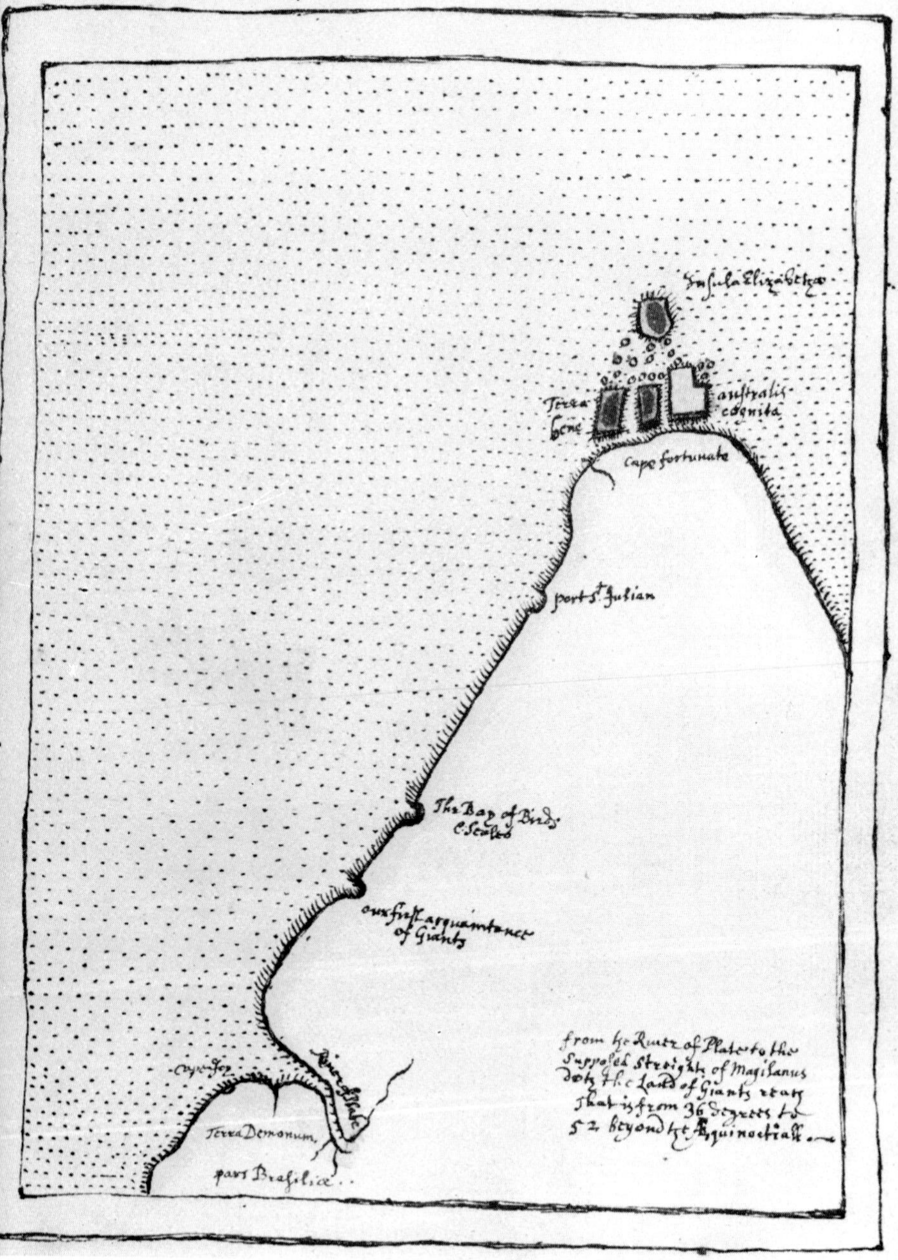

Insula Elizabetæ

Terra
bona

australis
cognita

Cape fortunate

port St Julian

The Bay of Birds
C Scales

our first acquaintance
of Giants

Capo Joy

Terra Demonum,
pars Brasiliæ

from ye Riuer of Plate to the
supposed Streight of Magellanus
doth the Land of Giants reach
that is from 36 degrees to
52 beyond the Æquinoctiall.

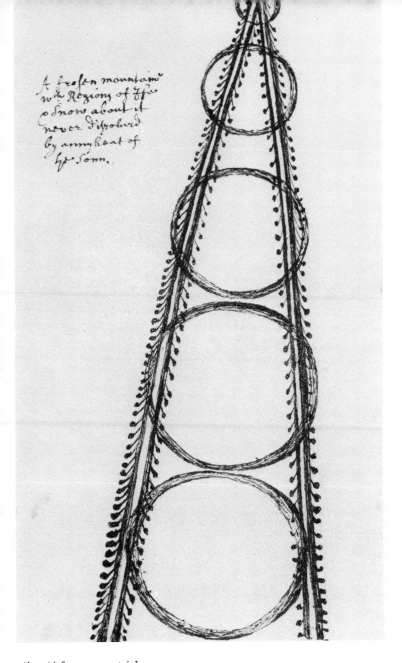

A frozen mountain
wth Regions of yͤ
ᵒ Snow about it
never dissolved
by anny heat of
yͤ Sonn.

Above 'A frozen mountain'

Opposite The southern end of South America and the Elizabethides

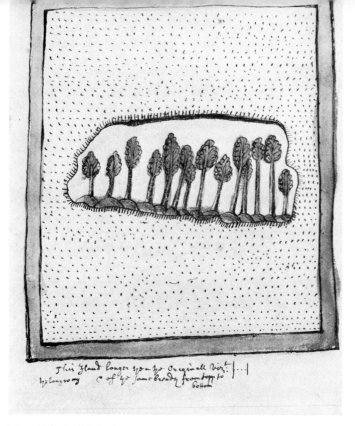

This Iland longer ypon the Originall viz: |...|
the longe way C of the same breadth from topp to
bottom

Map of Elizabeth Island

Map of Mocha Island

a Poole of fresh wahr
in the south parte of
the Ilond

this came cabins for the armourer and surgeon, while below, just above the ballast, was the magazine which so much impressed Nuño da Silva; above that, below the gun-room, was the master gunner's store.

As Nuño observed, there were seven gun ports on the deck above, but there were only five guns in the broadside, which would be wheeled into position as required. The for'ard guns tended to obstruct the handling of cables and so were stored separately except when the ship went into action – similarly the two quarter guns tended to obstruct the steerage and so were brought into position only when action threatened. This probably accounts for some of the discrepancies in the reckoning of her armament given by Don Francisco de Zarate and others whose acquaintance with *Golden Hind* was fairly brief; we may accept that of Nuño da Silva – eighteen guns all told, fourteen of them on this deck – as being accurate.

Most of the crew would have slept on the gun deck, with a small number in the diminutive forecastle, which contained a number of chests for 'dunnage'. One of these was hauled out on deck for Drake to sit on later in the voyage when he reprimanded the chaplain. The officers slept aft, with cabins for some of them leading off the after part of the gun deck, at whose after end was the gun-room where the master gunner and his mates dwelt, the forerunner of the midshipmen's habitat in the battleships of modern centuries. At the after end of the gun deck was the tiller, connected with the rudder, and the ship could be steered from here, where there was a compass, or by the whipstaff which projected from the tiller end into the half deck above. This half deck, extending for'ard as far as the mainmast, gave the ship her distinctive silhouette. Just for'ard of the whipstaff stood another compass; the helmsman received orders shouted down by the pilot standing just above him. It therefore stands to reason that Nuño da Silva, when fulfilling this function, had a good command of English, as is suggested by the factor of Guatulco, but by no other documentary source.

Alongside the helmsman's platform were cabins for the master and his mate and some of the gentlemen. The great cabin, used for meals and ceremonial occasions, the forerunner of the modern wardroom or merchant ship's saloon, was the aftermost space on the half-deck, from which a step led down into it. In the great cabin Drake's chair stood at the head of the table, with benches for his officers on either side – accommodating some ten or twelve all told. A bench seat ran round the stern against the stern gallery, which was entered from the great cabin through a door in the starboard side of the hull. As in Drake's personal cabin, there was a rack for weapons against the for'ard bulkhead, from which swords or pistols could be snatched up in an emergency. But of all the furnishings and equipment of *Golden Hind* none was more familiar to the crew than Drake's drum, that great red circuit on which were painted his arms. Its voice would roll round the ship and penetrate her deepest crannies, to summon all hands on deck for Drake to lean over the pool rail with some fresh command for them. It had sounded off Cape Virgins when the ship hove to to strike her topsails in honour of the queen and to receive the name *Golden Hind*.

The furnishings of Drake's own cabin were Spartan enough – a bunk, desk, table, chair and leather-covered sea-chest – the latter containing the precious documents relating to his voyage, including the draft instructions drawn up with the queen's approval, the precise wording of which was known to Drake alone. The furnishing and panelling were in oak and we may see the chest still, the interior of its lid adorned with paintings of the ship, in Berkeley Castle in Gloucestershire. The whole tone of these two cabins indeed reflected a rough and ready seafaring edition of the Drake drawing-room ashore still to be seen in Buckland Abbey.

Meals in the great cabin were a very formal occasion. Don Francisco de Zarate described how they ate off gilt-edged plates bearing Drake's arms, to the music of viols. San Juan de Anton reported 'I saw that the said Englishman was much feared by his men. He kept guards and when he dined they sounded trumpets and clarions.' Nuño da Silva observed that among the officers 'there were some of whom he made more account and had seated at his table, namely the master, pilot and doctor.' It was the sound of the viols and other musical instru-

ments sounding in the ship's great cabin which was so greatly
to astonish some of the Spanish settlers of Peru and to impress
the native chiefs of the East Indies.

Drake's pride in the arms which adorned his plates and guns
was also noted by Nuño da Silva; we may still see them to-day
in all their splendour carved above a fire-place in Buckland
Abbey. The Portuguese pilot wrote: 'On the bronze cannon
that he carried in the pinnace, there was sculptured the globe
of the world with a north star on it, passing over. He said these
were his arms and that the Queen had conferred them upon
him, commanding him to encompass the world.' The actual
patent giving formal grant of these arms was drawn up in the
year after Drake's return to England.

The bronze cannon carried in the pinnace was one of the
additional armament making up the eighteen. Spanish
prisoners of Drake noted with interest that *Golden Hind* carried a pinnace at her brow ready for launching and this was
an arrangement which as we have seen Drake had used with
advantage at Nombre de Dios, conveying pinnaces in sections
for subsequent assembly and launching. The general conclusion about the guns is that the main armament were demi-cul-
verins, with a bore of $4\frac{1}{2}$ in, firing ten pound cannon balls,
that she carried two long-range francolins for'ard on the forecastle and four breach-loading swivel guns, two on the forecastle and two on the quarter-deck, appropriately dubbed
'murthering pieces'.

Drake's navigation instruments were the best that the period
could provide and he was constantly adding to his store from
his captives. 'Francis Drake carried with him three books on
navigation,' said Nuño da Silva. 'One of these was in French,
another was Magellan's *Discovery* [but he could not say in
what language it was written]. Francis Drake kept a book in
which he entered his navigations and in which he delineated
birds, trees and sea-lions. He is an adept at painting and has
with him a boy, a relative of his, who is a great painter. When
they both shut themselves up in his cabin they are always
painting.' This referred of course to Drake's nephew John. It
is not surprising that the Spanish prisoners viewed this artistic

skill and *Golden Hind*'s growing gallery of portraiture of the coasts of the Spanish empire with consternation, for it would in due course enable others to follow in her wake.

Drake, in capturing Nuño da Silva in the Cape Verde Islands, had immediately taken from him his navigational equipment, including his chart, 'which,' he told the Spaniards later, 'did not include more of the Indies than the Rio de la Plata and the Cape of Good Hope', his astrolabe (one used by Drake is still preserved at Greenwich), his *libro de regimiento* or pilot's log, and his chart of the coast of Brazil

> ... which was in the Portuguese language; he had it translated into English and, as he navigated along the coast of Brazil, he went on checking it, from 24 degrees to which the Portuguese charts reach as far as the town which is called San Vicente. In point of fact Francis Drake wrote down all he had learnt and had heard related concerning the routes of the Portuguese, to the Islands of Cape Verde, the coast of Guinea, Santa Maria and the Indies, as well as the ports and land and sea forces of the Portuguese Indies.

The old Portuguese pilot bestowed his final accolade of praise on *Golden Hind* when he wrote, 'Taking it all in all, she is a ship which is in a fit condition to make a couple of voyages from Portugal to Brazil.'

But the draft plan of Drake's voyage, as far as it is now legible, provided for something even more exacting. The full text is today at best conjectural but reads something like this:

> ... shall enter the Strait of Magellan lying in 52 degrees of the pole, and having therefrom into the South Sea then he is to sail to the northwards so far as xxx degrees seeking along the said coast aforenamed like as of the other to find out places like to have traffic for the vending of commodities of her Majesty's realms. Whereas at present they are not under the obedience of any Christian prince so there is great hope of gold, silver, spices, drugs, cochineal and divers other special commodities, such as may enrich her Highness' dominions and also put shipping a-work greatly. And having gotten up as aforesaid in the xxx degrees in the South

Sea (if it shall be thought meat by the said Francis Drake to proceed so far,) then he is to return by same way homewards as he went out. Which voyaging by God's favour is to be performed in xiii months although he should spend v months in tarrying up the coasts, to get knowledge of the princes and countries there.

The said Francis Drake certainly 'thought it meat to proceed so far'; indeed in the light of what happened subsequently this was a most interesting blue-print for the voyage of *Golden Hind*.

9

Through the Straits of Magellan

The three ships now turned into the tortuous and fearsome waterway discovered by Magellan fifty-eight years before. The Portuguese navigator, whose true name was Magalhaes, was sailing in the service of the king of Spain and passed through from east to west in the year 1520, as the English were now about to do; he crossed the Pacific but his voyage ended disastrously in the Philippines where he was murdered by natives. The idea propounded by Dr Dee and other geographers, and accepted by Sir Richard Grenville, that *Terra Australis* was separated only by the Magellan Straits from the continent of South America was now about to be exploded by Drake.

The strait, wide at its eastern mouth, suddenly narrows, widens again, swings due south, divides into a series of fjord-like channels, then swings sharply north-westwards and narrows, passing into the Pacific between the islands of Santa Ines on the southern side and Desolation on the northern. Its horrifying magnificence was splendidly described by chaplain Fletcher and the other narrators in their rolling Tudor English; 'It is true which Magellan reporteth of this passage namely that there be many faire harbours and store of fresh water; but some ships need to be fraughted with nothing else besides anchors and cables, to find ground in most of them to come to anchor.'

The renaming of the ship seemed to have put them all in good humour to start with and this they certainly needed to negotiate such hazards. 'These things accomplished we joyfully entered into the Straight with hope of good success. We conjectured that, from the Cape whence we departed to the opposite land, on the other side against it, being a great Iland and high, and seemeth to make the mouth of a straight, that it was almost ten leagues or thereabouts by estimacion.' The 'great Iland and high' was Tierra del Fuego.

But afterwards we found the passange in some places four, in others three and two leagues broad, and where it was narrowest it was a large league. In passing alongst we plainly discovered that the same *terra australis*, left or set down to bee *terra incognita* before we come there, to be no Continent (and therefore no Streight) but between Islands and large passages amongst them.

Then followed a description of the awe-inspiring landscapes and the danger of the winds suddenly funnelling down the mountain clefts.

First the mountains being very high, and some reaching into the frozen region, did every one send out their several windes; somtymes behind us, to send us on our way; somtymes on the starboard side, to drive us to the larborde and so the contrary; somtymes right against us, to drive us further back in one houre than wee could recover again in many; but of all others this was the worst, that somtymes two or three of these windes would come together, and meat as it were, in one body, whose forces being becom one, did so violently fall into the sea, whirleing, or as the Spanyard saith, with a *tornado*, that they would pierce into the very bowells of the sea, and make it swell upward on every side; the hollows they made in the water, and the windes, breaking out againe, did take the swelling bankes so raised into the ayer, and being dispersed abroad, it rann down again a mighty raine. Besides this the sea is so deep in all this passage, that upon life and death there is no coming to anker.

Neither may I omit the grisly sight of the cold and frozen mountaines rearing their heads, yea, the greatest part of their bodies, into the cold and frozen region, where the power of the reflection of the sonn never reacheth to dissolve the ise and snow; so that the ise and snow hang about the spires of the mountains contrariwise, as it were regions by degrees, one above the other, and each exceeding another in breadth in a wonderfull order. From these hills distilled so sharpe a breath, that it seemed to enter into the bowels of nature, to the great discomfort of the lives of our men.

The 24th August, being Bartholomew Day, we fell with three islands, bearing triangle-wise one from another; one of them was very faire and large and of a fruitfull sorte, upon which, being next unto us and the weather very calme, our Generall with his gentlemen and certaine of his mariners then landed, taking possession thereof in her Majesties name and to her use, and called the same Elizabeth Island.

The other two he named appropriately Bartholomew Island, because it was that saint's day, and St George's in honour of the patron saint of England. A sinister note crept into the chaplain's description of the latter: 'In the island of *Saint George* we found the body of a man, so long dead before that his bones would not hold together, being moved out of the place where they lay.'

A happier description is that of the penguins, which the Englishmen saw here for the first time. Magellan had termed them 'geese'; they described them as 'less than a Goose but bigger than a mallard, short and well set together, having no feathers but instead thereof a sort of tight and matted down'. There were three thousand of them and the company easily killed all they needed for food. 'Their Beaks are like the Bills of *Crows*, they lodge and breed on land, where making Earths as Conies do they lay their Eggs. They feed on the Sea where they swim Incredible Swift.'

Drake was determined to take something back from this astonishing country to show his queen – he had evidently already made up his mind that he would not sail back that way, for Nuño da Silva wrote:

When half way through the Strait he cut down and carried in his ship the trunk of a tree which was fifteen or twenty handbreadths wide and so thick that it took two men, less one cubit, to engirte it. He ordered this trunk to be stored in the hold as ballast, saying that he was going to take it to the Queen of England as a sign that he had passed the Strait – which he had no need to do until his return voyage if he had contemplated returning that way.

The chaplain noted something of the condition of the no-madic natives observed ashore; men, women and children went naked with no apparent profession or trade such as tilling the ground or 'breeding of cattle, their total worldly goods being the barest necessities. I took an inventory of all the particulars of one as it seems the chiefest lord's house – 1 water pale, 2 drinking cupps, 2 boxes of stuff to paint, 2 wooden spitts, 1 pare of racks, 2 hatchetts, 1 knife, 1 fare floor of earth for a bed to lay upon without any cloathes.' Only their boats, 'made of large barke instead of other timber', attracted his praise: 'they are most artificiall, and are of most fine proportions, with a starne and foreship standing semicircular and well becometh the vessell.'

Then as *Golden Hind* reached the southernmost point of the strait, and had perforce to go about and head west north-west, Fletcher declared:

Passing with land in sight on both sides, we shortly fell with so narrow a straite, as carrying with it much winde, often turnings and many dangers, requireth an expert judgement in him that shall pass the same; it lieth West North West and East South East. But having left this strait a sterne, we seemed to be come out of a great river of two leagues broade, into a large and maine sea; having the night following an Iland in sight, which (being in height nothing inferior to the Iland *Fogo*, before spoken of) burneth (like it also) alofte in the aire, in a wonderfull sort, without intermission.

This would seem to have been Desolation Island, at the north-western end of which is Cabo Pilar and the entrance to the Pacific. As for the dimensions of the strait through which they had passed, 'by all our men's observations was concluded; that the entrance by which we came into the strait was in 52 degrees, the middest in 53 degrees 15 north, and the going out in 52 degrees 30 minutes, being 150 leagues in length.' This clearly indicated the 'V' shape of the strait and why the second half 'lieth West North West and East South East'.

Golden Hind had done remarkably well to get through in sixteen days exactly – Magellan had taken much longer.

> The sixth of September we left asterne of us all these troublesome Ilands, and were entered into the South Sea or *Mare del Zur*, at the cape whereof our Generall had determined with his whole company to have gone ashore, and there after a sermon to have left a monument of her Majestie ingraven in metall, for a perpetuall remembrance, which he had in a readiness for that prepared; but neither was there any anchoring, neither did the wind suffer us by any means to make a stay.

However the 'monument of her Majestie ingraven in metall' was to come in handy elsewhere on the American continent.

The Pacific was at first anything but pacific to the *Golden Hind*. Drake, from his tree in Panama, had once seen it and prayed to God to give him grace to sail in an English ship upon that sea. He now had his wish, but

> ... from September 7, the second day after our entrance into the South Sea (called by some *Mare pacificum*, but proving to us to be rather *Mare furiosum*), God by a contrary wind and intollerable tempest seemed to set himself against us, forcing us not only to alter our course and determination, but with great trouble, long time, many dangers, hard escapes and finall separating of our fleet, to yeeld ourselves unto his will.

Thus the chaplain in his usual felicitous way summed up the appalling buffeting to which the fleet was subjected.

It lasted 'full 52 days' till the end of October. 'In the time of this incredible storme, the 15 of *September*, the moone was eclipsed in Aries, and darkened about three points, for the space of three glasses.' For all that time 'we could not by any means recover any land (having in the meane time been driven so farre south as to 57 degrees and somewhat better).' This is to the south of Cape Horn and if any benefit can be said to have accrued from the ships being driven southward it is that Drake thereby discovered that no continent stretched up from the Antarctic but that to the south of South America all was open sea. 'The uttermost cape or headland of all these Ilands,' reads the narrative 'stands neere in 56 degrees within which there is no maine nor Iland to be seene to the Southwards, but that the Atlanticke Ocean and the South Sea meete in a most large and free scope.'

What momentous words were these! Drake's company had seen the Horn in weather conditions such as have destroyed many subsequent sailors, and it speaks volumes for the stoutness of *Golden Hind* that she came through. For this profound geographical discovery was marred by a dreadful disaster on the night of 30 September, when the *Marigold* with Captain John Thomas and all her crew disappeared, having without doubt foundered – indeed the chaplain and one of the crew of *Golden Hind* averred that they had heard the cries of drowning men above the roaring of the gale. When dawn broke only the *Elizabeth* was to be seen and the *Golden Hind* was to lose contact with her as well all too soon.

Eventually, on 7 October, they contrived to get back to Cabo Pilar at the western entrance of the Straits, very battered, and, as the chaplain picturesquely put it, 'with sorrie saile we entered harbour'. But even here there was trouble in store. 'We received within few howres of our comming to anchor so deadly a stroke and hard entertainment, that our Admirall left not onely an anchor behind her, through the violence and furie of the flawe, but in departing thence also lost the company and sight of our Vice-admirall, the *Elizabeth*.' A great deal has been written about the separating of the two ships; one account unkindly attributes it:

Partly to the negligence of those that had charge [of the *Elizabeth*] partly through a kind of desire that some in her had to be out of these troubles and to be at home againe; which (as is since knowne) they therefore by all means assayed and performed. For the very next day, *October* 8, reaching the mouth of the straits againe (which we were now so neare unto) they returned back the same way by which they came forward, and so coasting Brazil, they arrived in England *June* 2 the year following.

It may be that Winter had an unwilling crew; certainly he was deeply perturbed at his inability to find the *Golden Hind* again but whether through a misunderstanding or not he searched for her in the Straits instead of outside in the Pacific. He and Drake lit fires ashore in the vain hope of attracting each other's attention. Eventually, having navigated the fearsome waterway from west to east and re-entered the Atlantic, finding no sign of the *Golden Hind*, Winter sadly assumed that she was lost, and set course for England; he arrived at Ilfracombe in the summer and put it about that she had foundered with all hands. Drake, however, continued to hope that the *Elizabeth* was still somewhere in the South Sea and months later entrusted a safe-conduct to one of his released Spanish prisoners containing a message for Winter should he encounter him.

'So now our Admirall,' continues the narrative 'if she had retained her old name of *Pellican*, which she bore on departure from our country, she might have been now indeed said to be as a pellican alone in the wilderness.' Of the five ships which had set out from Plymouth, only one remained in the hostile Pacific and the poor *Golden Hind* was now destined to be buffeted once more back to Cape Horn. 'From this day of parting of friendes, we ran in among the Ilands before mentioned, lying to the Southward of America, through which we passed from one sea to the other.' It is clear that the ship sought refuge in the archipelago of Cape Horn itself, 'where, coming to anchor, we found the waters there to have their indraught and free passage ... among these Ilands making our abode'. The fearsome weather at this outpost of a vast Continent is graphically described.

> The winds were such as if all the bowels of the earth had been set at libertie, or as if all the clouds under heaven had been called together to lay their force upon that one

100

place. . . . Our anchors, as false friends in such a danger, gave over their holdfast, and as if it had been with the horror of the thing, did shrinke down to hide themselves in this miserable storme, committing the distressed ship and helplesse men to the uncertaine and rolling seas, which tossed them like a ball in a racket. In this case, to let fall more anchors would availe us nothing; for being driven from our first place of anchoring, so unmeasurable was the depth, that five hundred fathome would fetch no good.

So the *Golden Hind* drove about the archipelago of the Horn and her company learnt the hardest possible way much that earlier navigators and cartographers had wrongly assessed.

Here, as in a fit place, it shall not be amisse, to remove that error in opinions which hath been helde by many, of the impossible return out of the *Mare de Zur* into the West Ocean, by reason of the supposed Eastern current and Levant windes, which (say they) speedily carrie any thither but suffer no returne. They are therein likewise altogether deceived; for neither did we meete with any such current, neither had any such certain windes with any such speed to carry us through; but at all times in our own journie there, we found more opportunity to return back again into the West Ocean, than to goe forward into *Mare de Zur*.

Indeed the winds had blown them continually southward and eastward, when they wanted to go westward and northward; but delivery was at hand. 'Now, as we were fallen to the uttermost part of the Ilands, October 28, our troubles did make an end, the storm ceased and our calamaities (onely the absence of our friendes excepted) were removed.'

The sun reappeared at last and they remarked upon the briefness of the southern night in those late spring days. 'At those Southerly parts we found the night in the latter end of October to be but two hours long; the sun being yet above seven degrees distant from the Tropick; so that it seemeth, being in the Tropick, to leave very little or no night at all in that place.' They stayed two days in the archipelago of the Horn after the storm abated to refresh themselves and repair the *Golden Hind* and then on 30 October they set sail, 'shaping our course right north-west, to coast along the parts of Peru (for so the generall mappes set the course to lie).' In this the general maps then available were woefully wrong, as they were in many particulars where they had been drawn largely by guess-work. They 'chanced next day with two Ilands, being as it were store-houses of our liberal content' and on 1 November set out once again north-westwards, but found themselves drawing further away from the land. 'We soon espied that we might easily have been deceived ... we found that the generall mappes did erre from the truth in setting down the coast of *Peru*.'

What they termed 'Peru' covered not only the present-day state but also Chile. 'We found this part of *Peru*, all alongst to the height of *Lima*, which is 12 degrees South of the Line, to be mountainous and very barren, without water or wood for most part, except in certain places inhabited by the Spaniards and few others, which are very fruitfull and commodious.' Having found the mistake in the map, they kept close 'aboard the shore, as well of the broken land as of the mainland of India, till we fell in sight of an Island named Mucho'.

The name 'India' or 'Indies' was of course applied to south and central America indiscriminately since Columbus's time. In the draft plan for the voyage we have seen that the queen referred to the south of the continent as 'not being under the dominion of any Christian prince' and indeed the Spaniards had not as yet penetrated much further south, though they had reached a point on the mainland opposite 'Mucho', or Isla Mocha, which lies in thirty-eight degrees south, to the north of the Spanish settlement of Valdivia which *Golden Hind* did not enter. She anchored off the island on 25 November, having sailed a considerable distance up the coast of Chile before she encountered any opposition other than the forces of nature.

We found it to be a fruitful place, and all stored with sundrie sorts of good things; as sheep and other cattill, maize (which is a kind of graine whereof they make bread), potatoes and such other rootes. The inhabitants are such Indians as by the cruell and most extreme deceit of the Spaniards have been driven to flee the maine here, to releeve and fortifie themselves.

As the inhabitants of Mocha were refugees from Spanish oppression and those were the only Europeans they had seen, it was small wonder that they assumed the crew of *Golden Hind* had come to oppress them likewise.

Drake had taken a landing party ashore and they were marvelling at the 'Ostridges' of which there were many when suddenly the Indians launched an attack. 'The Generall himself was shot in the face, under his right eye, and close by his nose, the arrow piercing in a marvellous way in under "*basis cerebri*" with no small danger to his life; besides that, he was grievously wounded in the head.' Nuño da Silva had noted that Drake carried some scars from earlier encounters; he was now barely to survive. 'He has the mark of an arrow wound in his right cheek which is not apparent if one does not look with special care,' observed the old pilot. 'In one leg he has an arquebus ball that was shot at him in the Indies.' This landing at Mocha cost Drake in addition the lives of four men – those of his pilot and surgeon, Thomas Brewer and Thomas Flood, killed outright by the Indians, and two others who died of their wounds later – 'Great Nele' or Nils, a Dane (Little Nele a Fleming being luckier) and Diego, Drake's personal steward, 'a Black More' – that is a Cimaroon or escaped Negro slave from the Panama Isthmus. One of his men received twenty-five arrow wounds, another twenty-three; nine or ten all told were wounded.

After this unpleasant experience *Golden Hind* weighed anchor and sailed on; five days after her call at Mocha she anchored in 'Philips' Bay', or Bahia San Felipe, near Quintero, in '32 degrees or thereabouts'. She stayed there five days and picked up an Indian to serve as pilot – a man who knew the coast intimately, for Drake had now decided upon his first major onslaught on the ships of the king of Spain and wished to return south, having overshot Valparaiso, the port of Santiago, by about six leagues. The *Golden Hind* set sail on 4 December and next day, 'by the willing conduct of our new Indian Pilote, we came to anchor in the desired harbour about noon in the middle of the bay as far forward as the beach of Anton Gonzalez ... the harbour the Spaniards call *Valperizo* and the town adjoining it *St James* of Chili; it stands in 35 degrees 40 minutes.' In fact the city of Santiago de Chile lies some distance inland from Valparaiso, towards the looming chain of the Andes.

The call at Valparaiso was quite profitable, in kind if not in money; 'amongst other things we found in the towne diverse storehouses of the wines of *Chili*; and in the harbour a ship called the *Captaine of Moriall*, or the *Grand Captaine of the South, Admirall to the Ilands of Solomon*, loaden for the most part with the same kind of freight.' In a later report Pedro Sarmiento de Gamboa described the action as the Spaniards saw it:

> The Corsair sent his skiff with eighteen Englishmen, arquebusiers, archers and men with shields to seize a merchant ship that lay at anchor in the port and was named 'La Capitana' because she had served as such in the voyage of discovery to the Solomon Islands. She was about to sail for Peru and had on board five sailors and two negroes. The Englishmen entered her and took the sailors below and locked them up.

Thomas Moone, formerly captain of the *Christopher*, always ready for trouble, 'strake ye Spanish pilate with his fist of the face saying Abassho Pirra, which is to say in English, Go downe, dogge, and the poor Spaniards being sore afrayde went down into the houlde of the ship, all saving one of them, who leping out at the stern of the ship swam on shore.'

Pedro Sarmiento continued:

> Then some went to fetch their chief, the Corsair Drake, who went to 'La Capitana' and placed guards in her. Some men went ashore, and broke open the warehouses, where they found no gold but instead they only found wine, flour, salt pork, lard and suet. They took seventeen hundred jars of wine and whatever else they wanted and transferred all to La Capitana, in which they found twenty four thousand pesos of gold as was entered in the register carried by her

master and pilot, Hernando Guerrero. On Saturday 6th December at noon the English Corsair set sail, taking 'La Capitana' and the plunder with him. He placed twenty-five men in her to guard and navigate her.

Leaving a shocked Valparaiso astern *Golden Hind* headed south once more and next day, Sunday, reached Quintero again and dropped the Indian pilot who had proved so useful to them, but kept his chart to enable them to navigate from port to port. 'From Quintero they came to the bay of Tanguey to take on water and not finding any proceeded to the port of La Herradura where the ships cast anchor and took in a supply of water and pigs.' It was high time to trim *Golden Hind* and clear off the accumulation of marine growth after the desperate conditions of Cape Horn. On 19 December, a fortnight after the descent on Valparaiso, they found a bay which looked suitable, a short distance south of Coquimbo, or as they rendered it 'Cyppo', in 29 degrees 30 minutes. Unfortunately the Spaniards had settled Coquimbo fairly recently and it did not take long for the news of the presence of a heretic galleon nearby to reach their ears. 'We were immediately discovered by the Spaniards', who sent a force estimated at three hundred, of whom one hundred were actually Spanish, to attack the English landing party. Luckily the ship was not as yet careened and Drake recalled his men in safety to her, all save one Cornishman:

> Only one *Richard Minivy*, being over bold and carelesse of his own safety, chose either to make three hundred men, by outbraving of them, to become afraide, or else himself to die in the place; the latter of which he did, whose dead body being drawne by the Indians from the rocke to the shoare, was there manfully by the Spaniards beheaded; the right hand cut off, the heart plucked out; all which they carried away in our sight.

Such pointless mutilation of a dead comrade was just another example of the cruelty which Drake knew only too well. Nevertheless he did not allow it to influence his own treatment of the Spanish prisoners he was to take shortly.

Their welcome in this first bay having been so unpleasant, on 20 December they 'fell with a more convenient harbour' to the north of Coquimbo 'lying in 27 degrees 55 minutes south of the line'. The Spaniards reported later that 'the English ship nearly ran aground on a shoal near certain islands' and that for this reason did not enter the port of Coquimbo. In fact *Golden Hind* cast anchor off the north-west of the Islas de Pajaros (Bird Islands) and then sailed into the Bahia Salada where the 'convenient harbour' described was situated. She stayed forty days here, being careened, greased and re-rigged; Drake had a pinnace built and the guns which had hitherto been carried below placed on the *Golden Hind*'s deck. The careening, however, was not without incident; when he was about to lay her over she nearly capsized but, ever resourceful, Drake rescued her by use of the burton-tackle. Rather surprisingly the English accounts make no mention of this narrow escape but merely say, 'In this place we spent some time in trimming of our ship and the building of our pinnace as we desired.' From the description of the locality it would appear to be the one called by the Chileans 'Bahia Inglesa', with evident reason.

> In this bay we had such abundance of fish, not much unlike our gurnard in England, as no place ever afforded us the like (Cape Blanck only upon the coast of Barbary excepted) since our first setting forth of *Plymouth* that our gentlemen sporting themselves by day with four or five hooks or lines in two or three houres, would take sometimes four hundred, sometimes more at a time.

Golden Hind weighed anchor again on 15 January 1579 and, having failed to locate the river port of Copiago, three days later reached 'an island in the same height with the North Cape of the province of Mormorena' or Morro Morena. Next day the ship called at Morro de Jorje and then at Tarapaca, in the Pisagua River.

> Landing there we lighted upon a Spaniard who lay asleepe, and had lying in him thirteen barres of silver, weighing in all about four thousand Spanish duccats; wee would not (could we have chosen) have awakened him of his nappe;

but seeing wee, against our wills, did him that injury, we freed him of his charge, which otherwise perhaps would have kept him waking, and so left him to take out (if it pleased him) the other part of his sleepe in more serenity.

This incident is borne out by the Spanish account, which says the man had fallen asleep on his way from Potosi – many miles inland, in modern Bolivia – with three thousand pesos in silver, some 'native sheep' and a lot of sun-dried beef, called *chaqui*. The English account suggests that the 'native sheep' were with a different man and that shortly afterwards Drake went ashore again.

... and founde there a Spaniard and an Indian boy, and found with him eight Indian sheepe laden with vii or eight 100 lb weight of fine silver, and brought both the sheep and silver away with him on boorde, and he eat the sheep, but hee brought home the silver. These sheep had long necks like camels, and are very great, and will beare each of them 150 lb weight it they be loded. They are smooth bodyed, somewhat like a stag in body.

This is a very neat description of a llama.
A short way off,

... in 22 degrees 30 minutes, lay *Mormorena* another great towne of the same people over whom the Spaniards held government; with them our Generall thought meet to deal and therefore *January* 26 we cast anchor here. The next place likely to afford us any news of our ships (for all this way from the height where we builded our pinnace, there was no bay or harbour at all for shipping) was the port of the name of *Arica*, standing in 20 degrees, where we arrived the 7th of February ... in two barks here we found some forty and odd barres of silver (of the bignesse and fashion of a brickbatte, and in weight each of them about 20 pounds) of which we took the burthen on ourselves to ease them.

They found the silver 'lying open upon the wares, piled on one another three bares hye'. Pedro Sarmiento in his report said the two ships belonged respectively to Felipe Corco, in which they took thirty-three bars of silver and the other to Jorje Diaz in which they found no silver and to which they set fire. The inhabitants of the village were summoned by the ringing of bells and armed themselves. The English ship fired some artillery at the village. Then during the night something happened aboard *Golden Hind* which the Spaniards considered most odd: 'Trumpets were blown and musical instruments were played on board.' Drake was dining and celebrating in the usual manner.

In the morning they seized three fishing boats and in one of them Drake sent ashore three Spaniards and ten or twelve Indians captured in Chile. This magnanimous gesture was rewarded by the three Spaniards sailing along the coast ahead giving the alarm, but their energy did not last long enough for them to send the warning ahead to Callao de Lima and for that port Drake now set course with some haste. However, it would have been foolish to ignore booty *en route*. 'In our way to Lima we met with another barke at *Arequipa*, which had begun to load some silver and gold.' Arequipa in fact lies some distance inland from its port, Mollendo; according to Pedro Sarmiento's report, it was off Quilca that 'they took a trading bark, with some money and clothing, and transferred her crew to their ship'.

It was really amazing that the Spaniards had not seen fit to press on up the coast and warn Callao. Six days from Quilca, after a quick passage, *Golden Hind* entered the principal port of Peru. 'They reached the island of Lima,' reported the Spaniards 'and entered by the South Channel, between the island and the point, being piloted by the mariner Juan Greco of "La Capitana", who had been brought from Chili.' Juan Greco, as his name implied, was a Greek by birth, and had been pressed into Drake's service. 'They entered the port without being perceived, nor had any warning been received by the Viceroy on land or sea, such as could easily have been sent, for there had been ample time for doing so.'

It was between ten in the evening and midnight on 13 February 1579 that *Golden Hind*, followed by her pinnace and skiff, sailed into Callao. There were no less than thirty ships in the port, of which seventeen were ready for sea, 'including some of the most especiall ships in all the South Sea' and the

Golden Hind 'entered and anchored all night in the middest of them'. The horror in the Spanish ships may be imagined, when dawn broke and they realized who their new neighbour was. Drake's men wasted no time; nine ships were at anchor and they cut the cables of seven of them, so that they went drifting all over the place, running aground. The English enquired where Miguel Angel's ship *Nuestra Senora del Valle* was, 'where there were more than fifteen hundred barres of plate'. They cleared out her cargo but the Spaniards claimed afterwards that they were disappointed as the silver had not yet been brought aboard. The English account however is so specific as to give this the lie: 'the chest full of royalls of plate was flat, covered with black leather and only locked; it was above ii foote long, and 6/2 and ten inches deep; it was as full of them as could be thrust.'

Drake's men then turned their attention to a ship belonging to Alonso Rodriguez Batista. 'When the Englishmen reached the *San Cristobal*, which had just arrived from Panama with a cargo of Galician stuffs, they boarded her, shooting many arrows at her sailors and pilot. The said Alonso Rodrigues was wounded by an arrow; it is said that one Englishman was killed.' The English accounts merely give his name as Thomas. 'The English seized the ship with all her cargo, and taking her with their ship, pinnace and skiff, set sail around the island of the port towards the north and west.' It was important that they should do so, as they got the best of the wind, which the island tended to blanket, and so they had a head start of any possible pursuit. The shock to Spanish pride, morale and organization was intense but the takings themselves were only moderate, considering the large number of ships in Callao while fate, by dispersing the rest of his fleet, had prevented Drake doing the thing which above all others he had hoped to do.

For in the prison of the Inquisition at Lima, only a short distance inland, lay his friend, fellow-Devonian and former shipmate John Oxenham, captured when trying to lead the Cimaroons against the Spaniards in the Isthmus of Panama. Oxenham had been fired with the idea of sailing the Pacific but had intended to cross the Isthmus on foot and capture a Spanish ship on the Pacific side; the plan had failed and most of his men executed summarily as common pirates, but a more lingering fate was destined for him and his officers. Now the man whose birthplace lay below the western tors of Dartmoor would have given much to have rescued the man whose birthplace, South Tawton, lay below the northern tors, under the blue shadow of Cosdon, if only he could have! But he had one ship instead of five and eighty-five men instead of over two hundred, an insufficient force with which to attempt a raid on the capital of Peru. It lay too far inland for his tactics of Nombre de Dios to be repeated with success; he dared not risk the loss of the *Golden Hind* and her already precious cargo. Drake could but hope that the profound shock he had administered by his appearance in the Spaniards' private ocean would cow them into sparing Oxenham's life.

10

The taking of the Cacafuego

On the 16 February *Golden Hind* had sailed out of Callao, after two days' hectic activity, leaving astern of her a trail of chaos and confusion. Meanwhile the Spanish sailors who had got ashore had raised the alarm. The port governor despatched messengers in all haste to the viceroy at Lima, but Lima was two leagues from Callao and they did not arrive till 1 o'clock in the morning of the fifteenth. Having issued arms to all the male population the viceroy despatched General Diego de Frias Trijo to defend Callao 'and the King's money which was about to be embarked and consisted of more than three thousand pesos in bars of silver'.

All this took time, over twenty-four hours in fact, and by the time the Spanish forces reached Callao *Golden Hind* was already far out at sea, though still visible from the shore. After some deliberation Diego de Frias decided to put to sea in pursuit and embarked some three hundred men 'all with a great desire to chastise the Corsair' in two ships – Miguel Angel's *Nuestra Senora del Valle* and Cristobal Hernandez's *Nao dos Muriles*. The General embarked in the former, which became the *capitana* or flagship, with Pedro de Arana as Admiral or second-in-command in the latter. Among the officers was Pedro Sarmiento de Gamboa, the great navigator. He was nine years older than Drake, widely experienced in both Atlantic and Pacific. He had already fallen foul of the

Inquisition and been condemned to public penance and permanent banishment from the Indies, which the Archbishop of Lima, sensing the stupidity of wasting so good a seaman, wisely commuted. Pedro had a good idea of where Drake would be heading next and was critical of the leadership of the Spanish expedition; the landsmen and soldiers who commanded it did not view the situation with a sailor's eye and they declined to listen to Pedro.

Golden Hind was by his reckoning already four leagues distant when the Spanish ships eventually got under way. The *capitana* almost immediately made the mistake of keeping too close in to the island on her way out of the Harbour and thus lost the wind; the *Almiranta*, in which Pedro was, kept further from the island and so retained the wind, passing out ahead of the general's ship. The look-out in the *Golden Hind* reported to Drake that two Spanish ships had emerged from Callao astern of him. He thereupon asked his Spanish prisoners if they knew what ships these were. Their answer was that presumably they were vessels tacking about trying to save those that were still drifting after he had cut their cables.

This answer may have satisfied him for the moment, but not for long. Realizing that the ships were holding a following course 'the Corsair Francis realized the truth. Dissembling, he said to the sailors whom he had taken prisoner that he would now release them according to his previous promise.' So he ordered them into the pinnace to go over to the captured *San Cristobal*, tell his own men who were sailing her to return at once to *Golden Hind* and the Spaniards to return to Callao. What happened next may be gathered from Pedro's account. The easy-going Devonians manning the prize ship were in no hurry to obey their captain's orders, not realizing that they were being pursued or that there was any urgency, when suddenly the skiff came alongside and there was Drake himself leaping aboard and roaring at them to obey his orders. 'As these Englishmen delayed in returning, and as he saw that we were in pursuit,' wrote Pedro 'he jumped into his skiff and went to the vessel, wrangling with his men.' The recalcitrants all jumped into the pinnace in a hurry and left the Spaniards aboard the *San Cristobal*, following their furious captain back aboard *Golden Hind*. 'After collecting his men, the English-man spread his topgallant sails and took flight towards the north-west,' Pedro concluded.

With topgallants above her topsails *Golden Hind* could show most ships a clean pair of heels – certainly her Callao pursuers. As observed before, she did not normally carry topgallant mast and yards but they could be rapidly fitted as an emergency rig. The four or five liberated Spaniards sailed the *San Cristobal* back towards Callao and the *Almiranta* wasted some time speaking with them and taking Juan Greco aboard, but then gamely followed in pursuit. 'At sunset she [the *Golden Hind*] was almost out of sight, and had gained headway because our vessels were without ballast and could not carry much sail and pitched with the movement of the men, thus navigating very slowly.' It is a cumbersome and rather pathetic picture. 'Moreover the English ship, being further out at sea, caught a stiffer breeze and sailed on the wind. Notwithstanding this, although at dusk we lost sight of her, we did not give up pursuing her for a great part of the night.'

From Juan Greco, summoned over to the *Almiranta* from Drake's former prize, the Spaniards ascertained 'that the English vessel was large and strong, carried seventy or eighty men and many pieces of artillery, besides many fire-instruments.' This, coupled with the fact that the Spanish ships had no guns but only arquebuses, made General Diego de Frias Trijo think hard and 'moreover the most imperative reason for returning seemed to be that many of the gentlemen were very seasick and were not in a condition to stand, much less to fight. Nevertheless,' said Pedro Sarmiento witheringly 'there were many who were capable of doing both.' More time was wasted holding a conference aboard the *capitana* while she was hove-to. 'Finally, at the end of much discussion it was resolved to return to obtain reinforcements.' Unfortunately the viceroy did not accept this reason when his ships returned having accomplished nothing. In his fury at this second humiliation he imprisoned the general, punished some of the senior officers severely, reprimanded others and despatched a land force this time under General Luis de Toledo, with Pedro Sarmiento appointed 'sergeant major' to pursue the English up the coast.

113

The *Golden Hind* however was gone, by no means unrewarded, for her captain had learnt some vital intelligence during the raid on Callao. Even before he arrived there he had encountered off Valles a bark bound from Panama to Callao, belonging to one Francisco de Truxillo of Lima. From her captain, Gaspar Martin, Drake had learnt not only of the imminent arrival of the *San Cristobal* at Callao but also that a ship belonging to one San Juan de Anton, 'laden with much silver', had sailed a few days previously, bound for Panama but calling at a number of small ports *en route* to take on cargoes of flour. This ship's cargo would be the mainstay of that of the *flota* which would in due course be sailing from Nombre de Dios to keep King Philip's coffers filled; here was the prize above all prizes by which Drake could 'annoy him by his Indies'. When they were in Callao itself 'lastly we had intelligence of a certain rich ship which was loaden with gold and silver for Panama, that had set out of this harbour the second of *February*.' Her name was *Nuestra Senora de la Concepcion*, otherwise 'that gallant ship the *Cacafuego*, the great glory of the South Sea, that was gone from Lima fourteen days before us'.

Cacafuego was the rude Spanish seamen's nickname for the ponderous, unarmed floating treasure-house – *Shitfire* in basic nautical English. *Golden Hind* was now sailing northwards steadily with a favourable wind. 'We fell with the port of Paita in 4 degrees 40 on *February* 20, with the port of Saint *Helen* (Santa Elena) and the river and port of *Guayaquil* February 24.' The port lies some miles up the river, whose banks are low-lying, where the coast of Ecuador makes a bulge to the west. Even with the greatest chase of his life before him Drake could not resist a certain 'brigantine out of Guayaquil' and hove to temporarily to seize eighty bars of gold and a great golden crucifix from her 'together with a great quantity of ropes to store in his own ship'. Her owner was Benito Diaz Bravo and she was captured off the rivers of the Quiximies (or Cojimies, as now spelt) between Capes Pasado and San Francisco, some five leagues south of the latter.

The Spaniards estimated the value of the brigantine's gold, which they said belonged to private merchants, at fifteen thousand pesos; the Englishmen also helped themselves to 'all the clothing and food which they found in certain trunks'. Drake's expert eye told him the ship was a flyer. He 'made experiments in sailing with the bark, but as she sailed faster on the wind than his own ship he wrapped her sails around her anchor and cast them into the sea so that she could not sail ahead and raise the alarm.' The simplicity of this device was typical of Drake. Outsail the *Golden Hind*? Never! one can hear him say. But having stripped Bravo and his crew of the means of rapid movement, he did not abandon them to their fate. He allowed them to return to their ship and gave them a little coarse linen to make a jury rig, under which Bravo sailed his ship to the port of Manta. There, in due course, he reported to Pedro Sarmiento de Gamboa that 'like a shameless man who fears not God nor man, the Corsair made many arrogant speeches, saying that San Juan de Anton could not escape him'.

General Luis de Toledo and Pedro Sarmiento in fact reached Paita on 10 March, a fortnight after the *Golden Hind* had dashed in and out, not even anchoring, such was Drake's haste to catch the treasure ship. 'We passed the line the twenty-eighth,' wrote Fletcher and immediately north of the equator they were to be rewarded. Drake had offered a prize of his gold chain to whoever should first sight the *Cacafuego* and his own nephew, John Drake, won it and wore it proudly afterwards: 'this did John Drake descry on St David's Day, being the first of March, about iii of the clock in ye afternoon and boarded her about v of the clock.' Francis Petty, one of the gentlemen on board the *Golden Hind* wrote: 'It followed that John Drake, going up into the top, descried her about three of the clock.' The revised narrative put it slightly differently.

The first of *March* we fell with Cape *Francisco*, where, about midday, we discried a sayle ahead of us, with whom, once we had spoken with her, we lay still in the same place about six days to recover our breathe again, which we had almost spent with hasty following, and to recall to mind what adventures had passed since our late comming from Lima;

115

but especially to do *Iohn de Anton* a kindnesse, in freeing him of the care of those things with which his ship was laden.

For a graphic account of the taking of the *Cacafuego* we may turn to the reports of San Juan de Anton to the viceroy and of John Drake himself, when in later years he had the misfortune to fall into the hands of the Inquisition, which interrogated him on repeated occasions. He told them that when he first sighted the *Cacafuego* the sun was high; his uncle did not want to give the game away by overhauling his victim too rapidly and decided to postpone the attack till nightfall. But the Spanish lookout would almost certainly have descried the *Golden Hind*'s canvas astern of him and if she suddenly furled her sails in the middle of the day he would have smelt a rat. How should he pursue slowly while giving the appearance of full speed? As usual, Drake was ready with a seaman's answer and in order to get way off the *Golden Hind* without reducing sail he towed astern 'Spanish pots used for oyle' and as John Drake told the Inquisitors 'he hung out many cables and mattresses which went dragging along. He lowered his sails and hid his pinnace on the offside of the galleon.' The bit about lowering the sails conflicts with other accounts and it must be remembered that John Drake was trying to recall precise details of events years after they occurred.

When darkness fell all the impediments were cut adrift and the *Golden Hind* swiftly overhauled her victim. They were now near Punta La Galera, the *Golden Hind* being nearer the land, and the *Cacafuego*'s captain very naturally took her, as Drake intended, for a coasting bark on passage from Guayaquil to Panama. At about 9 o'clock *Golden Hind* crossed his course and came alongside; San Juan de Anton dipped his ensign in the tropical gloom but she did not respond. 'What ship is that?' he called, coming to the side. No response, then a voice roared back '*Nuestra Senora de la Concepcion*! We are English! Strike sail, or we send you to the bottom!' 'What English? Who dares bid me strike sail? Never! Come aboard and strike sail yourselves!' the astonished San Juan responded bravely.

Drake's men were not slow in accepting his invitation. As Domingo de Lizaya, the *Cacafuego*'s 'writer' later reported to the Viceroy: 'Then the said vessel fired her heavy artillery twice – the first shot carried away the mizzen-mast of San Juan de Anton's ship and the other passed high up near the main-mast. Then they immediately fired many arquebuses and a launch, filled with Englishmen, came alongside San Juan de Anton's ship and they entered her because she was powerless to resist.'

San Juan de Anton and his bo'sun Sancho were taken over to the *Golden Hind*; when they came aboard, Drake was just removing his helmet and coat of mail. He embraced the *Cacafuego*'s captain and consoled him 'Be patient, for such is the usage of war'; then he gave orders for him to be locked in the poop cabin with twelve men to guard him. Meanwhile 'about thirty Englishmen, armed with swords, shields and arquebuses remained as guards aboard San Juan de Anton's ship. They locked into her below the poop all the passengers and crew . . . and kept them under guard.'

Drake now had the *Cacafuego* sailed well out to sea, away from the prying eyes on shore or from vessels on the coasting trade route, and 'on the following day they opened the chests and taking all the silver and gold they found in them, transported it to the Englishmen's ship, the captain whereof is Francis Drake. They said that he is a native of Plymouth and is married there.' The English records stated, 'We found in her some Fruits, Conserves, Sugars and a great Quantity of Jewels and Precious Stones, 13 chests Royalls of Plate, 80 lb weight of gold, 26 Tons of uncoyned Silver, value about 360,000 pesos. We gave the Master a little linnen for these commodities.' Small wonder that Drake's 'voyage was made' by this one ship which the Spanish called *Nao rica*, the rich ship, or that Elizabeth, Hatton and the others were eventually to receive four thousand per cent on their investment in the voyage. Small wonder also that the damage to King Philip's treasury was catastrophic.

The two ships lay alongside each other for six days all told while the transfer of cargo proceeded. While San Juan de Anton was on board the *Golden Hind* he naturally tried to find out as much as he could about the ship, her complement and Drake's personal interests. Drake seemed to have no wish to be reticent, but rather to be intentionally expansive. Drake told him 'that he had come to rob by command of the Queen of England and carried the arms she had given him and his commission'. Then his anger at Spanish cruelty broke out. He knew very well, he declared, that they had killed and hanged many Englishmen at Panama and 'that four of the same company were now alive at Lima'. These were of course Oxenham and his officers. 'Tell the Viceroy of Peru,' Drake went on 'not to hang them for if he does I swear it will cost the heads of three thousand men of Peru, all of which heads I will cast into the port of Callao by Lima.' San Juan de Anton of course reported this, as Drake intended he should. The viceroy heeded and let Oxenham live until a year had passed and Drake was far away, heading for home – then, when he knew he was safe, he executed his prisoner.

San Juan de Anton steered the conversation into more palatable channels and asked, a trifle artlessly, how did Drake intend to return home? There were three ways, Captain Francis replied: 'One was the way he had come, the other was the pass of Vallano.' This referred to a crossing of the Isthmus of Panama. San Juan de Anton replied 'that off there the way was closed'. 'Thereupon the said Captain Francis would not say any more, and locked up the map of the world on which he had been demonstrating.'

San Juan and the bo'sun observed *Golden Hind* keenly. They estimated her complement to be eighty, '60 of whom were good for fighting; 12 were gentlemen cadets' – *gentiles hombres caballeros* as San Juan de Anton put it. He saw fifteen, the bo'sun twelve pieces of heavy cast iron artillery, of which the latter said five were on each side and two at the poop, two of which were of bronze, and a great deal of ammunition and weapons – pikes and arquebuses in the poop-cabin, more pieces of bronze in the ballast, and 'many other things in the way of armour to be worn under one's linen or hat in warfare' – in short the *Golden Hind* was a veritable floating arsenal. He noted, however, that she 'is covered with seaweed and greatly needs to be careened and cleaned'.

The fate of San Juan de Anton and his officers and crew was very different to that meted out to the English prisoners at San Juan de Ulua or to the crew of John Oxenham. 'On Saturday the 7th March he set all the prisoners free and told San Juan de Anton he could go where he wished.' Before they left there were two incidents worthy of note.

> The Pylate's name was Don Francisco, who had two cupps of silver gilt clene over, to whom Drake at his departure said as followeth; 'Seignior Pilate, you have ii cupps and I must needes have one of these' wch the Pilate yeelded unto willingly, because he could not chuse. When Don Francisco the Spanish pilate departed from Drake hee saide 'Captaine our ship shall be called no more the Cacafogo but the Cacaplata, and your ship shall be the Cacafogo' whereat Drake and his men laughed heartily and let the Spaniards depart.

It all seemed very good-humoured, gentlemanly stuff. As for San Juan de Anton, Drake handed him a safe-conduct to give to Captain Winter of the *Elizabeth* should he perchance fall in with him. Drake apparently still hoped that Winter was somewhere in the Pacific, but the wording of the document also suggests that he gave it to the Spaniards deliberately to confuse his enemies. It eventually came into the hands of the Inquisition and in July 1579, four months later, 'the licentiates Cerezuela and Ulloa, in their morning session' used it in the examination of an Englishman named John Butler 'in the prison of the Inquisition in the City of Lose Reyes' (Lima). They got him to translate it into Spanish for them; translated back into English it read approximately thus:

> Safe conduct. On board the ship named the Golden Hind on the sixth of March 1579.
> Master Winter. If it please God that by a favourable chance Your Honour should meet San Juan de Anton, I pray you treat him well, according to the word I have given him. If Your Honour should be lacking in any of the things that San Juan de Anton carries, pay him double their value in the merchandise that Your Honour carries. Give orders that none of your soldiers are to do him harm or wound him.

What we determined about the return to our country will be carried out if God so wills, although I greatly doubt whether this letter will reach your hands, I abide as God knows, consistently praying to the Lord who holds you and me and all the world in his keeping to save or to damn. I give him thanks always. Amen. This my writing is not only for Winter but also for Mr Thomas, Mr Charles, Mr Coombe, Mr Anthony and all the other good friends whom I commend to Him who redeemed us all with His Blood. I have faith in God that he will not inflict more toils upon us but will help us in our tribulations. I beseech you, for the love of Jesus Christ, that if God permits you to suffer affliction, you do not despair of the great mercy of God, for the great Prophet says that the Lord grants and gives new life. May God thus have mercy and show his compassion – to Him be glory, honour, power and empire for ever and ever, amen.

I your mournful captain whose heart is very heavy for you.

FRANCIS DRAKE.

San Juan de Anton returned to his now empty ship and set course north-east into the Bay of Panama, while he observed *Golden Hind* standing away to the north-north-west. She remained in sight for a couple of days before she vanished into the immensity of the Pacific.

11

Don Francisco de Zarate

Spanish America was in a ferment as a result of *Golden Hind*'s exploits. Rumour and counter-rumour were rife; where would she strike next? The consensus of opinion among the lands-men was that Drake would attack shipping at Panama or land and try to emulate Oxenham. Pedro thought Oxenham's un-happy experience would be the very thing to deter Drake from doing the same, and of course he was right. Pedro insisted that Drake had no outlet save by the coasts of Nicaragua and New Spain 'which will also have been told him by the Portuguese pilot he carries. For the latter is well acquainted with the coast as he has navigated it for a long time.' Pedro then developed the theory that Drake would seek the North-West Passage home. He would not run the gauntlet of the Spanish ships which were now alerted all the long way down the coasts of Peru and Chile to the Straits through which he had come; the weather, too, was propitious for the northern route. 'From this present month of March onwards until September sum-mer and the best season prevail as far north as Cap Mendocino in forty-three degrees,' wrote Pedro Sarmiento. Cape Mendo-cino is on the coast of California. From this cape stretch westward into the Pacific the submarine highlands called the Mendocino Escarpment. Pedro was one of the few Spanish navigators to have sailed that far; there were no Spanish settle-ments there as yet.

This would be the quickest route for getting from this sea to his country and while this route is not familiar to the pilots here, because they do not ordinarily navigate in the region, it is not unknown to the cosmographers and particularly to the English who navigate to Iceland, Bacallaos, Labrador, Totilan and Norway. For them it is familiar and they are not afraid of navigating very far north.

No doubt he had such men as Frobisher, Davis and Gilbert in mind. The Spaniards said that Drake had a magic mirror in which he could see the movement of ships a thousand miles away; conversely it might be said that Pedro Sarmiento de Gamboa had a magic mirror which showed where *Golden Hind* would sail next, so accurate were his forecasts. He had unstinting admiration for Drake as his conclusion shows: 'A man who has had the spirit to do what he has done will not be lacking in courage to persevere in his attempt, especially as he can take advantage at present of it being summer in the polar regions.'

Pedro was absolutely right – these were Drake's initial intentions – but as before his superiors ignored him. They wasted time futilely hunting round the Gulf of Panama and then despatched Pedro southwards, through the Straits and into the Atlantic where, by an unkind blow of fate after all his efforts, he was captured by another Devonian, Captain Whiddon, and taken as a prisoner of war to England. Meanwhile the price of ignoring his warnings was about to be paid and the first of the subjects of the viceroy of New Spain, Drake's old enemy, was about to become his victim.

On 15 March *Golden Hind* was off the coast of Nicaragua and there captured a bark belonging to Rodrigo Tello, bound for Panama. In the words of Nuño da Silva, Drake

> ... sent the crew ashore in his pinnace, retaining possession of the ship and her pilot, Alonso Sanchez Colchero, who was a pilot on the China route and had been sent to Panama by the Viceroy of New Spain. Colchero was on his way thither with several important charts, as well as some despatches from the Viceroy and from His Majesty to the Governor residing in the Philippines. Francis Drake valued these highly

and said he would take them to his Queen. He carried this
pilot with him from March 13 when he took him prisoner
until April 4 and discussed with him matters concerning
navigation.

The strength of the 'discussion' is doubtful; of all the
prisoners taken by Drake, the most hostile and uncooperative
was undoubtedly Colchero. When the rest of Tello's people
were allowed to go ashore Drake refused to release him, saying
he was a pilot on the route to China and he needed him to help
him navigate there. Evidently Drake had already determined
on a return round the world if he could not find the North-West
Passage. Colchero denied that he was a pilot, saying he was
only an ordinary sailor and a poor man with wife and children.
Drake told him 'not to plague him by speaking such non-
sense' and that he would hang him if he said any more. This
'hanging' was not execution, but a form of maritime torture
by which the obstinate victim was drawn up by a rope to the
mainyard and then lowered into the sea up to the neck before
being drawn up and lowered again. Later, when the ship came
off Realejo in Nicaragua, Drake wanted to enter the port and
asked Colchero to take him in over the bar. The Spaniard refused, saying he had never been into the harbour, at which
Drake ordered him to be 'hanged'. 'Twice they placed a rope
round his neck and drew him up from the deck, but when they
saw he was exhausted, they left him alone.'

Colchero also alleged that Drake tried to bribe him, 'with
many promises of silver and gold', to go with him to England
and become a Lutheran. 'When he saw that Colchero was
adamant, he said "You must be a devoted servant of King
Philip, and a great captain".' Whether this was embellished for
the sake of his Spanish masters is not clear, but certainly Colchero was a devoted servant of King Philip and refused to
be swayed by pressure despite his advancing years. Colchero
also claimed that Drake put him ashore without any money,
but he neglected to mention what another of the Spanish
prisoners, Diego de Messa, affirmed – that when put ashore
with the rest of Tello's men he was entrusted with a letter to

Colchero's wife in which Drake had allowed him to enclose fifty pesos in reals.

The following day, 16 March, *Golden Hind* anchored off the island of Cano, 'setting ourselves for certaine dayes in a fresh river'. But all was not well: 'while we abode in this place, we felt a very terrible earthquake, the force whereof was such that our ship and pinnace, riding very neere an English mile from the shore, were shaken and did quiver as if it had been laid on dry land' – but once again the stoutness of the *Golden Hind*'s construction saw her through.

Giusepe de Pareces, a passenger in Tello's ship, described how the Englishmen had boarded her from a launch and taken them to the *Golden Hind* – 'a vessel with high sides lying in a cove'. As soon as the launch reached the ship Drake had her artillery transferred to the said bark with the heaviest of the chests and then cast on the banks of the river the bars of silver carried in his ship. As she rose out of the water he had her careened and caulked both sides. After the ship had been careened, he set sail. Pareces also tried to learn the identity of Nuño da Silva: 'Captain Francis spoke in his praise, saying he was an excellent pilot,' but Nuño declined to speak to the Spanish prisoners; he 'only looked at them and laughed to himself'.

Drake now decided to keep out of sight of ships and land, so as to preserve an element of surprise.

> From here we parted the 24th day of the month forenamed, with full purpose to work the nearest course, as the winde would suffer us, without touch of land a long time; and therefore passed by the port of Papagaia [this lies in the Golfo de Papagaia, or Gulf of Parrots, in Costa Rica] the port of Vale, of the most rich and excellent balm of Jericho; Quantepico, and divers others, as also certain gulphes hereabout which without intermission send forth such continuall and violent windes, that the Spaniards, though their ships be good, dare not venture themselves too neere.

Having safely passed these dangers, *Golden Hind* lay well of the coast, waiting to pounce on her next unsuspecting victim.

Don Francisco de Zarate, a wealthy Spanish captain, cousin of the Duke of Medina Sidonia, sailed out of Acapulco in

Mexico on 23 March 1579 in his ship *Espirito Santo* and set a course south-east for Panama. Ten days later he was off Acajutla, 'close to the volcanoes of Guatemala'. The night of Friday the third to Saturday 4 April was clear, with a moon, and suddenly, half an hour before dawn, when he was 'two leagues to seward of the land', they heard the flap of canvas and 'saw, by moonlight, a ship very close to ours. Our helmsman shouted to her to stand away and not to come alongside. To this they made no answer pretending to be asleep. The helmsman shouted louder, asking where the ship hailed from. They answered "from Peru" and that she belonged to Miguel Angel, which is the name of a well-known captain on that route.' Miguel Angel was of course the owner of *Nuestra Senora del Valle* which the *Golden Hind* had encountered in Callao. To allay suspicion Drake had forced the Spanish pilot Colchero to do the hailing so that they should not be betrayed by an English accent. 'The spokesman in that ship was a Spaniard, whose name I will tell Your Excellency later on,' Don Francisco hinted darkly in his report to the viceroy.

In a moment more *Golden Hind* was alongside him, grappling the *Espirito Santo,* the English swarmed aboard and Don Francisco found himself captured and transhipped.

In a very short time we arrived where their general was, in a very good galleon, as well mounted with artillery as any I have seen in my life. He had more to say in praise of her when he had sailed in her for a little, for as an educated and observant man he missed nothing.

I found him promenading on deck [Don Francisco continued] and approaching him I kissed his hands. He received me with a show of kindness and took me to his cabin where he bade me be seated and said 'I am a friend of those who tell me the truth, but with those who do not I get out of humour. Therefore, (as this is the best road to my favour) you must tell me how much silver and gold your ship carries?' I answered 'None'. He repeated his question. I replied 'none, only some small plates that I use and some cups. That is all that is in her.'

In fact, according to the English reports, the ship 'was laden with lynen, cloth and fine China silks, and there were also in her divers chests full of fine earthen dishes, very finely wrought, of fine white earth brought by the Spaniards from the country of Chyna, which dishes the Spanyards greatly esteem. Of these dishes Drake took four chests full of them.' He also took 'Packs of fine lynen cloth and good store of taffeta and other fine silks'.

Drake 'Kept silent for a while, and then, resuming the conversation, asked if I knew Your Excellency. I said "Yes". "Is any relative of his or thing belonging to him in this ship?" "No, senor." "Well, it would give me greater joy to come across him than all the gold and silver of the Indies. You would see how a gentleman should be made to keep his word." I made no reply to this.'

What the viceroy of New Spain must have thought on reading this may be imagined. He would see that Drake had not forgotten nor forgiven his blatant treachery at San Juan de Ulua and perhaps even his stern and fanatical heart missed a beat. Drake was now on his very doorstep, with the advantage of surprise and a record of devastating success behind him. Certainly a clerk annotating the text of the letter at some later stage thought it funny and made a sardonic and significant note 'Ojo! A Don Martin Enriquez' in the margin.

Drake then rose

    ... and bidding me go with him, led me to a cabin situated in the poop below deck, where there was a prison which they term 'the ballast'. In it, at the far end, was an old man. Drake said to me 'Sit down, this is the place where you will have to remain.' I took this in good part and was about to sit down when he stopped me and said; 'I do not wish you to try this just yet, I only want you to tell me who that man in there is.' I answered that I did not know him. 'Well' he answered 'know that it is a pilot named Colchero, whom the Viceroy was sending to Panama to convey Don Goncalo to China.' He then had the pilot released from the prison and we all went up on deck.

This was the man, Don Francisco added, who had hailed him from the *Golden Hind* before his ship was captured.

Don Francisco had no criticism of his treatment at Drake's hands, rather the reverse. 'We talked a good while before it was time to dine. He ordered me to sit next him and began to give me food from his own plate, telling me not to grieve, that my life and property were safe. I kissed his hands for this. . . . Of my belongings he took but little. Indeed he was quite courteous about it.' The English reports said, 'The owner of the ship having very costly apparell, earnestly entreated Drake, and besought him not to take away from him his apparell, which he promised not to do, and the gentleman gave him a falcon of gold with a great emerald in the breast thereof for his favourable dealing with him.'

Charles Kingsley in *Westward Ho!* makes the falcon figure in the story of John Oxenham, whom he had made the lover of Don Francisco's wife and father of Ayacanora, who ultimately married Amyas Leigh. It was through her recollection of the falcon with 'the great green stone' that Salvation Yeo recognized his 'little maid' once more. Kingsley wove fiction with fact, but in Don Francisco's own words 'Certain trifles of mine having taken his fancy, he had them brought to his ship and gave me, in exchange for them, a falchion and a small brazier of silver, and I can assure Your Excellency that he lost nothing by the bargain. On his return to his vessel he asked me to pardon him for taking the trifles, but they were for his wife.' Indeed the falcon with the emerald in its breast was duly presented to Mary Newman in Plymouth Sound a year and a half later.

The handling capabilities of *Golden Hind* particularly impressed Don Francisco. 'His vessel is a galleon of nearly 400 tons, and sails perfectly,' he wrote. Even allowing for differences in Spanish and English methods of calculation, this was clearly an exaggeration but it may have been done to impress the viceroy with the hopelessness of resisting such a leviathan. 'The enemy ship carried her bark at her prow, as if she were being towed' – an allusion to the method of stowing the pinnace when not in use.

The capture of the *Espirito Santo* took place in the early hours of Saturday so that Don Francisco's second day on board the *Golden Hind* was Sunday. Not only did this enable him to see the English at their devotions but also to see the ship and her captain in all their finery.

On the following day, which was Sunday, in the morning he dressed and decked himself very finely and had his galleon decorated with all her flags and banners. She is manned by a hundred men [he continued] all of service and of fighting age, and all are as practised therein as old soldiers from Italy. Each one takes particular pride to keep his arquebus clean. The captain treats them with affection and they treat him with respect. He carried with him nine or ten gentlemen, the sons of English gentlemen. These form a part of his council which he calls together for even the most trivial matters, although he takes advice from no one. But he enjoys hearing what they say and afterwards he issues his orders.

English forms of discipline, at once friendly yet strict, must have seemed strange to a high-born Spaniard, accustomed to the rigid caste system which, far from sanctioning the calling together of a council on trivial matters, left the captain in icy isolation, scarcely deigning to communicate with the ship's officers. Nevertheless Don Francisco saw straight to the heart of the matter. Drake humoured his officers by letting them have their say but it did not alter his judgement one iota – he made up his mind and did what he wanted just the same, a benevolent despot indeed.

'The aforesaid gentlemen sit at his table as well as the Portuguese pilot whom he brought from England' (an error, since Nuño da Silva was captured in the Cape Verde Islands) 'who spoke, not a word all the time I was on board.' No doubt Nuño felt that the less he had to do with Spaniards the better, after so long aboard the *Golden Hind,* and subsequent unhappy events were to prove him absolutely right.

'He is served on silver dishes with gold borders and gilded garlands, in which are his arms. He carried all possible dainties and perfumed waters. He said that many of them had been given him by the Queen. None of these gentlemen took a seat or covered his head before him, until he urged them repeatedly to do so.'

Reverting to the *Golden Hind* herself, Don Francisco continued: 'This galleon of his carries about thirty heavy pieces of artillery and a great quantity of firearms with the requisite ammunition and lead.' Then a further thought about Drake came to him, so that he interspersed recollection of captain and ship alternately.

> He dines and sups to the music of viols. He carries trained carpenters and artisans, so as to be able to careen the ship at any time. Besides being new, the ship has a double sheathing. I understand that all the men he carries with him receive wages because, when one ship was plundered, no man dared take anything without his authority. He shows them great favour, but punishes the least fault. He also carries painters who paint for him pictures of the coast in its exact colours. This I am most grieved to see, for everything is depicted so naturally that anyone who uses these paintings as a guide cannot possibly go astray. I understand from him that he had sailed from his own country with five vessels, four sloops (of the long type) and that half of the armada belonged to the Queen.

During his short time aboard the *Golden Hind* Don Francisco had learnt of the Doughty affair and noted the presence of Thomas's brother John still on board; as this was most intriguing he reported it to the viceroy. He related that Drake had arrived off the Magellan Straits two months before he intended to pass through:

> ... during that time there were many great storms. So it was that one of the gentlemen, whom he had with him, said to him; 'We have been a long time in this strait and you have placed all of us who follow or serve you in danger of death. It would therefore be prudent of you to give order that we return to the North Sea [the Atlantic] where we are certain of capturing prizes, so that we can give up seeking to make new discoveries. You see how fraught with difficulties these are.' This gentleman must have sustained the opinion with more vigour than seemed proper to the General. His answer was to have the gentleman carried below and put in irons. On another day, at the same hour, he ordered him to be taken out and to be beheaded in the presence of them all. The length of his imprisonment was no more than was

necessary to substantiate the lawsuit that was conducted against him.

'All this he told me,' went on Don Francisco, 'speaking much good about the dead man, but adding that he had not been able to act otherwise because this was what the Queen's service demanded.' This significant phrase has been echoed in countless situations in the service of the crown ever since. 'He showed me the commission he had received from her and carried with him' – '*monstrome las provisiones que della traya*' as the original has it. A Spanish nobleman like Don Francisco de Zarate would never have fabricated this in a report to the viceroy – it would in any case have been no advantage to him – and this gives the lie to the school who say that Drake never held the queen's commission for his voyage.

I tried to ascertain whether any relatives of the dead man had remained on board. They told me there was only one, who was one of those who ate at his table. During all this time I was on board, which was fifty-five hours, this young man never left the ship although all the others did so in turn. It was not that he was left to guard me – I think that they guarded him.

The perspicacious Don Francisco was no doubt right yet again and Drake did not entirely trust John Doughty not to betray him. But of all Don Francisco's descriptions of his captor and of the *Golden Hind* the most telling is the last sentence of his letter to the Viceroy: 'I managed to ascertain whether the General was well liked and all said that they adored him.'

From the *Espirito Santo* Drake only took the pilot, whom he wanted to take him into the harbour of Guatulco, and 'a proper negro wench named Maria' who had been Don Francisco's personal property and was to come in useful as a comfort for the crew of the *Golden Hind* during the long trans-Pacific voyage. Then he let Don Francisco return to his ship and sail her whither he would. He headed for Realejo, nowadays called Corinto, on the coast of Guatemala; thence on Holy Thursday, 16 April 1579, Don Francisco hastily despatched his illuminating report to the viceroy of New Spain.

12

A shock for New Spain

'The next haven which we chanced with on April 15 in 15 degrees 40 minutes was *Guatelco*, so named of the Spaniards who inhabited it, with whom we had some entercourse, to the supply of many things which we desired, as chiefly bread and a pot as big as a basket full of reals of plate.' Guatulco was more properly named Aguatulca, but this very gentlemanly account gives no inkling of the actual sense of tremendous shock that the inhabitants of the little place experienced when they suddenly found *Golden Hind* in their harbour and Drake and his men wreaking havoc ashore.

Gaspar de Vargas, chief *alcalde* of Guatulco, reported afterwards to the viceroy that on Holy Monday 1579, at 8 o'clock in the morning he was informed by some of the crew of a ship belonging to Juan de Madrid, which was in Guatulco laden with stuffs for Zonzonate and due to sail the following Wednesday, that they had just seen two sails near the entrance to the port, one large, one small. They thought the larger was a ship expected from Peru and the other a pearl fisher.

Two hours later, the *alcalde* continued, both ships began to enter harbour and 'it became apparent that the larger one was, as everyone says, of more than three hundred tons.' Allowing for Spanish measurements again the apparent exaggeration may be natural enough for almost immediately the report continued:

131

They entered the port with great determination and the larger ship cast anchor. She was a strong, leaded ship, double sheathed, of 200 tons. The bark, which turned out to be a launch, and the ship's boat, filled with men, began to come very suddenly in a resolute manner towards the shore. Then only was it understood that it was the English Corsair that he turned out to be.

The *alcalde* went to meet them with a few Spaniards and some Indians who were decorating the church for Holy Thursday and Easter. They tried to oppose the English landing and succeeded in so far that 'the boat, which carried more than forty archers and arquebusiers, was delayed until the launch began to discharge its artillery, which was supported by the arquebuses in the boat'. The 'launch' must have been the ship's pinnace, which as we have seen carried her own armament. The Spaniards were soon forced to abandon the town and withdrew up the hill behind. 'What is most and above all to be deplored,' wrote Gaspar de Vargas piously 'is the shamelessness with which they with their knives hacked into pieces the sacred images and crucifixes.' They then returned to *Golden Hind* laden with plunder: 'As far as we could see they carried off three persons, who were the curate, his relative the mayor of Suchitepec, named Miranda, who had come to spend Holy Week in the port, and a certain Francisco Gomez, factor.' The *alcalde* also noted the presence of Nuño da Silva: 'The Portuguese speaks the English language as if it were his own and he is the General's all in all.'

Francisco Gomez Rengifo, the factor to whom the *alcalde* referred, was the author of an interesting report to the viceroy regarding his brief stay on board *Golden Hind*. He reported that Drake said to him:

You will be saying now this man is a devil, who robs by day and prays by night in public. This is what I do, but it is just as when King Philip gives a very large written paper to your Viceroy, Don Martin Enriquez, telling him what he is to do and how he is to govern; so the Queen, my Sovereign lady, has ordered me to come to these parts. I do regret to possess myself of anything that does not belong exclusively to King Philip or to Don Martin Enriquez, for it grieves me that their vessels should be paying for them. But I am not going to stop until I have collected the two million that my cousin John Hawkins lost for certain at San Juan de Ulua.

San Juan de Ulua! how that name must have burned itself into Drake's soul and into that of Don Martin Enriquez. Drake sent him an even more pointed message by the pilot Colchero, whom he set ashore here: 'if he should ever see His Lordship the Viceroy he was to tell him to be on his guard against him or other Englishmen, for they were going to burn him and all that belonged to him for having broken his word to John Hawkins at San Juan de Ulua.'
As soon as Drake's men got ashore

> ... they went to the town house, where they found a judge sitting in judgment, being associate with two other officers, uppon three negrose that had conspired the burning of the towne, and Drake took the prisoners and the judges and brought them on shipboard together, and set one of the prisoners, who was willing to stay in the country, on lande, who fled into the woods to save himselfe; but the other two negrose he kept with him a great space.

They were indeed singularly fortunate, in being saved in the nick of time from Spanish justice and were eventually conveyed right across the Pacific to find a new home there. 'When Drake had the three principall Spaniards of the town he caused the chief judge to command all the townsmen to avoyd, that he might safely water there, and also take the spoyle of the towne.' The irrepressible Tom Moone 'tooke a Spanish gentleman as he was flying out of the towne, and riflinge him hee found a chain of gold about him.'
Golden Hind remained at Guatulco three days. Because it was their last call in Spanish America and particularly because it was situated in Don Martin Enriquez's territory, the only place raided therein, Drake seems to have allowed his men particular licence. They behaved as pure iconoclasts in the church, smashing statues and images, even, according to Spanish reports, wiping the sweat off their faces with altar cloths. On board the *Golden Hind* the bo'sun broke a crucifix before

the scandalized eyes of the Spanish prisoners, telling them they could not regard that as God – it was only wood and metal.

Nor was Drake himself blameless in his behaviour at Guatulco. On the last morning there, Holy Thursday, 16 April, he suddenly turned to Nuño da Silva and ordered him to leave the ship and go ashore – as the unfortunate old pilot himself said, 'he cast the said Nuño da Silva into the ship of Juan Gomez without leaving him anything whatsoever in payment of all he had taken from him and without having previously shown any intention of leaving him anywhere on the outward voyage.' Several witnesses had said that Drake and Da Silva had become firm friends. What Nuño's emotions must have been as he saw the *Golden Hind*, his floating home for fifteen months, sweep out of Guatulco at 3 o'clock that same afternoon, leaving him to the Spanish wolves, may be imagined. It was a far cry from his being Drake's 'all-in-all' as the *alcalde* had described him only a few days before, and despite the admiration which one must feel for Drake in so many respects, the marooning of Nuño da Silva among his enemies appears inexcusable. One may perhaps seek a reason, if not an excuse; it was Drake's last call in Spanish America and if he found the North-West Passage and returned by it to England he would be carrying a Catholic back to a Protestant country; if he went across the Pacific he might encounter the Portuguese and Da Silva would be in even greater trouble than with the Spaniards. Or it may simply have been that the *Golden Hind* was now entering waters where Nuño would be no further use as a pilot – Drake had so much wanted Colchero on this part of the voyage – and so he would be one extra unproductive mouth to feed under certain conditions.

The truth will never be known but the three years' hell which awaited Nuño da Silva may be laid at Drake's door. The *alcalde*, as surprised as Nuño was to meet him again, promptly had him arrested and sent off on his long journey to Mexico City where the viceroy, who had worked himself into a fine fury as report after report of Drake's depredations came pouring in, was awaiting him with feline malice. On 17 May he wrote to his colleague, Don Francisco de Toledo, viceroy

134

of Peru: 'Up to the moment I have not seen the pilot, but I have had men stationed along the road at intervals and I expect him hourly. When he arrives I shall manage, by fair means or foul, to make a minute investigation about the voyage and the Corsair's design in leaving him behind. At present I have my suspicions about the affair.'

Don Martin Enriquez was adept at foul means and the inference of his letter was that Nuño had been left ashore as an agent of Drake, perhaps to draw suspicion off from his next intended point of attack. In fact when Nuño de Silva arrived in Mexico City the viceroy interrogated him very closely without a break for almost a day and a half, but in the end appeared to be convinced of his sincerity. The next step was however to hand him over to the Inquisition, as he was suspected of having become a Lutheran during his long voyage in *Golden Hind*.

Meanwhile New Spain was in a state of shock, rumour chasing rumour, Spaniards chasing shadows while the author of their chaos cheerfully observed, 'And now having reasonably, as we thought, provided ourselves, we departed from the coast of America for the present'.

The viceroy of New Spain was now harvesting the dragon's seed he had sown at San Juan de Ulua eleven years before, and he did not find it palatable. First and foremost, he must know more of this impudent Englishman, for as yet his information was scrappy; news said that the attack had been on Acapulco, on the coast of Mexico, whereas it had really been on Guatulco in Guatemala. Don Martin decided to interrogate the Englishmen still in his power.

Miles Phillips and Paul Horsewell of the *Jesus of Lübeck* had reached the end of the confinement in a convent to which they had been sentenced at the *auto da fe* in Mexico.

When our time was expired we were again brought before the Inquisitors [wrote Miles] and had our fools' coats pulled off and hung up in the church. Every man's name and sentence was written on his coat, with the words added – *An heretic reconciled*. The coats were also there of men burned, upon which was written – *An obstinate heretic burnt*.

Then we were allowed to go free, yet not so free but that we knew all our actions were spied upon.

The methods of totalitarian regimes do not change.

Some married negro or half-caste women. For my own part, I could never settle to marry in the country, though many fair offers were made to me. Therefore I decided to become apprenticed to a silk weaver. So I remained at my craft for three years and at the end of that time news came that some Englishmen had landed with a great force at Acapulco and were coming to Mexico to despoil it. This caused a great stir among the Spaniards.

Then Paul Horsewell and I were sent for by the Viceroy, who demanded of us whether we knew an Englishman named Francis Drake, who was brother to John Hawkins.

This error on his part gave them at least a chance to prevaricate. 'To which we replied that Captain Hawkins had only one brother, a man of sixty years or thereabouts, who was now governor of Plymouth.' Then came the direct question, which merited a lie:

Then he asked if we knew Francis Drake, and we answered no.

While this was happening, news came that the Englishman had gone. Nevertheless a strong force of soldiers was sent to Acapulco and I was sent with this force as an interpreter. When we came to Acapulco we found that Captain Drake had left a month before our arrival. Yet our captain put his men aboard two or three small ships, taking me with him, sailed southward towards Panama. Then we met other ships which told us that Drake was clean gone from the coast, and so we returned to Acapulco. Next day we began our journey towards Mexico, and arrived there some weeks after our leaving.

The Spanish fixation that Drake had gone south was their cardinal error, involving a lot of useless expense. If they had listened to Pedro Sarmiento they might have done better and might even have forestalled Drake at Guatulco. Pedro, on arrival at Manta where he had seen the ship which Drake had

Drake at the court of the ruler of Ternate

Golden Hind on the rocks off Celebes, from Nicola van Sype's map of the circumnavigation

An engraving of the knighting of Drake on board the *Golden Hind*

Two silver medals engraved with Mercator's world map showing Drake's circumnavigation with a dotted line

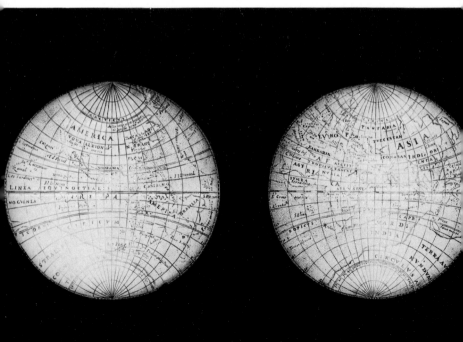

The cup given to Drake by Queen Elizabeth to encase the coconut which he had brought back to present to her

The 'Drake Chair', made from the timbers of *Golden Hind* when she was broken up, which was given to the Bodleian Library, Oxford, in 1662 by Joh Davies of Camberwell, keeper of naval stores at Deptford dockyard

Drake's drum, decorated with his coat of arms and crest and a pattern of studded nails

Drake's seal

The astrolabe made for
Drake by Humphrey
Cole

Drake's chest from the
great cabin of the
Golden Hind

Above Buckland Abbey, Devon, Drake's house

Left Drake's coat of arms in Buckland Abbey

Opposite An interior view of Buckland Abbey

Opposite above left Elizabeth Sydenham, Sir Francis's second wife

Opposite above right Sir Francis Drake, painted by an unknown artist

In autumn 1974 a historically authentic replica of the *Golden Hind* will sail from Plymouth, Devon, following Drake's original route to Panama and thence to San Francisco. This picture shows a shipwright tightening a clamp on the planking near the stem or bow during the building of the *Golden Hind* replica

Two shipwrights preparing the keel to receive the half-frames or ribs during the building of the replica of Drake's famous ship

robbed of her sails, reasoned that the *Golden Hind* would head direct for the coast of Nicaragua and advised the admiral to sail thither instead of following the coast all round to Panama. The admiral agreed but General Luis de Toledo was not convinced. 'He had no instructions,' he said, with that slavish adherence to the rule-book which has been the downfall of so many military commanders. So the Spaniards concentrated on Panama while Drake was wreaking havoc further north.

It was Gaspar de Vargas, the magistrate at Guatulco, who assumed that the *Golden Hind* was heading for Acapulco and wrote as much to the viceroy. It lay a hundred leagues further up the coast so he despatched a messenger at top speed to warn the town 'so that even if he has to kill horses in doing so, he should reach that port before the ship, so that the necessary precautions can be taken'. Rumours that Drake had already landed there reached the viceroy before the *alcalde's* letter, which was ten days under way. In that letter de Vargas proposed that he should embark four hundred men in two ships, one of them belonging to the king of Spain, and lie in wait for *Golden Hind*.

> I think beyond doubt he will set course for Acapulco, because it seems that he had come from Zonzonate where he must have done no small damage on his way and in the ports wither two vessels laden with cargo went from that port. One belonged to Sebastian Ruiz, the other to Don Francisco de Zarate. It is suspected that he met these because, according to the sailors, the ship is so low in the water that she appears as though she must be laden with gold, silver and merchandise. All this is conjecture, but it may be true.

Some of it was, although some vital parts were not. Two days after Gaspar de Vargas despatched his letter, Don Francisco de Zarate sailed into Realejo in the *Espirito Santo* and another letter was on its way to the viceroy. Don Martin wrote on the evening 23 April – the day that the *alcalde's* report reached him – the first of a series of letters to King Philip, in one of which he made the significant observation 'On these coasts there is no mode of defence'. They were ancient history by the time they reached the Escorial and the king evidently did not think any action was called for on his part, for his secretary 'laid by' the letters in the best civil service tradition, merely annotating them, 'No need to reply. Place with other papers on Drake'.

The stir and fruitless activity went on for months but no one could answer the vital question, where had Drake gone? The licentiate Valverde, President of Audiencia of Guatemala, had a belated brain-wave and despatched a fleet towards California, which he considered the most likely direction. They came back empty-handed and he had to explain why he had sent them. As late as 16 April 1580 he sent a report to King Philip explaining his reasons for despatching 'Your Armada with orders to pass beyond New Spain and New Galicia and to go to the Californias, the Gulf of Vermejo' (this was the old name for the Gulf of California). There were four routes, he conjectured, by which Drake could return to England: the strait of Los Bacollaos ('stockfish'), which was the supposed North-West Passage, the existence of which was admitted to be uncertain, or by way of China, or by Vallano – the Panama Isthmus – or by the Straits of Magellan, by which he had come.

Valverdè gave the king five reasons why he thought Drake would find the China route too difficult; first, the navigation would be long and troublesome and he would have to pilot and coast all the world in order to return to England; secondly, that he could not convey in his ship all the provisions needed for eighty men for so long a voyage, even if she carried no cargo other than victuals; thirdly, that he would have to call at or pass within sight of Portuguese ports 'when he would be seized or chastised by the armadas there – on reaching Asia, he would also run the risk of the Turks'. This chose to ignore the fact that *Golden Hind* might avoid both. Valverde went on to explain that military men tended to dissemble in order to throw the enemy off the scent; Drake's strength lay in telling the Spaniards the truth, which was the last thing they were likely to believe.

Valverde's fifth reason was that Drake had put ashore at Guatulco

Nuño da Silva, a most experienced Portuguese pilot, most skilful in the art of navigation and the knowledge of the heavens, whom he had brought with him for fifteen months. Now it would have been in his interest to have taken him further, for he was a friend of his and he would need his counsel and ingenuity in so long a voyage, so much so that he would never have left him behind had he intended to return by way of China.

This might of course be the explanation for Drake's landing Nuño at Guatulco – to throw the Spaniards off the scent as to his future intentions.

Valverde indeed concluded that Drake would in all probability return via the Magellan Straits, first because he knew them already, secondly – as had been learnt from Nuño da Silva – they were navigable both ways and not in only one direction as the Spaniards had previously assumed. He further assumed wrongly that the weather further north was less propitious from May to October than outside those months – the exact opposite of what Pedro Sarmiento de Gamboa knew to be the case.

Probably the Corsair has wintered on the coast, in the region of the Californias [wrote Valverde] in one of those small bays or deep coves that are there or off one of the adjacent islands. He may be there with the idea of returning in the month of November when the following winds could assist her. His sole consideration will be to allow time to pass, so that the coasts will be as unguarded and unprepared as when he came.

As further evidence of Drake's intentions he cited, very illogically, that the English had seized the entire stock of Indian women's petticoats in Guatulco, 'disregarding a large quantity of valuable silk clothing'. Valverde could not imagine either that Drake would, from the Mexican coast, follow the route to China which Magellan took in the *Victoria* all those years before – and this despite the fact that a year ago, on 29 March 1579, Captain Juan Solano, the lieutenant-governor of Costa Rica, had told Valverde himself that Drake said, 'he had ordered his captains to meet him, at a certain date, at Macao and Goa, in the Portuguese Indies, so as to proceed to his own country.' This was perhaps bluff, inferring that Winter was still in the Pacific; in any case Valverde did not believe it.

The Inquisition had wasted no time, once the viceroy had finished his interrogation, in turning on Nuño da Silva. The first report of their questioning of him is dated 23 May 1579, a few days after his arrival in Mexico and is headed 'Summary of the confession of the pilot – deposition by Nuño da Silva as to how he was made prisoner'. Nuño was repeatedly interrogated. The Inquisitors were certain he must have accepted heresy during the long time he was in an English ship. They were still at it nearly a year later when on 9 February 1580 the Chief Inquisitor sent a commission to Fra Andre de Aguiare at Acapulco to examine Juan Pascual, a seaman about to sail for China.

> Your Reference has already received notice of the cause of detention, in this Holy Office, of Nuño da Silva, the Portuguese pilot who was for so long a time with Francis Drake, the Englishman and Lutheran, who went about committing robberies on the coast of the South Seas. We have received a report that this pilot joined the English Lutherans in performing the rites and ceremonies of their sect. Information about this could be obtained from a certain Juan Pascual, a seaman who is now in that port and is about to sail for China by the first vessel. The English took the said Juan Pascual from Don Francisco de Zarate's ship and landed him at Guatulco, where he was taken.

Pascual indeed endeavoured under interrogation by Fra Aguiare to inculpate Nuño da Silva to save his own skin, although he was a compatriot, a native of Vilanova in the Algarve. He twisted his evidence sycophantically so that the Inquisitor should hear what he wanted. On board *Golden Hind*, he said, the English prayed twice a day and Nuño with them, but he could not say whether the pilot said the same prayers as the Englishmen did. He had to admit however that the Spanish prisoners were not forced to take part in the 'Lutheran devotions' which he described by saying that 'the said Drake knelt on his knees on a cushion in front of a table and chanted in a low voice and all the others responded to him. The other Spaniards withdrew and went to the prow of the ship, but, twice a day, the said Nuño da Silva prayed with the rest, and listened to their sermons and held a book like a "Book of Hours" in his hand.' The Spaniards were allowed 'to tell their Christian beads as they were accustomed to do' but 'Drake made them eat meat on Fridays and in Lent'; but he admitted that this was because they were Lutherans and gave them to eat what they ate themselves – a good enough reason in a ship at sea.

The Inquisitors pressed Pascual to say that Drake had ill-treated his prisoners but he had to admit that he had never seen him harm anyone; Pascual did allege, however, that the crew of *Golden Hind* went in terror of their captain and passed him with hat in hand if they met him, bowing low with eyes downcast to the deck.

As to Nuño da Silva, the old pilot, although tortured on the rack and threatened with the confiscation of all his possessions, stoutly refused to admit that he had done more than receive holy communion twice in accordance with the rites of the English Church. Eventually even the Inquisitors were persuaded to let him go, but not until 1583, a full four years after his initial arrest by them, and then at King Philip's personal command. Evidently the truth of what Drake was like, what conditions were like aboard the *Golden Hind* and how Nuño da Silva had comported himself there during his enforced stay of fifteen months had at last permeated to high places in Spain. Perhaps too Philip sensed the need to improve his 'image' in Portugal which he had taken over forcibly in 1580. Nuño was given money for his return from Mexico to Spain and 'no man' – significantly, it was emphasized, 'not the jayler of the Holy House in Seville' – was 'to molest him'. So much for the Inquisition, who dared not gainsay the king. Sea employment was once more offered to Nuño da Silva, 'but first he is to visit his family'; and so the old pilot, now aged sixty-three, ended his days in the trade he loved, conning ships from the pilot's platform above the whipstaff – though no doubt with many memories, some probably nostalgic, of his days in *Golden Hind*.

Most of the others got off more lightly. Don Francisco de Zarate, having despatched his comprehensive letter to the viceroy immediately on landing at Realejo, got in his blow first before news of Drake's escapade at Guatulco reached Don Martin Enriquez. It seems that Zarate suffered no penalty for his acquaintance with Drake; as a cousin of the Duke of Medina Sidonia, future commander of the Armada and a leading grandee of Spain, even the Inquisition would have thought twice about attacking him. The authorities were a bit more suspicious about San Juan de Anton – after all, he had lost a vast amount of treasure from the *Cacafuego*. There may also have been some foundation for the theory that he had spent some time in his youth in England and that 'de Anton' is the Spanish rendering of 'Southampton'. He had to make a very detailed deposition to exculpate himself and was also called upon to give a full explanation to Pedro Sarmiento de Gamboa, appointed by the viceroy to investigate the whole affair.

But profound though the effect on some individuals was, the voyage of *Golden Hind* had had a far more devastating influence on Spanish hegemony in general. For the first time another power had challenged Spanish supremacy in the Pacific, had actually attacked Spanish shipping in the ports of Peru and New Spain and had shown the Spanish authorities and the Inquisition that they were not always safe to persecute with impunity. 'This province is greatly disturbed,' wrote Don Garcia de Palacios, the royal judge in Guatemala 'and I believe that in Peru and Tierra Pirme' (the Spanish Main) 'it must be the same.' From Realejo he wrote to the Captain-General of the Fleet 'It would be just that a man who had the audacity to do what he did, and rob so much silver and gold, should be hindered from enjoying it and carrying it to his own country, as a tit-bit for his countrymen.' The said Captain-General of the Fleet, Don Christobal de Eraso, wrote to the judge of the royal court in Panama from Nombre de Dios: 'I have particularly looked into the account given by San Juan de Anton of the voyage made by this Corsair; I am filled with amazement at the boldness he has displayed. I have held a council meeting of the captains, pilots and cosmographers of the Armada and with the map in hand tried to see by what route the Corsair might go out again.' The Spanish aristocrats could hardly believe it; a relative of the captain-general, Don Miguel de Eraso y Aguilar, wrote to King Philip from Cartagena: 'It is a thing that terrifies one, this voyage and the boldness of this low man (for it is said that his father was a shoe-maker).'

The viceroy of Peru had not dared to act against his English prisoners while there was a likelihood of *Golden Hind* suddenly reappearing and Drake fulfilling his threat of three thousand Spanish heads being cast into the port of Callao. But by 20 February 1580, it was decided that the *Golden Hind* must be far away and the Inquisitors in Lima 'ordered that Captain John Oxenham be brought from the said prison and in the presence of the Chief Clerk he took the oath in due form and promised to speak the truth'. They now proceeded to interrogate closely the man who had been the prisoner of the secular and religious powers of Spain for nearly three years. What state he was in by them, submitted as he had been to torture, one cannot say, but his answers seem to have been fearless and straightforward.

Questioned as to whether, while in England or since he had left there, he had heard or understood that Queen Elizabeth or any other person had entertained the project to arm a certain number of vessels for the purpose of establishing settlements or for other purposes on the coasts of the North Sea, or in the region of the Strait of Magellan or on the coast of the South Sea, he answered that four years ago an English knight named Richard Grenville, who lives at a distance of a league and a half from Plymouth [no doubt by this Oxenham was referring to Buckland Abbey] and is very rich, applied to the Queen for a licence to come to the Straits of Magellan and pass to the South Sea in order to search for land or some islands where to found settlements, because in England there are many inhabitants but little land. The Queen gave him the licence and witness saw it. It is very splendid. The said Grenville bought two ships and was about to buy two or three more when the Queen revoked the licence, because she had learnt that beyond the Strait of Magellan there were settlements made by

Spaniards, who might harm them. They said Grenville sold the ships, after the licence had been taken from him. Prior to that he had spoken to witness many times, trying to persuade him to accompany him, but witness did not wish to do so. Grenville's project was to found a settlement on the River Plate, then to pass through the Straits and establish settlements wherever a good country for such could be found.

Witness thinks that if the Queen were to give a licence to Captain Francis Drake he would certainly come and pass through the Strait, because he is a very good mariner and pilot, there is no better one than he in England to do it. [It would appear from this that Oxenham had no knowledge of Drake's recent presence in Callao so that evidently the viceroy had not mentioned his reasons for seeking his advice on how to melt down church bells for ammunition.] Witness thinks that the Queen will not, as long as she lives, grant the licence but that after the Queen's death there will certainly be someone who will come to the Strait.

Questioned as to how many ships it would be possible for Francis Drake to come with to the Strait Oxenham answered that with the aid of his relatives and companions Drake might be able to bring two or three vessels, but that, after discovering a good country, they would be able to come with more ships. Witness said that Captain Francis discussed the subject with him.

Questioned whether they had discussed how, and by what route, they were to return to England after having passed through the Straits, he said that it seemed to him that it was by the same Strait, but others said that there was a route through another Strait that passed into the North Sea, but nobody knows this for a certainty or had passed through it.

The document concluded with the sinister observation, 'With this the examination ceased. The prisoner was sent back to his cell.' The sinister note was echoed in the Inquisitors' final report dated after an *auto da fe* held in Lima on 29 October 1580. 'Trial of John Oxenham, Captain of the English who, coming for the purpose of committing robberies, entered Vallano near Nombre de Dios. It was voted that he be admitted to reconciliation, but sentenced to perpetual captivity, which term is to be spent in His Majesty's galleys, in service at the oars without wages and with confiscation of property.' Such then was the churchmen's heartless sentence, but the secular authorities also had their card to play.

Meanwhile Thomas 'Xervel' as they called him, master of the ship, was 'admitted to reconciliation but sentenced to perpetual captivity with confiscation of property and to ten years of service, without wages, in the galleys. After ten years he is to be confined somewhere in this city, in the locality designated to him.' As for John Butler,

> pilot of the said English ship, it had been voted (after having examined him under torture) that he be taken out in the public *auto da fe*, that he abjure *de vehementi* and be absolved for the major excommunication which he had incurred and that he serve in the galleys of His Majesty, for six years, at the oars, without wages.

> It has already been communicated to Your Lordship how these three Englishmen (and another, a youth, who is a brother of the said John Butler) had been brought by us to these prisons from the royal prison where they had been taken by those who brought them from Vallano. We therefore return them to the same royal prison where, after they had been there for a few days, the Criminal Magistrates passed a sentence upon them and the said John Oxenham, Thomas Xervel and John Butler were hanged. The said youth who calls himself Henry Butler was sentenced by the magistrates to perpetual service in the galleys.

Thus ended the sad venture of John Oxenham, subjected with his officers and men to the full cruelty of the two-pronged Spanish terror machine. Drake did not get the news until his return to England and it merely strengthened his almost fanatical resolve to humiliate that proud nation. The cruel irony was that *Golden Hind* had been unable to save Oxenham when she was in Callao on the very doorstep of Lima.

13

New Albion

While the Spaniards were speculating wildly and chasing shadows, *Golden Hind* set course 'directly into the sea, whereon we sayled five hundred leagues in longitude, to get a wind'. Between 16 April, when she sailed from Guatulco, and 3 June, when she reached forty-two degrees north latitude, she covered 'fourteen hundred leagues in all'. Then, 'in the night following, we found such alteration of heate into extreme and nipping cold, that our men in general did grievously complaine thereof, some of them feeling their health much impaired thereby.'

Forty-two degrees coincides almost exactly with Cape Mendocino, which Pedro Sarmiento had mentioned as the point as far as which the best season prevailed until September.

> We seemed to be in the frozen Zone rather than in any way so neere unto the sun [wrote the chaplain] for it came to that extremity, in sailing but two degrees further to the north-west in our course, that though sea-men lack not good stomachs, yet it seemed a question to many of us, whether their hands should feed their mouths or rather keep themselves within their coverts for the pinching cold that did benumme them.

The geographers were once again proved to be wrong by Drake's discoveries. They had assumed that the west coast of America ran virtually north-east from Cape Mendocino until the North-West Passage was reached, but

> The land in that part of America, being farther out into the West than we before imagined, we were neerer on it than we were aware; and yet the nearer still we came unto it the more extremitie of cold did sease upon us. The fifth day of *June* we were forced by contrarie windes to run by the shoare, which we then first descried, and to cast anchor in a bad bay, the best roade we could for the present meet with.

The narrative continues to describe the 'extreme gusts and flawes' that beat upon them, 'which if they ceased and were still at any time, immediately upon their intercession there followed the most vile, thick and stinking fogges, against which the sea prevailed nothing'. Such fogs are all too familiar a feature of the Golden Gate area to this day, but wherever this 'bad bay' was they could not stay in it, so *Golden Hind* endeavoured to tack on to the north 'in the extremity of the cold (which had now utterly discouraged our men), the winds directly bent against us, having once gotten us under sayle again, commanded us to the Southward whether we would or no'.

The ship had reached the latitude of modern Vancouver before she put about. 'From the height of 48 degrees, in which we now were, to 38 we found the land, by coasting along it, to be but low and reasonable plaine; every hill (whereof we saw many, but none verie high) though it were *June*, and the sunne in his nearest approach unto them, being covered with snow.' As to the North-West Passage, they had of course seen no sign of it and chaplain Fletcher, musing on what they had discovered in their voyage to the Canadian coast, observed:

> We conjecture that either there is no passage at all through these Northern coasts (which is most likely), or, if there be, that yet it is unnavigable. Adde hereunto, that though we searched the coast diligently, even unto the forty-eighth degree, yet we found not the land to trend so much as one point in any place towards the East, but rather running on continually North-west, as if it went directly to meet with Asia.

How very nearly right they were! and now *Golden Hind* had

sailed down the coast of modern Oregon and was approaching California from the north-north-west. 'In 38 degrees 30 minutes we fell with a convenient and fit harborough and on *June* 17 came to anchor therein.'

Controversy has raged ever since the settlement of the American West and still continues as to where this 'convenient and fit harborough' was exactly – was it inside or outside the Golden Gate, within San Francisco Bay or in the Point Reyes peninsula? The majority inclines to the opinion that it was Drake's Bay, just inside Point Reyes Head, which sticks out sharply from the protruding peninsula, 'a dark wedge of land for ever thrust like a great lance point against the burnished breastplate of the Pacific', as a modern writer has described it. Coming close-hauled round this from the north-north-west *Golden Hind* would have found herself suddenly under the lee of this headland, the most projecting promontory in all her exploration of the north-west American coast. However, 'on the third day following, viz. the 21, our ship having received a leake at sea, was brought to anchor neerer the shoare, that, her goods being landed, she might be repaired.' The most widely accepted location for this further move is Drake's cove, or Drake's Estero, an estuary a mile in from Point Reyes Head, which would be entirely sheltered and indeed the description of the surroundings, 'white banks and cliffs which lie towards the sea' certainly fits, for these cliffs are very much in evidence in the sweep of Drake's Bay and are reminiscent of the Sussex coast in the vicinity of the Seven Sisters.

The *Golden Hind* had barely anchored and Drake and his landing party gone ashore than their presence attracted the astonished delight of the local Indians, who had never seen white men before and regarded them as gods.

> Their men for the most part goe naked; the women take a kind of bulrushes, and kembing it after the manner of hemp, make themselves thereof a loose garment, which being knitte about their middles, hanges downe about their hippes, and so affordes to them a covering of that which nature teaches should be hidden; about their shoulders they weare also the skin of a deere, with the haire upon it.

The Indians addressed Drake as 'Hioh'. From the signs of reverence which accompanied this they inferred that it meant 'god' or 'king' and the gallant Captain Francis, though doubtless flattered, could not as a good Protestant accept the former and as a good subject of Her Majesty hardly the latter. He made it plain that he wished to see their chief

> ... and among the rest the king himselfe, a man of goodly stature and comely personage, attended with his guard of about a hundred tall and warlike men, this day, viz *June 26*, came down to see us. Before his coming were sent two ambassadors or messengers to our Generall, to signifie that their *Hioh*, that is their king, was coming and at hand ... they by signs made request to our Generall, to send something by their hands to their *Hioh* or king, as a token that his coming might be in peace. Our Generall willingly satisfied their desire; and they, glad men, made speedy return to their *Hioh*.

The Indians, however, were determined that Drake should become their overlord.

> They made signs to our General to have him sit down; unto whom both the king and divers others made several orations, or rather indeed if wee had understood them, supplications that he would take the Province and kingdom into his hand, and become their king and patron; making signes that they would asigne unto him their right and title in their whole land, and become his vassals in themselves and their posterity.

The king, the chaplain noted, wore a splendid crown of feathers and now,

> ... joyfully singing a song, set the crowne upon his [Drake's] head, inriched his neck with all their chaines, and offering unto him many other things, honoured him by the name of *Hyoh*.
>
> These things being so freely offered, our Generall thought not meet to reject or refuse the same, both that he would not give them any cause of mistrust or disliking him (that being the onely place, wherein at this present we were of

necessite inforced to seek relief of many thinges.) Where-fore, in the name of and to the use of her most excellent Maiesty, he tooke the scepter, crowne and dignity of the said countrie into his hand.

Once the *Golden Hind*'s careening and caulking was com-plete, Drake, taking his gentlemen adventurers and a large number of seamen with him, went up into the interior to see the Indians' villages. 'The inland we found to be farre different from the shoare, a goodly country, and fruitfull soyle, stored with many blessings fit for the use of man.' The fauna also fascinated them

> ... large and fat Deere which there we saw by the thousands ... besides a multitude of a strange kinde of Conies, by farre exceeding them in number; their heads and bodies in which they resemble other Conies, are but small; his tayle, like the tayle of a Rat, exceeding long; and his feet like the pawes of a Want or mole; under his chinne, on either side, he hath a bagge, into which he gathereth his meate, when he hath filled his belly alreade, that he may with it either feed his young, or feed himselfe when he lists not to travaile from his burroughe; the people eate their bodies, and make great account of their skinnes, for their kinges holidaies coate was made of them.
>
> This country our General named *Albion*, and that for two causes; the one in respect of the white banckes and cliffs, which lie towards the sea; the other, that it might have some affinity, even in name also, with our own country, which was sometime so called.

So 'New Albion' it became and was so referred to for some time by geographers: 'the Spaniards never had any dealing, or so much as set a foote in this country, the utmost of their discoveries reaching onely to many degrees Southwards of the place,' wrote Fletcher and indeed their conquest of California did not take place till two centuries later, though after *Golden Hind* had gone individual Spanish navigators did penetrate the waters round San Francisco Bay.

There followed an event whose repercussions have echoed into modern times.

Before we went from thence, our Generall caused to be set up a monument for our being there, as also of her majesties and successors right and title to that kingdome; namely, a plate of brasse, fast nailed to a great and firme poste; whereon is engraven her graces name, and the day and year of our arrivall there, and of the free giving up of the province and kingdome, both by the king and people, unto her maiesties hands; together with her highnesse picture and armes, in a piece of sixpence current English monie, shewing itself by a hole made of purpose through the plate; underneath was likewise engraven the name of our Generall, etc.

So the British Empire in America was founded not where most people thought and indeed on the far side from the Roanoke of Raleigh and Greville; it was centuries before people of British stock were to reach it again and who knows what legal rights might have existed and exist still regarding New Albion, taken over 'in her maiesties name'! Only documentary proof of this existed for centuries and then, by an incredible chance, in our own century a plate similar to that described was discovered by a chauffeur driving his employer's car between Point Reyes and San Francisco; the latter however had no interest and the chauffeur jettisoned it, only for it to be found again, much nearer San Quentin and the inner waters of San Francisco Bay, by a young man seeking a picnic spot. He had the good sense to take it to the University of California and their forensic tests pronounced it to be genuine. It is in their keeping today and a facsimile hangs in Buckland Abbey.

Its wording, clearly visible on the original, almost exactly fulfils the description given by the chaplain:

BE IT KNOWN UNTO ALL MEN BY THESE PRESENTS JUNE 17 1579 BY THE GRACE OF GOD IN THE NAME OF HER MAJESTY QUEEN ELIZABETH OF ENGLAND AND HER SUCCESSORS FOREVER I TAKE POSSESSION OF THIS KINGDOM WHOSE KING AND PEOPLE FREELY RESIGNE THEIR RIGHT AND TITLE IN THE WHOLE LAND UNTO HER MAJESTIES KEEPING NOW NAMED BY ME AND TO BE KNOWNE UNTO ALL MEN AS NOVA ALBION —

FRANCIS DRAKE

The location of its second discovery has prompted the theory that the landing took place inside San Francisco Bay and some very erudite argument has been adduced to show that this was so. The only strange point, if this were so, is that Fletcher's revised narrative makes no mention of the Golden Gate and given as he was to precise and colourful descriptions one would have thought that he would not have failed to notice such a notable topographical feature with the same enthusiasm which he showed for those in the Cape Verde Islands or Magellan Straits.

Golden Hind had remained five weeks in all in her 'convenient and fit harborough' and the chaplain related how she sailed away on 23 July 1579, to the accompaniment of a great display of grief by the Indians who 'being loathe to leave us, presently ranne to the top of the hill to keepe us in their sight as long as they could' and lit bonfires, presumably as a sacrifice, to their white *Hioh* and his great sea-bird. On the following day they came to some islands 'which lay at no great distance from our place of landing'. These they named the Islands of St James, and they are almost certainly the modern Farallon Islands, which lie well out to sea west-south-west of the Golden Gate. Fletcher described them as 'having on them plentifull and great store of Seales and birds'.

Golden Hind sailed thence on 25 July:

> ... and our Generall now, counting that the extremity of the cold not only continued, but increased, the Sunne being gone further from us, and that the wind blowing still (as it did at first) from the North West, cut off all hope of finding a passage through these Northern parts, thought it necessarie to loose no time; and therefore with general consent bent his course directly to runne with the Ilands of the Moluccas.

With the wind on her starboard beam out into the Pacific she flew, away from the American continent and the turmoil further south: 'and so, having in our view but aire and sea, without the sight of any land for the space of full sixty-eight days together, we continued on our course through the maine Ocean.'

14

To the Spice Islands

It was 30 September before they sighted any land, in the shape of some islands 'lying about eight degrees north of the line'. From the description of what befell there it had long been assumed these must be the Ladrones, but it is now more widely accepted that one of the Palau group must have been the island in question.

Here the landing party from *Golden Hind* was attacked by natives, who, 'having stones good store in their canowes, let flie a maine of them against us. It was farre from our Generalls meaning to requite their malice by like' but in order to scare them 'he caused a great peece to be shot off, not to hurt them but to affright them. Which wrought the desired effect against them, for at the noise thereof they every one leaped out of his canowe into the water, and diving under the keele of their boates, staied them from going any way till our ship was gone a good way from them.' Then they all raced for the shore 'and so we left that place, to be knowne hereafter by the name of the *Island of Theeves*'. Magellan had similarly named islands the 'Ladrones', or 'robbers'.

Till 3 October *Golden Hind* was unable to emerge from the extensive archipelago but from then until the sixteenth she held on her course, 'where we fell with four Ilands standing in 7 degrees 5 minutes to the Northward of the Line. We coasted then till the 21 day and then anchored and watered upon the biggest of them, called Mindanao. [These were of course the Philippines]. Mindanao is very extensive and of curious shape and it took some six days to clear it.' On 22 October the *Golden Hind* passed between two islands 'some six or eight leagues' southward of it and a couple of war canoes came out in the hopes of speaking to her, 'but there arose so much wind from the north' that she carried straight on on her southerly course.

The next landfall was Talao or Talau in 3 degrees 40 minutes, followed by a group of three others, then on 1 November '*Ile Suaco*, in 1 degree 30 minutes'; then two days later she entered the archipelago of the Moluccas, the Spice Islands to which they had looked forward so eagerly during all their long voyage across the Pacific. 'There are four high pitched Ilands,' wrote Fletcher 'their names are *Ternate, Tidore, Matchan* and *Batchan*' – or to give the last two their modern spelling, Mahian and Batjan – 'all of them very fruitfull and yeelding abundance of cloves, whereof we furnished ourselves of as much as we desired at a very cheap rate.' *Golden Hind* took on about six tons of spices all told and then set sail. Passing the large island of Gillolo 'we directed our course to have gone to Tidore, but in coasting about a little island belonging to the King of *Terenate, November* 4, his deputy or Viceroy with all expedition came off to our ship in a canow, and without any feare or doubting of our good meaning came presently aboard.'

The sequel to this was that the king of Ternate himself visited the *Golden Hind* – 'the manner of his coming as it was princely so truly it seemed to us very strange and marvellous'. So great was the respect in which he was held by his own people that neither his viceroy nor any of his counsellors 'durst speake unto him but upon their knees, not rising againe till they were licenced'. Drake was very pleased at being so honoured and determined to give his royal visitor a fitting welcome: 'Our ordinance thundered, which were mixed with a great store of small shot, among which sounding our trumpets and other instruments of musick.' The king was delighted, but preferred not to go aboard *Golden Hind* himself; instead 'requesting our musick to come into the boate, he joyned his canow to the same, and was towed at least a whole howre together, with the boats at the sterne of our ship.' This incident is depicted by de Hondt or Hondius in a vignette in his map, which shows four native canoes being towed at the stern of *Golden Hind*.

In Ternate was a castle built by the Portuguese but the present king and his brother had driven them out, for, according to Fletcher, 'they cruelly murthered the king himselfe (father of him who now reigns)' in 'seeking to settle a tyrannous government'. 'The Portugall was wholly driven from that Iland,' he continued 'and glad that he keeps a footing in *Tydore*.'

While the ship was anchored at Ternate she received a visit from a most interesting personage, 'a goodly gentleman' who brought an interpreter and came 'to view our ship and to confere with our Generall; he was apparrelled much after our manner, most neate and courtlike.' He told the Englishman that he was only a stranger to the Spice Islands himself, being a native of the province of Paghia in China. His name, he said, was '*Parsaos*, of the familie of *Homber*, of which familie there had eleven reigned in continuall succession these two hundred years.' Parsaos marvelled at the ship having come so far and asked Drake to give him full details of 'the occasion, way and manner of his coming so far from England thither, with the manifold occurrences that had happened to him in the way'. Drake, to his great pleasure, told him all he wanted to know and he then begged the English captain to visit China before sailing any further westward. 'Hereupon he took occasion to relate the number and greatness of the provinces' and told how 'in *Suntien* which is the chiefest Citie of *China*, they had brasse ordnance of all sorts above two thousand years agoe'.

Enticing though this glimpse of ancient Chinese civilisation must have been, Drake would not be deflected. He had told the Queen to expect him home by August 1579 and that date was already long past: 'So the stranger parted sorrie that he could not prevaile in his request, yet exceeding glad of the intelligence he had learned.'

One wooded island in the vicinity of Ternate, as yet

uninhabited received its first settlers in the oddest manner, which, if their descendants persisted into later centuries, must have set an ethnic puzzle. 'At their departure Drake left behind him uppon this Iland the two negroes which hee tooke at Aguatulca, and likewise the negro wench Maria, shee being gotten with childe in the ship, and now being very great, was left here on the Iland, which Drake named the Ile Francisca after the name of one of the negrose.' So Don Francisco de Zarate's Negro girl found a new home an ocean away from her former one and two oceans away from the continent whence her forebears hailed.

The island was the scene of a petty blaze between Drake and one of the crew. 'Here Drake quarrelled with Will Legge, taking occasion by that means to take from him a wedge of gold, weying 20 lbs; but because hee would make some shew of honest dealing he called for a chisel, and gave the gould a marck, and said he would give it to Legges wife the value thereof at his arrival in England.'

Golden Hind sailed from Ternate on 9 November: 'Considering that our ship for want of trimming was now growne foule, that our cashe and vessels for water were much decayed, and that divers other things stood in need of reparation; our next care was, how we might fall with such a place where with safetie we might a while stay for the redressing of these inconveniences.' They had last careened the ship in New Albion, four months before and an ocean away; moreover 'the lack of wind persuaded us it was the fittest time that we could take. With this resolution we sayled along till *November* 14' when they came upon a little island to the south of Celebes 'standing in 1 degree 40 minutes towards the pole antartick; which being without inhabitants, gave us the better hope of quiet abode.' So *Golden Hind* dropped anchor; the place proved ideal, and they stayed twenty-six days all told, setting up a smith's forge 'both for the making of some necessarie shipworke and for the repairing of some iron-hooped caskes'. *Golden Hind* was entirely self-sufficient; they careened her and 'performed our other business to our content'. While there they noticed at night very large bats which 'flie with marvellous swiftnesse' and 'huge multitudes of a certain kinde of

Crayfishe of such a size that one was sufficient to satisfie four hungry men at a dinner'. The name 'Crab Island' obviously suggested itself and was duly bestowed and, very pleased with their temporary abode, they set sail on 12 December 1579, setting course westward.

The archipelago of modern Indonesia, even in these days of echo soundings and refined charts, present a formidable array of islands, islets and reefs to baffle and bewilder the mariner. To the first English ship to negotiate these waters it was to prove an almost fatal hazard. Fletcher wrote: '*December* 12 we put to sea, directing our course towards the west; the sixteenth day we had sight of the Iland *Celebes* or *Silebis*, but having a bad winde and being intangled among many Ilandes, we could not by any means recover the north of *Silebis*, or continue our course further west, but were enforced to alter the same towarde the south.' Even so he spoke of their course being 'very dangerous by reason of many shoales, which lay farre off, here and there among the Ilands' inasmuch that in all their voyage from England they 'never had more care to keep ourselves afloate . . . thus we were forced to beate up and down with extraordinary care and circumspection till *January* 9, at which time we supposed that we had at last attained a free passage and the wind being enlarged, followed us as we desired with a reasonable gale.'

A stern wind, no islands in sight ahead, apparently deep water under the keel – one can almost hear them sigh with relief after nearly a month's frustrations – all seemed set fair 'when we on a sudden, when we least suspected, no shew or suspition of danger appearing to us, and we were now sailing onwards with full sailes, in the beginning of the first watch of the said day at night, even in a moment our ship was laid up fast upon a desperate shoale, with no other likelihood in appearance, but that wee with her must perish'.

So in the middle of the night there had been a terrible crunch under poor *Golden Hind*'s keel and there in the darkness she lay, her sails flapping and useless, held fast with a list to starboard, as the 'watch below' came tumbling up on deck horrified. It is in such straits that those who follow the sea know whether men love their ship and *Golden Hind*'s personality had evidently imposed itself firmly even on her chaplain, who was not a seafaring man by profession. She spoke to him, as a ship in danger can communicate like a wounded animal. 'As touching our ship, this was the comfort that shee could give us, that shee herself lying there confined already upon the hard and pinching rocks, did tell us plaine, that she continually expected her speedy dispatch, as soon as the sea and windes should come.'

Meanwhile Drake had not wasted a moment. Directly the chaplain had led them in prayer 'our Generall (exhorting us to have the especiallest care of the better part, to wit the soule) incouraged us all we bestir ourselves, shewing us the way thereto by his own example'. He had the pumps 'well played' and the *Golden Hind* was pumped clear of water; to the relief of everyone her normal leaks did not increase, and it was evident that her gallant timbers were still sound. The parson added piously, 'which truly we acknowledged to be an immediate providence of God alone, inasmuch as no strength of wood and iron could have possible borne so hard and violent a shocke as our ship did, dashing herself with full sail upon the rockes, except the extraordinary hand of God had kept the same.'

When dawn broke and the ship was still intact they 'again renewed our travail to see if we could not presently find any anchor hold, which we had formerly sought in vain'. But the second attempt proved as fruitless as the first. They now all agreed to cast themselves on God's mercy, and 'had a Sermon, and the Sacrament of the bodie and blood of our Saviour celebrated' but 'after this sweet repast was thus received, lest we should seem guilty in any aspect for not using all lawfull means we could invent, we fell to one other practice yet unassayed, to wit the unloading of our ship by casting some of her goods into the sea'.

The Flemish cartographer Nicolas van Sijpe, whose map, printed in 1582, was corrected and approved by Drake himself, gives a graphic vignette of the scene – *Golden Hind* fast upon the submerged rock, with a sea-anchor out and barrels of cargo drifting away from her. The canny Drake confined himself to throwing overboard some of the cloves from Ternate and a number of guns, but preferred to trust to divine providence before ditching the precious silver and gold. He did not trust in vain for on 10 January the wind suddenly slackened and *Golden Hind* rolled off into deep water.

Francis Fletcher described what happened with his usual felicity:

> The manner of our delivery was onely thus; the place where-on we sate so fast was a firm rocke in a cleft, whereof it was we struck on the larboard side. At low water there was not above six foote depth in all on the starboard, within little distance as you have heard no bottom to be found; the brize during the whole time that we were stayed, blew some-what stiffe directly against our broadside, and so perforce kept the ship upright. It pleased God in the beginning of the tyde, while the water was yet almost at lowest, to slacke the stiffness of the winde and now our ship, who required thirteen foot water to make her fleet, and had not at that time on the one side above seven at most, wanting her prop on the other side, which had too long alreadie kept her up, fell a healing towards the deepe water, and by that meanes freed her keele and made us all glad men.

It had been a near thing; after all the dangers of shipwreck and gale in the Straits of Magellan and round the Horn, all the dangers of capture and death at the hands of Spain, and of earthquake in central America it would have been a miserable end to lose their ship from grounding on this lonely reef. Fletcher described it as 'at least three or four leagues in length; it lies in 2 degrees, lacking three or four minutes, south lati-tude' but its shape must have been curious indeed, dropping so steeply from the point where the *Golden Hind* lay that she could find no hold for her anchors.

'Of all the dangers that in our whole voyage we met with, this was the greatest,' he wrote, but he very naturally did not describe what happened to him next. Evidently on that fateful day of stranding, 9 January, he had been indiscreet enough to voice the opinion that their predicament was a divine judg-ment on their sins, notably Drake's in executing Doughty. One did not criticize the supreme commander thus, any more

than in the modern navy it is wise to stand on the quarter-
deck of the flagship and denounce the methods of the admiral.
While danger was imminent Drake had his hands full and
ignored Fletcher; once the *Golden Hind* was safe, he struck.

He had the chaplain seized and padlocked by the leg to the
hatch-covers before him, while he himself sat cross-legged on a
sea-chest hauled out of the forecastle 'with a pair of pantouffles
in his hand'. No doubt it was an incongruous sight, but the
wretched chaplain, remembering Doughty, must have quailed.
'Francis Fletcher,' the captain roared 'I do here excommunicate thee out of the Church of God and from all benefits and
graces thereof and I denounce thee to the devil and all his
angels.' Here was the 'master under God' speaking – asserting
indeed an even greater authority as the Head of the Church,
and no doubt as the queen's sole representative in the Java
Sea Drake so regarded himself. Should Fletcher dare to appear
on the foredeck he went on, he would have him hanged, while
as a final indignity he caused the parson to wear a placard
reading: 'Francis Fletcher, the falsest knave that liveth.' The
humiliation of the man whose cure of souls was the ship's
company may be imagined but he seems to have borne no
rancour and to have accepted it with becoming fortitude,
perhaps because Drake did not bear malice long and after a
few days' uncertainty released and 'absolved' him to return to
his normal duties. The lesson of unquestioning obedience had
however been taught and learnt.

15

'*Be the Queen alive and well?*'

'The day of this deliverance was the tenth of *January*' 1580, but they were not quite clear of trouble yet. Two days later, 'being not able to hoist our sayles by reason of the tempest, we let fall our anchors upon a shoale in 3 degrees 30 minutes.' Another two days later, they again cast anchor at an island in 4 degrees 6 minutes where they spent a day. 'After this we met with foule weather, westerly wind and dangerous shoals.' The southernmost cape of Celebes lay in 5 degrees from the line, but try as they would they could not clear it. On 20 January *Golden Hind* was forced to run to a small island from which she got away as best she could, but for weeks to come she was still thrashing about the Indonesian archipelago. On 8 February she was hailed by two canoes which directed them 'to their towne not far off named *Barativa*; it stands in 7 degrees 13 minutes South of the line.' They were able to trade with these natives and sailed again on 10 February, passing a 'green Iland' to the south two days later and 'five bigge Ilands which lay in the height of 9 degrees 40 minutes' on 16 February. It was the same story for the next fortnight, passing islands, anchoring occasionally until on 12 March the ship came into clearer water at last on the coast of a large island which 'we found to be the Iland *Java*, the middle whereof stands in 7 degrees 30 minutes beyond the equator.'

Drake and some of his gentlemen and seamen went ashore

and 'presented the king (of whom he was joyfully and lov-
ingly received) with his musicke'. This approach had already
paid dividends with the king of Ternate and even the Spaniards
had been impressed by the culture of this 'corsair' who ate
to the music of viols. In native eyes Drake's behaviour was a
far cry from the oppressive methods of the Spanish and Portuguese. 'In this Iland there is one chief but many undergoverns
or petty kings,' continued Fletcher 'whom they call *Raias*, who
live in great familiaritie and friendship with one another.'
Golden Hind received a visit from Rajah Donan, 'coming
aboard us in requitall of our musick which was made to him,
presented our Generall with his courtly musick'. It was a
charming example of inter-racial understanding and the
Englishmen took their leave from the East Indies in an atmos-
phere of unrestrained goodwill.

Drake had carefully avoided the Portuguese outposts – he
had no wish for a confrontation, his quarrel being with the
king of Spain, under whose dominion the unfortunate kingdom
of Portugal was now about to pass – and with his voyage made
he determined to shape the quickest course home. *Golden
Hind* weighed anchor from Java on 'the 26th of *March*, and
set course West South West directly towards the cape of
good hope, or *Bon Esperance*, and continued without touch
of ought but aire and water till the 21 of May, when we espied
land (to wit, a part of the maine of *Africa*), in some places
very high, under the latitude of 31 degrees and half.'

This uneventful voyage, aided by favourable winds right
across the Indian Ocean, must have been very pleasant after
all the dangers and tribulations through which *Golden Hind*
had come. Her African landfall was in the vicinity of modern
Durban and so 'we coasted along till *June* 15, on which day,
having very fair weather, and the wind at South East, we
past the Cape itself, so neere in sight that we had been able with
our peeces to have shot to land.'

So, swept along by the Agulhas Current, *Golden Hind*
headed once more into the waters of the Atlantic from which
she had been absent nearly two years. Steadily and unevent-
fully she sailed north, keeping out of both the Spaniards' and
the 'Portugals'' way. '*July* 15 we fell with land again about

Rio *de Sesto'* – the River Cess in modern Liberia – 'where we saw many negroes in their boats fishing, whereof two were very neere us, but we cared not to stay.' *Golden Hind* however needed water and so 'on the 22 of the same month we came to *Sierra Leone,* and spent two days watering in the mouth of the *Tagoine,* and then put to sea again; here also we had oisters, and plenty of lemmons, which gave us good refreshing.'

She crossed the Tropic of Cancer on 15 August, 'having the winde at Northeast and we fifty leagues off the nearest land' and a week later was 'in the height of the Canaries'. Drake avoided all the scenes of his earlier exploits and was not seeking homeward-bound Spanish treasure-ships now; they all had one thought only in their minds – Devon! And so on 26 September the look-out cried 'Land ho!' and everyone rushed up on deck and to the cross-trees and indeed, far ahead, there rose out of the sea the unmistakable blue curve of Dartmoor. As *Golden Hind* drew nearer its features become more distinct – the great ridge of Shell Top and Shavercombe, to the west the isolated volcanic cone with the tiny building which they knew to be the church on Brent Tor.

Golden Hind seemed to race forward, carried like them all by an emotion almost too great to be borne. The features of the lower land now became distinguishable – dear old Rame Head and the long coast of Cornwall stretching away to the Gribbin, backed by the higher land of Mount Edgcumbe, and to starboard the heights of Staddon, the cliffs of Wembury and the looming mass of Bolt Tail. To seaward of Rame Head were some Plymouth fishermen and John Drake watched as his uncle went to the poop rail to shout a greeting in his rolling Devon voice and to ask the vital question 'Be the Queen alive and well?'

For the first time in three years Devon accents, not of his crew, answered him. Yes, she was still alive and well – happily for him, for were she dead the great exploit might not have found favour with her successor. What day was it? Monday. But by the ship's reckoning it was Sunday – she had rounded the world and lost a day! 'Monday . . . in the reckoning of those that had stayed at home in one place or countree, but in our computation the Lorde's day,' wrote Fletcher. There was

163

16

Sic parvis magna

The autumn evening light lay gently on the Sound and St Nicholas Island. The news was round Plymouth like wildfire and people streamed on to the Hoe to cheer. Drake was home! They had expected him a year ago, which was when the queen had been told by him he would be and as the months wore on the pessimists had said *Golden Hind* would never see her home port. Yet there she was, weather-beaten it is true, but sturdy and well-found, somewhat down by the bows due to the king of Spain's silver. The first boat off from the shore, pulling hard towards her as she lay at anchor behind the island, bore the familiar figure of Mary Drake, and beside her the mayor of Plymouth. The *Golden Hind*'s captain handed her over the side and they rushed into each other's arms.

When their kisses and hugs relaxed a little Drake welcomed the mayor and asked him what news of the queen. None yet, the mayor answered; it would be wiser to lie low until her attitude were known, for the Spanish ambassador had complained bitterly of Drake's exploits, and his enemies had not been slow to whisper calumnies against him. So it was decided to leave the ship where she was but to take most of the treasure ashore and place it for safe keeping at Radford, the ancestral house of Drake's good friend, Christopher Harris. From the landing near Mount Batten the packhorses toiled in relays up to Radford House. Then Drake lay low, as the mayor

165

advised, and Mary stayed on board the *Golden Hind* with him. With his usual innate wisdom he sent off John Brewer to the Queen to announce his return and others to Sir Christopher Hatton, suggesting that Elizabeth might care to inspect some of the 'samples' he had brought back with him.

Meanwhile intense diplomatic activity was going on in London and Mendoza, the Spanish ambassador, wasted no time. On 23 October 1580, immediately after Drake's return he drew up a list of alleged depredations and misdemeanours, presenting them to Walsingham with a demand for satisfaction and the punishment of Drake. This was passed on to the latter, who submitted his case to a Devon magistrate and the man he chose was none other than Edward Tremayne, of Colla-combe Barton near Lamerton. Tremayne was an old friend of Sir Christopher Hatton and came from Drake's own part of Devon, the area between Dartmoor and the Tamar only a few miles from Tavistock. He had suffered torture on the rack under Queen Mary when it had been hoped to make him inculpate the Princess Elizabeth. He pounced speedily on the exaggerations by which the Spaniards spoiled their own case and, having interviewed Drake himself and practically all the fifty-nine surviving members of *Golden Hind*'s company, he sent his report in a mere fortnight later, on 8 November.

I do think mete also to inform Your honour that Mr Drake made me acquaynted with certaine matters grievouslie objected against him by the Spanish Ambassador uppon the perticulers whereof he praied me to examyne bothe the gentlemen and others of his companie the which I thought reasonable to yelde unto and thereupon drave the interroga-tions. Following, viz. (firstly) whither Mr Drake and his companie had taken from the king of Spaine and his subjects in goulde and silver to the value of one million and halfe or not.

Secondly, whither they have in their voyage taken any shippes or vessells of the said King or his subjects and after sunk them with their men or maryners or not.

Thirdlie whither they had at any time in any fight killed any of the said King's subjects or had cut off their hands or armes or otherwise with any crueltie mangled any of them. The answers unto which interrogations as they have confessed and delivered unto me with their own handes and as I herde them all to affirme, I do send unto your Honour.

By which you maie soon see how much things be influenced beyonde the truthe!

He then listed the evidence of Lawrence Eliot, confirmed by that of John Chester, George Cary and George Fortescue, four of Drake's gentlemen, and all westcountrymen. The only missing ones were Francis Fletcher, the chaplain, Thomas and John Drake, his relatives and John Doughty. Eliot's evidence ran

To the fyrst I say that to the valeu I cann say nothinge, the thing being invidious unto me: only sylver and some goulde there was taken, but how moche I know not: but a verrie small some in respecte of that that is reported.

To the second, I confesse that there were shyppes taken: but that any weare sunk with their men and mariners, yet is altogether untrewe.

To the thirde that to my knowledge there was no Spaniarde slaine by any of us, or had their armes or hands cutt off, or otherwise by any creweltie mangled or maimed. Only one man I remember was hurt in the face, which our Generall caused to be sent for and lodged him in his owne shipp, sett him at his own table, and would not soffer him to depart before he was recovered and so sent him safe away!

There follow a list of forty-five names of the crew who testified similarly. Indeed Mendoza's accusations of killing and maiming Spaniards are so false as to be absurd; the total non-English casualties of the circumnavigation amounted to one Patagonian Indian, plus the Spaniard hurt in the face, which may refer to either Giusepe de Pareces or to San Juan de Anton, master of the *Cacafuego*. English casualties were heavier: four died as results of wounds inflicted by the Spaniards, two were shot by Patagonians and two by Indians, while the sea accounted for the entire crew of the *Marigold* and the crew of one pinnace: privations, illness or disease carried off ten more of the eighty-five who left Plymouth in the *Golden Hind*. Fifty-nine returned.

Mendoza added a footnote to his list of robberies which again did not help his case. 'Also I fynde deposed to be taken by reporte and not registered, these parcells followinge – 500 m 36 pezos.' Drake's comment was to the point, displaying a seaman's knowledge of seamen's ways: 'Sir Francis Drake dothe utterlye denye that either he had or yet even dyd to any parcell of those pezos unregistered, but verelye thinketh that the same beinge hydden under the baliste of the shippe are kept from the merchants by the maryners of the shippes wherein they were laden.'

Walsingham accepted Tremayne's report and showed it to the queen, who cut Mendoza short when he complained further. He described Drake bitterly as 'the master thief of the unknown world', and there were many who hoped the queen would have Drake's head to appease the Spaniards, but she was made of sterner stuff than her successor who was prepared to sacrifice Raleigh for a similar reason.

In due course she sent Drake a command that she wished to see some of his samples, that he should fear nothing and that he should sail *Golden Hind* round to Deptford as she intended to visit the ship. So the silver was brought again from the vaults at Radford and loaded once more into the *Golden Hind*. With her sails bending to the wind she tacked gracefully out of the Sound to the cheers of the populace on the Hoe and getting to wind out of Rame Head, sailed away up Channel, sped on by the good wishes of Devon.

She made a quick passage to the Thames and brought up opposite the Tower of London, beneath whose sombre walls the king of Spain's treasure passed to its final place of safety. Then they took the *Golden Hind* across to Deptford and waited for the queen.

It was a fine spring day, 4 April 1581, when Gloriana came, attended as usual by a great assembly of courtiers, including a delighted Christopher Hatton and by a number of diplomats, among whom the French ambassador was conspicuous by his presence and the Spanish ambassador by his absence. Even now they were not quite certain what Elizabeth was up to, as she had ordered a sword to be brought to 'strike off Drake's head'. Some people thought she meant to do it and indeed Drake himself was not entirely certain that she did not intend at least to imprison him. As Stow wrote in his Annals, 'Yet Captain Drake all this while being therewithal and by his friends much encouraged rested doubtfull of the event, untill the Day that the Queene's Majesty came aborde his weather beaten Barke.' Drake had decked the *Golden Hind* not only with her habitual St George's flag, but with a brave display of royal banners – the red and gold lions of England with the blue and gold fleur de lys of France. A hush of expectancy fell, as the queen, carried in her chair by her gentlemen-at-arms headed by Sir Christopher Hatton as vice-chamberlain, approached the ship. Drake was at the gangway to kneel in greeting as the figure stepped daintily over the side of *Golden Hind*.

'And in the next yeare following, to wit 1581 on the 4th of Aprill' wrote Stow 'her Majesty dining at Deptford in Kent, after dinner entered the ship, which Captain Drake had so happily guided round about the world, and being there a bridge her Majesty had passed over brake, being upon the same more than 200 persons, and no man hurt by the fal.'

Stow goes on to describe the queen – 'she was tall of stature, strong in every limbe and joynte, her fingers small and long, her voyce loud and shrill, shee was of an admirable readie wit' and indeed she now showed it. First in negotiating the gangway, she contrived to lose a gold and purple garter. When the French ambassador rushed forward and picking it up, begged to be allowed to keep it, she laughingly replied that she could not keep her stocking up without it.

'But you may do another service for me,' Elizabeth added, 'Drake, kneel down' and she motioned that the sword she had brought 'to strike off his head' be given to her. Then, as the famous captain knelt and surveyed the boards of his own quarter deck, with superb political finesse, she handed the sword to the French envoy, the Sieur de Marchaumont motioning to him what to do, and as she touched Drake on the shoulder, her loud clear voice rang out 'Arise, Sir Francis Drake!' 'She did make captaine Drake knight in the same ship,

169

for reward of his service,' wrote Stow, while young John Drake who was watching, later told the Inquisitors into whose hands he fell 'She named Captain Francis, Sir Francis, which is the same as "Don" and received him well, showing him great honour'.

The officers and men of *Golden Hind* raised a great cheer, echoed by the crowd ashore. Drake, relieved and delighted, rose, and Mary Newman, that simple westcountry girl, found herself propelled forward by her husband's strong arm to curtsey to the queen and to be presented for the very first time as Lady Drake.

Elizabeth had an affection for Devonians – she liked their soft rolling speech, and never sought to ridicule it, or rid them of it at her court. She once observed that, 'They were all born courtiers with a becoming confidence.' Now she bade the greatest of them all to show her over *Golden Hind* and so, with a 'becoming confidence' Drake led her from stem galley to forecastle, from great cabin to ballast. The ship must be preserved, she said, for posterity to admire always, and immediately gave orders for a dry dock to be built 'and to make a house where the ship could be preserved as a memorial'.

So a dry dock was built, with brick walls seventy-five feet long by twenty-four feet broad, just enclosing the hull of the *Golden Hind*, whose upperworks and masts rose above it as do those of *Cutty Sark* in her dry berth at Greenwich to this day. The queen came to dinner on board (and this gave Ben Jonson the idea of making a character in one of his plays say 'We'll have dinner in Sir Francis Drake's ship that hath gone round the world'). She also gave orders for the formal grant of arms to Drake and the grant is dated 16 June 1581.

Whereas it hath pleased the Queen's most excellent Majesty graciously to regard the praiseworthy deserts of Sir Francis Drake knight, and to remunerate the same in him, not only with the honourable order of knighthood and by sundry other demonstrations of her Highness's especial favour, but also further desirous that the impressions of her princely affection towards him might be as it were immortally derived and conveyed to his offspring and posterity for ever, hath assigned and given unto him arms and tokens of honour answerable to the greatness of his deserts and meet for his place and calling: that is to say Sable and fess wavy between two stars argent: the helm adorned with a globe terrestrial: upon the height whereof is a ship under sail, trained about the same with golden hawsers by the direction of a hand appearing out of the clouds, all in proper colour with the words '*Auxilio Divino*'. These arms with the words *Sic Parvis Magna* have been registered, and the grant signed by Robert Cooke, Clarencieux king of arms.'

This was confirmation of the arms which Nuño da Silva had seen upon the cannon in the *Golden Hind*.

John Drake, in his deposition to the Inquisition (in circumstances under which he would be unlikely to exaggerate) – said apropos Drake and the queen, that 'there was a day on which he conversed with her nine times and people said "that no one had ever enjoyed such an honour"'. Indeed Elizabeth showed the greatest interest in every particular of the voyage. Drake presented her with the log-book and the paintings which he and John had made, but she was avid for more.

She invited him to the Palace of Greenwich again and again. And so, there was the Devon farmer's son walking turn and turn about in the palace garden – a far cry from the cottage at Crowndale – with Henry VIII's daughter. She questioning, ever questioning, he answering and explaining. Could this really be the rough seaman who listened to the sigh and rustle of Elizabeth's stiff brocaded skirts beside him? Apt indeed were the words the herald chose for him – '*Sic parvis magna*' – 'Great things have small beginnings'.

On New Year's Day, 1582, the Queen presented Drake with a splendid goblet on a slender stem, its top rounded in the form of a globe. It had been made by a Swiss silversmith, Abraham Gessner of Zürich, ten years before and it was now engraved with a map of the world and a picture of the *Golden Hind*.

Meanwhile the *Golden Hind* lay in her final berth at Deptford and the English people from far and near swarmed over her to see the ship in which an Englishman first ventured into the Pacific to strike a blow at the monolithic might of Spain. Nor did the heralds neglect her any more than her master. Her likeness appears to this day on the arms of his own county of Devon, as it did on his own arms. The motto, too, in his arms – *Auxilio Divino* ('by God's help') – that providential aid by which the ship bore him round the world.

One distressing epilogue to the circumnavigation was the legal action brought against Drake by John Doughty, who prosecuted him in the Earl Marshal's court for murdering his brother in Patagonia. Sir Francis contended that such a case lay outside the jurisdiction of the Marshal and he applied for a writ from the Court of Queen's Bench to stay with the proceedings. The Lord Chief Justice earned some unpopularity by ruling that Doughty was entitled to proceed and it cannot have been pleasant for Sir Francis to have the case hanging over his head, but there, in fact, the matter rested, for Drake never went for trial as young Doughty was found to be involved in underhand dealings with the Spanish. Realising there was now no chance of restitution from the English government, a group of Spanish merchants attempted to come to terms with Drake himself and their agent in England, Pedro de Zubiaur, became thick with John Doughty. It came out that when chances of negotiating with Sir Francis for a return of part of his plunder were hopeless, there was a plot to murder him. Doughty had written a letter which ran 'when the Queen did Knight Drake she did then Knight the arrantest Knave, the vilest villain, the falsest thief and the cruelest murderer that ever was born'; and then a servant of Hatton's reported he had heard Doughty swear he would kill him. Such threats were common form in Elizabethan England, but Doughty and another English contact of de Zubiaur were arrested and on the rack revealed that Philip II had offered a reward of 20,000 ducats to anyone who would either kidnap Drake and send him to Spain, or bring his head to the Escorial on a charger. Doughty was prepared to make the attempt himself. For all his boasted connexions with Lord Burghley, he failed to gain release from his cell in the Marshalsea Prison.

of Winchester College in the year 1580. Of the ship Jonson made one of his characters say: 'We'll have our provided supper brought aboard Sir Francis Drake's ship that hath encompassed the world, where with full cups and banquets, we will do sacrifice for a prosperous voyage.'

The year after his return from the circumnavigation, immediately following up his knighthood, Drake purchased the house which was his heart's desire – none other than Buckland Abbey, or, as its new owners had called it, Buckland Grenville. Sir Richard would never have sold it to Drake had he known, but Sir Francis cunningly contrived that his good friends Christopher Harris of Radford and John Hale did the negotiations for him. Thus it was only when the sale was a *fait accompli* that Grenville realized it was the upstart from Tavistock who was the true owner. So Francis and Mary Drake moved in – the humbly born Cornish maid was now Lady Drake, mistress of one of the finest houses in Devon. It had cost £3,400, an immense sum in 1581, and Drake was one of the few men who could afford it. The following year he was granted the manor of Sherford by the queen, and he purchased the manor of Yarcombe in East Devon from his distant kinsmen, the Drakes of Ashe, near Musbury. This famous clan, which later married into the Churchills and produced John, Duke of Marlborough, ancestor of Sir Winston, had not deigned to acknowledge their younger cousin of Tavistock until he suddenly became a millionaire and the national hero: then they were quite ready to sell him Yarcombe.

Alas! Mary Drake was not to enjoy being mistress of the great house for long. The marriage register of St Budeaux has a note against the entry in July 1569 referring to the register of deaths of 1582 and against 25 January 1582/3 appears the burial of 'The Lady Marie Drake, wife of Sir Francis Drake, knight'. So she was buried on the hilltop at St Budeaux by the church where she was married, looking across to Saltash where she was born, simple in death as she had been in life.

The widower at Buckland meanwhile was in the forefront of local affairs, for the brief period that he was away from the sea. Plymouth had made him its mayor for the first time in 1581, and he set up a compass on the Hoe to show seamen and landlubbers the way to the fabled West. By 1583 he was a Member of Parliament, sitting for Bossiney near Tintagel on the north Cornish coast, later to become one of the 'rotten boroughs'.

1585 marked an important event in Drake's life – his second marriage. The lady of his choice was Elizabeth Sydenham, the beautiful young daughter of Sir George Sydenham of Combe Sydenham in Somerset, a gracious Tudor house in the Quantock Hills. The Sydenhams were an old family who would not originally have contemplated Drake as a husband for their daughter, but now he was world-famous, a knight and a millionaire to boot. West country tradition says that Elizabeth had been one of Queen Elizabeth's ladies-in-waiting and that Drake first met her at court at Syon House, when he went up to London with his pack horses laden with Spanish treasure, and later when he sailed *Golden Hind* to Deptford.

Local legend tells another story. This was that Elizabeth Sydenham, dismayed by Drake's apparent total disappearance at sea (which could in her case have been only on the comparatively short West Indies voyage) was persuaded by her parents that he was dead and that she should marry another. As she was about to enter the church at Monksilver on her wedding day a cannon-ball fell at her feet. It was a sign that Drake was still alive, she declared, and she refused to go on with the ceremony. Fanciful rubbish? Perhaps – but at Combe Sydenham until a few years ago they exhibited an ancient cannon-ball said to be the one concerned. Some scholars have considered it a meteorite.

In any case Drake married Elizabeth Sydenham, most probably in London, in February 1585. The queen apparently raised no objection as she did in the case of Walter Raleigh and Elizabeth Throckmorton. Drake installed his new bride in Buckland Abbey, where she became a most efficient and popular lady of the house. We can still see today the splendid drawing room there where they entertained the gentry of Devon and the queen's admirals.

In 1583 Drake purchased the manor of Sampford Sperrey, high up on Dartmoor below the grey rocks of Pu Tor to the west of the valley of the River Walkham and this, together with the manors of Sherford and Yarcombe, and Buckland

Abbey, he granted to Elizabeth's trustees on her wedding day. One further purchase of note was a London house – a fine mansion in Dowgate Ward near the River Thames, known as The Herbor, which had once belonged to Margaret Pole, Countess of Salisbury. Drake needed a residence in the city for attending Parliament and court as well as for his dealings with merchants and bankers. Lady Drake, too, enjoyed visits to the capital where she could entertain in style. She was to outlive Sir Francis and after his death married Sir William Courtenay of Powderham Castle, a widower.

The rest of Sir Francis Drake's story belongs to national history. In 1585, as he was preparing a fleet to sail to the Moluccas on a military expedition, Philip II ordered the arrest of all English merchant ships in Spanish and Portuguese ports in reprisal for the depredations of Drake and others across the line. This was taken by Queen Elizabeth as a declaration of war and so the fleet was diverted to the Peninsula to embark stranded English merchants before proceeding to the West Indies to strike further blows at Spanish power. With twenty-nine warships under Drake's command, this was the largest naval force Elizabeth had yet sent to sea. No English merchants at Vigo were prepared to leave until their accounts had been settled and not one of them realized that this was the end of an epoch, that after years of uneasy peace there would be a war with Spain in Europe that would outlast the queen's reign.

After a notable demonstration of maritime supremacy in Vigo Bay, with colours flying, the fleet departed and no Spaniard dared to give chase. 'If the influence of sea-power on history is what has been claimed for it,' wrote Sir Julian Corbett, three generations ago, 'then this moment marks an epoch.' Thence to the Caribbean, where Drake sacked San Domingo, the capital of Hispaniola and the administrative hub of the Spanish dominions in the Americas. Next he took Cartagena, stripping the port of its defences. Finally he called at Raleigh's infant colony in Virginia, offering Ralph Lane, the governor, either a ship with supplies or a passage home. Lane bravely chose to stay, but when a terrific gale battered the ship Drake had assigned to him, he reluctantly decided to embark for England with all but fifteen of the Roanoke settlers. The whole expedition had been a tremendous fillip for English morale. 'Truly, Sir Francis Drake is a fearful man to the King of Spain,' wrote Lord Burghley, when the fleet's triumphs were reported at court, for he had inflicted terrible wounds on the Spanish Empire.

No less dramatic was the Cadiz expedition in the Spring of 1587 'to impeach the provision of Spain' and prevent an armada from being sent against England. 'The winds command me away,' Drake wrote, as he sailed. 'Pray unto God for us that He will direct us in the right way; then we shall not doubt our enemies, for they are the sons of men.' In Cadiz harbour he destroyed thirty-one Spanish ships and captured six others, 'with very little loss, not worth mentioning'. He took the castle of Sagres on the Algarve coast, with neighbouring forts, as a base for watering English vessels and a key point on a very busy shipping route. Lisbon proved too heavily defended to allow an attack to be made, so Drake followed up intelligences to hunt down in the Azores the *San Felipe*, a great carrack, belonging to Philip II himself, returning from the East Indies with a precious cargo worth £114,000. If burning Cadiz was reckoned singeing the king of Spain's beard, then the capture of the *San Felipe* was a triumph of a different order. 'It taught others that carracks were no such bugs, but they might be taken,' as Richard Hakluyt fruitily put it. The prize made known in London the extensive, undreamt of, range of East Indian commodities. The fact that as the century closed an English East India Company was granted a royal charter of foundation, foreshadowing the development of a great imperial ideal, owes much to Drake's seizure of King Philip's great vessel. From the anchorage at Cadiz Sir Francis had written a characteristic letter to his old friend John Fox that shows his Christian humility in executing what he was convinced was the divine will, and saying that the victory belonged not to himself but to all the faithful: 'Master Fox, whereas we have had of late such happy success against the Spaniards, I do assure myself you have faithfully remembered us in your good prayers and therefore I have not forgotten briefly to make you a partaker thereof.' He called on Fox to continue his supplication and thanksgiving 'that we may have continued peace in Israel' and signed his letter 'Your loving friend and faithful son in Christ Jesus'. As a postscript he added, 'Our enemies are many, but our Protector commandeth the whole world. Let us all pray continually that our Lord Jesus will hear us in good time mercifully.' In fact, before the letter reached England, Fox had died, snapping a link with Drake's Protestant origins, and with his father, the vicar of Upchurch.

Next spring Drake was anxious to repeat the success of the Cadiz raid by a further expedition to the Peninsula, since attack was the best means of defence; yet Howard of Effingham, the lord high admiral, would not risk leaving the Channel undefended. Drake was adamant and when his pungent memoranda persuaded the queen of the importance of his plan she summoned him to court. While away from Plymouth his men sent a characteristic letter to him, showing the great affection in which he was held. 'All in generality do greatly desire your return ... and so we commit you to the Lord of Lords, who preserve and keep you all.' Admiral Howard now changed his tune and appointed Sir Francis his vice admiral for the campaign. He had feared the unruly sea-dog might find it hard to play second fiddle, yet to his delight he found him behaving 'most dutifully', and he reported this to Secretary Walsingham, suggesting the national hero be sent a warmly worded letter of thanks. Indeed, it was Drake who was almost universally regarded as the inspiration of the seamen and the effective commander of the grand fleet.

At last ninety ships left the Sound on 7 July racing towards the Bay of Biscay, 'to fight with them much better cheap upon their own coasts', though when the wind shifted from the north-east to the south, they had to return home, reaching Plymouth on the day that Medina Sidonia left Coruña, being borne towards England on the same wind. When news reached Plymouth on 19 July that the Spaniards were off the Lizard, it may be, as Thomas Fuller first related many years later, that Sir Francis continued his game of bowls on the Hoe, saying 'We have plenty of time to finish the game and beat the Spaniards too.' From the first moment of the campaign, as Medina Sidonia's impregnable crescent of vessels moved north-east along the Channel, the English gained the weather gauge, and they held it throughout. It was Drake who (to the envy of many) on the first night seized as his own prize the *Nuestra Señora del Rosario*, and later on nearly captured the *Gran Grifon*. It was Drake who, remembering his experiences at San Juan de Ulua and at Cadiz, proposed sending fire-ships against the enemy fleet anchored in Calais Roads, offering his own *Thomas* as a personal sacrifice. When subsequently the change of wind saved the fleeing Spaniards from certain destruction on the perilous shore of the Netherlands, so that they could make for home via the North Sea, the north of Scotland and the west coast of Ireland, Sir Francis dashed off a note to Walsingham, before giving chase. 'There was never anything pleased me better than the seeing the enemy flying with a southerly wind to the westwards. . . . I doubt it not but ere long so to handle the matter with the Duke of Sidonia as he shall wish himself at St Mary Port among his orange trees.' Lord Howard of Effingham paid tribute throughout to Drake's great experience and infectious courage so that most contemporaries at home and abroad regarded the defeat of the Armada as essentially *his* victory.

Then in 1589 came his not so successful expedition with Sir John Norris to Portugal in an attempt to place Don Antonio on the throne that Philip of Spain had seized. The queen's resultant displeasure caused him to withdraw to Devon, where Plymouth showered him with honours, and where (a legend in his own lifetime) he galloped down from the headwaters of the Meavy high on Dartmoor, with a stream of crystal-clear water following at his horse's hooves. There was plenty of work to absorb his energies at Plymouth, but he fervently hoped England could return to the offensive at sea, in Europe and beyond, and he prayed that he might be allowed once again to play a leading role, even if the queen could never forgive him for the ill success of the Portugal voyage.

Finally came the last sad chapter, the expedition to the Indies and Spanish Main in 1595, with Hawkins and Drake in 'joint command', ill yoked. Everything went wrong. The ports were better defended and sickness was rife in the fleet. As the ships came to anchor off Puerto Rico, John Hawkins died and with his last words asked that a legacy of £2,000 might be offered to Her Majesty to salve his conscience for his share in persuading her to send the ill-fated expedition. Drake still inspired universal confidence: 'I will bring you to twenty places more wealthy and easier to be gotten [than Puerto Rico],' he assured them and *en route* he would revisit the haunts of the Main he knew so well. He seized Rio de la Hacha, where he had suffered that early reverse under John Lovell, and now felt honour had been satisfied. Two days after Christmas he took Nombre de Dios a second time, but the treasure was pitifully small. He told his men he would not make course for home until he had gold in quantity, but in the Mosquito Gulf he went down with dysentery and had to take to his cabin. There was no hope for him and on 28 January 1596 Sir Francis died just as his fleet was coming to anchor at Nombre de Dios. Here in the bay he was buried with his drum beating a lament and the cannons firing; it was a fitting burial ground as it was 'almost in the same place where he began to grow famous to the world by his fortunate successes'.

Drake's drum, celebrated in Sir Henry Newbolt's lines, at least is still in Devon for all to see, standing on a plinth of red velvet in the hall Sir Richard Grenville built at Buckland. The famous drum that sounded aboard the *Golden Hind* to summon Drake's crew according to tradition still sounds when England is in danger.

In the Drake treasure-house of Buckland are other mementoes of the *Golden Hind*, notably the splendid red, gold and blue banners – the lions of England and the lilies of France – which flew at her topmasts the day Queen Elizabeth came aboard at Deptford in April 1581, to knight her captain.

The man whose crest gave the ship her name had likewise gone from strength to strength. Great men had confided in him – during Drake's absence at sea Walsingham had sought his advice from the Low Countries, and Sir Amyas Paulet from his embassy in Paris on the matter of the queen's projected marriage to the Duke of Alençon.

He had lavished money on Holdenby House, to prepare it for a visit his royal mistress never made. Burghley wrote, 'Sir, I may not pass out of this good house without thanks on your behalf to God, and on mine to you, nor without memory of her Majesty, to whom it appeareth this goodly, perfect, though not perfected work is consecrated.' Holdenby made a great impression on all who visited it. Sir Thomas Heneage wrote to Sir Christopher, 'If the praise of a house consist in the sea, beauty and use both within and without . . . Holdenby shall hold the pre-eminence of all the modern houses I have known or heard of in England.' In the month Drake returned, Hatton wrote back to Heneage that he was leaving his other shrine, 'I mean Holdenby, still unseen until that holy saint may sit in it, to whom it is dedicated.' In fact Elizabeth never went there and a newer house now stands on the site, but two great gateways bearing the date 1583 are still to be seen, indicating the spaciousness of the Holdenby Hatton built for her. Hatton had done well, though, out of the *Golden Hind*'s voyage – he received £2,300 or ten times as much in modern money – over 4,000 per cent on his investment.

In 1584 he introduced a bill for the Safety and Preservation of the Queen's Royal Person, and another to banish Jesuits. Of all the great men of the realm none was more aware of the dangers from without and of subversions within, none more eloquent in bringing this home to his compatriots. His speeches in Parliament were famous, though in later centuries appreciation waned, and it has been left to modern writers to resuscitate them. 'Hatton is yet another discovery,' wrote Sir John Neale in *Elizabeth and her Parliaments*, 'that a man so long, and apparently so firmly installed in legend as a Queen's plaything, should emerge with the stature he displayed in handling Parliament, is quite unexpected.'

Speech followed great speech: on 24 February 1585 on the Parry Plot; on 14 November 1586 on Mary Queen of Scots; on 22 February 1587 on the imminence of invasion by the Spanish Armada. He took part in several major treason trials, including that of Mary at Fotheringay; it was he who persuaded her to recognize the court. Then ten days after Drake's raid on Cadiz, on 29 April 1587, Elizabeth appointed him lord chancellor, and he rode in splendid procession from Ely Place to the Law Courts – although 'the gown-men grieved thereat', as Fuller put it, because he was not a lawyer by profession. But

Hatton did not try to run before he could walk: he modestly took advice, and 'though the Queen had her misgivings about the appointment', Hatton vindicated her trust magnificently. On 28 October 1587 he made a speech in the Star Chamber on the danger of the coming invasion which 'for its eloquence, its emotion, and its shining, confident patriotism, as well as a withering contempt for the enemy' was deemed 'not unworthy of a place in the treasury of England's best'. He was always the perfect foil and support for the dare-devil actions of Drake.

While the latter was fighting the Armada in *Revenge*, Hatton was in command of his troops at Tilbury, where the queen received them. On 3 August she dined with him at Ely Place. Then, after the defeat of the Spaniards, another signal honour came his way, when on 3 October 1588 he was appointed chancellor of Oxford University, and threw himself into the task with an enthusiasm and thoroughness that astonished the dons, who had expected just another figure-head. On 4 February 1589 Elizabeth attended Parliament and heard Hatton, in his capacity as lord chancellor, make an impressive speech on the importance of sea-power to England, telling his hearers that 'Our Navy ... is the greatest bulwark of the Kingdom.'

Spenser delighted in his speeches:

> So you, great lord! that with your counsel sway
> The burden of this kingdom mightily:
> With like delights sometimes may eke delay
> The rugged brow of careful policy.

Christopher Ockland in his 'Elizabetha' referred to him as 'Splendidus Hatton'.

But his health was failing, and on 11 November 1591 the queen came to his bedside at Ely Place and fed him with her own hands. Nine days later the greatest bearer of the golden hind died and was buried in St Paul's. His estates passed to his godson, Christopher, of Long Stanton, Cambridge, where so many golden hinds still grace the family tombs.

And what of the *Golden Hind* herself? She lasted in her dock at Deptford till 1662. Pepys recorded a visit to her, though he

Epilogue

remarked on the rottenness of her timbers, which made the auctioneers decide, regretfully, to have the famous ship broken up. Nevertheless, after three hundred years, portions of her actual woodwork may still be seen in a few places. In the Bodleian Library at Oxford, where Sir Christopher Hatton was once chancellor, stands a beautiful chair, its polished oak black with age, made from the ship's timbers, and bearing two plates with inscriptions. The first records that it was made from the remains of Drake's ship and donated to the library by John Davis, keeper of naval stores at Deptford dockyard in 1662. The second, hanging from the back of the chair, has verses written by Abraham Cowley in the same year, one side in Latin, the reverse in English, reading:

> To this great ship which round the Globe has run,
> And matcht in Race the Chariot of the Sun
> This Pythagorean Ship (for it may claim
> Without Presumption so deserv'd a Name,
> By knowledge once, and transformation now)
> In her new shape this sacred Port allow.
> Drake and his Ship, could not have wisht from Fate
> A more blest Station, or more blest Estate
> For lo! a Seate of endless reste is giv'n
> To her in Oxford, and to him in Heav'n.

Smoother and not so black is the great table that normally adorns the hall of the Middle Temple, used on great occasions, a short distance from the hall of the Inner Temple, in which, very appropriately, the portrait of Sir Christopher Hatton hangs.

So favourite a name did she bear that it has continued in use to the present day, though its earliest re-use was a mere three years after she was laid up at Deptford, when it was borne by the largest of the fleet in which Sir Humphrey Gilbert, half-brother of Sir Walter Raleigh, sailed to Newfoundland in 1583. Had he not transferred from her to the smaller *Squirrel* he might have survived the voyage; as it was, the last recorded words he uttered would have made a good motto for the original *Golden Hind* herself – 'We are as near to God by sea as by land.'

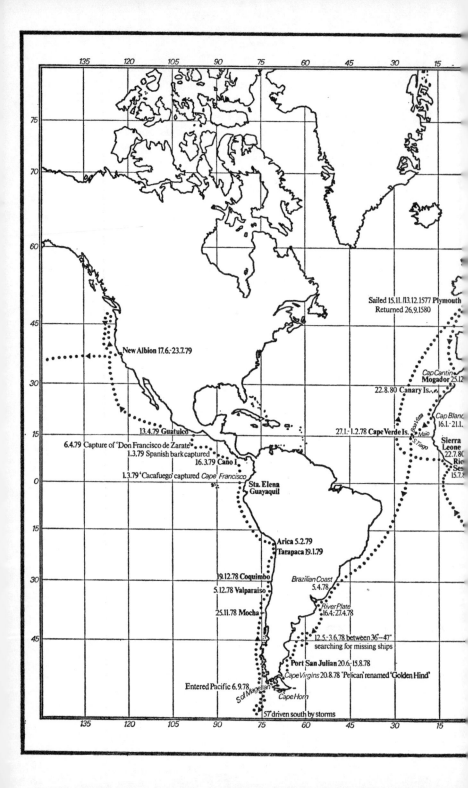

Sailed 15.11./13.12.1577 Plymouth
Returned 26.9.1580

New Albion 17.6.-23.7.79

Cap Cantin
Mogador 25.12

22.8.80 Canary Is.

Cap Blanc
16.1.- 21.1.

13.4.79 Guatulco

27.1.- 1.2.78 Cape Verde Is.

Boa Vista

6.4.79 Capture of 'Don Francisco de Zarate'

Sierra
Leone
22.7.80

1.3.79 Spanish bark captured

St Tiago

Maio

16.3.79 Cano I.

Rio
Ses
15.7.8

1.3.79 'Cacafuego' captured Cape Francisco

Sta. Elena
Guayaquil

Arica 5.2.79
Tarapaca 19.1.79

19.12.78 Coquimbo

Brazilian Coast
5.4.78

5.12.78 Valparaiso

River Plate
16.4.- 27.4.78

25.11.78 Mocha

12.5.- 3.6.78 between 36°-47°
searching for missing ships

Port San Julian 20.6.-15.8.78

Cape Virgins 20.8.78 'Pelican' renamed 'Golden Hind'

Entered Pacific 6.9.78

S of Magellan

Cape Horn

57° driven south by storms

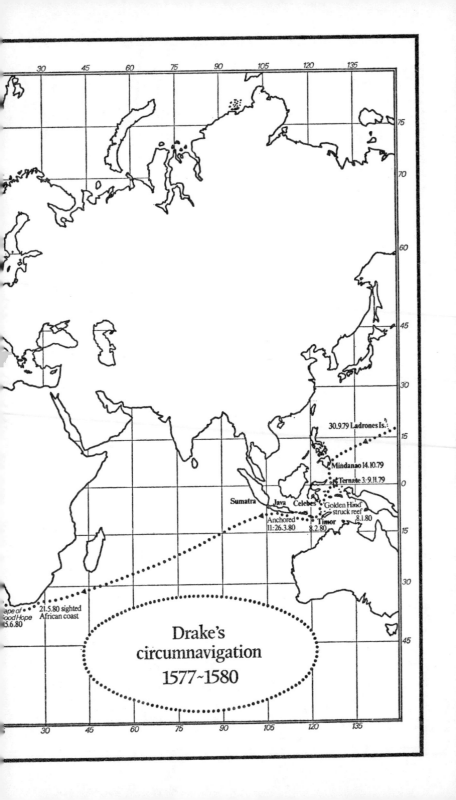

75

70

60

45

30

15

30.9.79 Ladrones Is.

15

Mindanao 14.10.79

Ternate 3-9.11.79

0

Sumatra   Java   Celebes   'Golden Hind'
                              struck reef
Anchored   Timor   8.1.80
11:26.3.80   8.2.80

15

30

ape of   21.5.80 sighted
ood Hope African coast
5.6.80

Drake's
circumnavigation
1577~1580

45

30   45   60   75   90   105   120   135

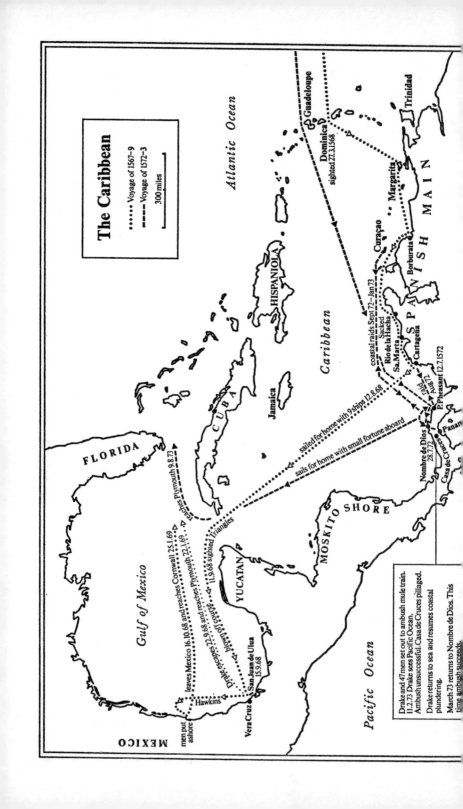

The Caribbean

· · · · · · Voyage of 1567–9

– – – – – Voyage of 1572–3

300 miles

Atlantic Ocean

Guadeloupe

Dominica sighted 27.3.1568

Trinidad

Margarita

Curaçao

S P A N I S H   M A I N

Borburata

HISPANIOLA

Caribbean

coastal raids Sept 72–Jan 73

Sacked
Rio de la Hacha
Sa. Marta

Cartagena

raid Aug 72

CUBA

Jamaica

sailed for home with 9 ships 12.8.68

sails for home with small fortune aboard

Nombre de Dios 28.7.72

P. Pheasant 12.7.1572

Panama

Casa de Cruces

MOSKITO SHORE

FLORIDA

Gulf of Mexico

reaches Plymouth 9.8.73

leaves Mexico 16.10.68 and reaches Cornwall 25.1.69

22.9.68 and reaches Plymouth 22.1.69

11.9.68 sighted Triangles

Drake escapes

blown off course

San Juan de Ulua
15.9.68

Vera Cruz

YUCATAN

men put
ashore

Hawkins

MEXICO

Pacific Ocean

Drake and 47 men set out to ambush mule train.
11.2.73 Drake sees Pacific Ocean. Ambush unsuccessful. Casa de Cruces pillaged.
Drake returns to sea and resumes coastal plundering.
March 73 returns to Nombre de Dios. This time ambush succeeds.

Bibliography

General

Andrews, K. R., *Elizabethan Privateering* (London, 1964)

Black, J. B., *The Reign of Elizabeth, 1558–1603*, vol. 6 in *The Oxford History of England*, revised edition (London, 1959)

Boxer, C. R., *The Portuguese Seaborne Empire* (London, 1969)

Braudel, F., *The Mediterranean World in the Age of Philip II*, English edition (London, 1972)

Keevil, J. J., *Medicine and the Navy*, vol. 1, 1200–1649 (London, 1957)

Newton, A. P., *The European Nations in the West Indies, 1493–1688* (London, 1933)

Oppenheim, M., *A History of the Administration of the Royal Navy and of Merchant Shipping in Relation to the Navy, 1509–1660* (London, 1896, reprinted 1961)

Oppenheim, M., *The Maritime History of Devon*, a reprint of an article written for the *Victoria Country History of Devon*, with an introduction by W. E. Minchinton (London, 1968)

Parry, J. H., *The Spanish Seaborne Empire* (London, 1966)

Rowse, A. L., *The Expansion of Elizabethan England* (London, 1953)

Taylor, E. G. R., *Tudor Geography, 1485–1583* (London, 1930)

Waters, D. W., *The Art of Navigation in England in Elizabethan and Early Stuart Times* (London, 1958)

Wernham, R. B., *Before the Armada: the Growth of English Foreign Policy, 1485–1558* (London, 1966)

Bibliography

Biographies of Drake

The most recent lives are those by Christopher Lloyd (London, 1957), Ernle Bradford (London, 1965), George Malcolm Thomson (London, 1972) and Neville Williams (London, 1973). The most detailed biography is Sir Julian Corbett's *Drake and the Tudor Navy* (two volumes, London, 1898), from which he distilled his short life in the *English Men of Action* series (London, 1902). Hans P. Kraus, *Sir Francis Drake* (Amsterdam, 1970) is valuable for its extensive range of illustrations from contemporary material. Lady Eliott-Drake, *The Family and Heirs of Sir Francis Drake*, vol. 1 (London, 1911), provides important family background.

Narratives and Documents

Richard Hakluyt, *The Principal Navigations, Voyages and Discoveries of the English Nation*, first published in 1589, has been reprinted in a facsimile edition by D. B. Quinn and R. A. Skelton in two volumes for the Hakluyt Society, Extra Series, no. 39 (London, 1965). Richard Hakluyt brought out further editions of his best-seller in 1598, 1599 and 1600. The standard edition is that prepared by Professor Sir Walter Raleigh for the Hakluyt Society in twelve volumes (London, 1903–5), but there is also a serviceable Everyman edition in eight volumes (London, 1907; reprinted 1962, with an introduction by John Masefield).

The key narratives and documents relating to Drake's voyage round the world are printed with an important commentary by John Hampden in *Francis Drake Privateer* (London, 1972). This includes the whole of Sir Francis Drake's (the seaman's nephew) *The World Encompassed* (London, 1628), and the narratives of John Cooke and John Winter. More exhaustive is the material printed by Henry R. Wagner, *Sir Francis Drake's Voyage Around the World: Its Aims and Achievements* (San Francisco, 1926); among the narratives here is the account by Francis Fletcher, the chaplain. N. M. Penzer has edited *The World Encompassed* with other records (London, 1926), while Zelia Nuttall's *New Light on Drake* for the Hakluyt Society, Second Series, vol. 34 (London, 1914), provides English translations of a great many documents in Spanish from the archives in Mexico, Seville and elsewhere, including the report of Nuño da Silva and the depositions of John Drake. Martin A. S. Hume, *Calendar of Letters and State Papers relating to English Affairs preserved in the Archives of Simancas, 1558–1603* in four volumes (London, 1892–9) adds significant detail.

The Golden Hind

Periodical Literature about the Circumnavigation and the 'Golden Hind'

Among a host of articles the following are the most important:

Andrews, K. R., 'The aims of Drake's expedition, 1577–80' in the *American Historical Review*, vol. 73 (New York, 1968);

Callender, Geoffrey, 'Drake and his detractors' in the *Mariner's Mirror*, vol. 7 (London, 1921). which is concerned with defending Drake over the Doughty affair;

Prideaux Naish, F. C., 'The mystery of the tonnage and dimensions of the Pelican/Golden Hind' in the *Mariner's Mirror*, vol. 34 (London, 1948);

Prideaux Naish, F. C., 'The identification of the Ashmolean model' in the *Mariner's Mirror*, vol. 36 (London, 1950), which establishes beyond reasonable doubt that the model in the Ashmolean Museum, Oxford, is a model of the *Golden Hind*;

Robinson, Gregory, 'A forgotten life of Sir Francis Drake' in the *Mariner's Mirror*, vol. 7 (London, 1921), the biography being that in G. W. Anderson's *Captain Cook's Voyages*, etc. (London, 1784);

Robinson, Gregory, 'The evidence about the Golden Hind' in the *Mariner's Mirror*, vol. 35 (London, 1949), which fully discusses the vessel's dimensions and armament;

Robinson, Gregory, 'The Trial and Death of Thomas Doughty' in the *Mariner's Mirror*, vol. 7 (London, 1921), which is a rejoinder to Callender's article, cited above;

Senior, W., 'Drake at the suit of John Doughty' in the *Mariner's Mirror*, vol. 7 (London, 1921), provides evidence about John's attempts to charge Drake in the English courts for the murder of his brother;

Starr, Walter A., 'Drake landed in San Francisco Bay in 1579. The testimony of the Plate of Brass' in the *California Historical Society Quarterly*, vol. 41 (1962). Earlier articles by H. E. Bolton, D. S. Watson, R. B. Haselden and A. L. Chickering in the September 1937 issue of the *Quarterly* discussed the authenticity of the brass plate discovered in 1936;

Taylor, E. G. R., 'The missing draft project of Drake's voyage, 1577–80' in *Geographical Journal*, vol. 75 (London, 1930);

Taylor, E. G. R., 'More light on Drake, 1577–80' in the *Mariner's Mirror*, vol. 16 (London, 1930), prints John Winter's report of June 1579.

Other Lives

Froude, J. A., *English Seamen in the Sixteenth Century* (London, 1895) is still worth reading, although much new information has since then come to light. Among recent biographical studies the most relevant are:

Brook, E. St John, *Sir Christopher Hatton* (London, 1946);

Rowse, A. L., *Sir Richard Grenville of the 'Revenge'* (London, 1937);

Unwin, Rayner, *The Defeat of Sir John Hawkins* (London, 1960);

Wallace, William M., *Sir Walter Raleigh* (London, 1959);

Williams, Neville, *Elizabeth I, Queen of England* (London, 1967);

Williamson, James A., *The Age of Drake* (London, 1938);

Williamson, James A., *Sir John Hawkins, the Time and the Man* (London, 1927);

Williamson, James A., *Hawkins of Plymouth* (London, 1969).

Index

Index

Cornelius ('the Irishman'), burnt by Inquisition, 23

Courtenay, Sir William, Lady Drake's second husband, 176

Cowley, Abraham, verses on Drake and his ship, 123

Cox, Richard, Bishop of Ely, 42

'Crab Island', Celebes, 156-7

Crowndale Farm, Tavistock, Devon, birthplace of Francis Drake, 2-3

Cuttill, Thomas, sailor on 1577 expedition, 77

Dartmoor, Devonshire, 1, 33

da Silva, Nuño, see Silva, Nuño da

Davis, John, presents chair to Bodleian Library, 183

Deane, John, sailor in 1577 expedition, 77

de Clare, Amicia, Countess of Devon, founder of Buckland Abbey (1273), 3, 46

Dee, Dr John, astrologer and geographer ('the Welsh wizard'), 34, 47

de Ferrers family of Devon, 3

de Fortibus, Isabella, Countess of Devon, x

de: all Spanish names ending in 'de' are entered under the last part of the name, for example Pedro Sarmiento de Gamboa is entered as Gamboa, Pedro Sarmiento de

Delgadillo, captain of garrison, San Juan de Ulua, 11, 12-13, 14

Deptford, on River Thames, visit and knighting of Drake by Queen Elizabeth, xviii, 168-71; building of Golden Hind, 87; preservation of Golden Hind, xviii, 182-3

Desolation Island, Magellan Straits, 97

Devon, Countess of, see de Clare, Amicia, de Fortibus, Isabella

Devonshire, county of England, ix-xi, xiii, 1-3, 5, 25, 28, 33, 45-6, 170, 174; see also Buckland Abbey; Dartmoor; Plymouth

Diego, Drake's negro steward, killed at Mucho, 103

Dominica, island of W. Indies, 9

Doughty, John, brother to T. Doughty, 129-30; prosecutes Drake for murder of T. Doughty, 172; arrested, tortured, confesses to dealing with Spaniards, imprisoned, 172

Doughty, Thomas, xv, 43-4, 50; commander of Mary, 62; commander of Pelican, 62-3; removed to Swan, 64; endeavours to cause dissension on Swan, 66; trial for mutiny, and execution, 75-84; Francis Fletcher punished for reference to, 159-60

Drake, Edmund, father of Francis Drake, xiii-xiv, 2, 3-4

Drake, Elizabeth (Elizabeth Sydenham), 175-6

Drake, Francis, 'El Draque', (1541-96), birth, xiii, 2; motives for attacks on Spain, xix-xxi; early life, 3; apprentice sailor, 4; first voyage to Spanish Main, 5-6; command of Judith, 8; slaving voyage with Hawkins, 9-24; marriage, 25; attack on Nombre de Dios, 26-33; first sights Pacific, 30; tactical use of pinnaces, 31, 91, 106, 109, 127; returns to Plymouth 1573, 33-4; service in Ireland 1575, 33-4, 75; meets Hatton, presented to Queen, 44; plans voyage to Pacific, 45, 92-3; summary of voyage round the world, xiv-xviii; 1577-80 expedition, ships disabled by storms at outset, 50-1; exploits on Cape Verde Is., 54-9; crosses Atlantic to Brazil, 60-7; S. American coasting experiences, 65-71; Doughty's trial and execution, 75-84; equipment etc. of Golden Hind, 85-93; decision not to return by Atlantic route, 97; Drake wounded in Mucho, 103; attacks on W. coast of S. and Central America, 104-34; discovers 'New Albion', 146-52; crosses Pacific, 152-3; in E. Indies, 153-62; returns to Plymouth, 164-6; knighted, 169; honoured by Queen Elizabeth, 171; his treatment of prisoners, xix, 58, 141, 166-7; becomes MP, 1583, 175; second marriage, 1585, 175; Vigo Bay, 176;

193